William Nicholson

Memoirs and travels of Mauritius Augustus, Count de Benyowsky

Consisting of his military operations in Poland, his exile into Kamchatka, his escape and voyage from that peninsula through the northern Pacific ocean, touching at Japan and Formosa. Vol. 2

William Nicholson

Memoirs and travels of Mauritius Augustus, Count de Benyowsky
Consisting of his military operations in Poland, his exile into Kamchatka, his escape and voyage from that peninsula through the northern Pacific ocean, touching at Japan and Formosa. Vol. 2

ISBN/EAN: 9783337191962

Printed in Europe, USA, Canada, Australia, Japan

Cover: Foto ©Andreas Hilbeck / pixelio.de

More available books at **www.hansebooks.com**

MEMOIRS AND TRAVELS

OF

MAURITIUS AUGUSTUS COUNT DE BENYOWSKY.

VOL. II.

THE

MEMOIRS and TRAVELS

OF THE

COUNT DE BENYOWSKY.

CONTINUATION OF THE JOURNAL OF A VOYAGE FROM THE PENINSULA OF KAMCHATKA TO MACAO IN CHINA.

MONDAY, August 15th, 1771: the veſſel aground at the Iſland of Uſmay Ligon. After a lethargic ſleep of four hours, I was awakened by the care of my aſſociates, who had uſed continual friction. As ſoon as I recovered my ſenſes, Mr. Panow informed me that we were on an Iſland inhabited by a people in a high ſtate of civilization, from whom I was about to receive a viſit; and a very ſhort time after, Mr. Cruſtiew acquainted me that two of the iſlanders were then at the entrance of my tent. I received them in the beft manner I could, and was in hopes of making myfelf underftood in the Japanefe language, by means of Mr. Bofcarew, whom I ordered to be called. All our efforts, however, were entirely ufelefs. They only fhook their heads, as a fign that they did not underftand us: but one of them prefented a paper to us, on which I perceived fome Latin letters. I received it with avidity, and it was with great pleafure that I read its contents in the Latin language to the following purport.

"The Health of our Lord Jefus to the Reader."

" In the year 1749, on the 24th of May, I arrived in this ifland, with three other companions of the fociety of Jefus, and being hofpitably received by the inhabitants, I fixed my abode here to propagate the word of God. The chiefs of this ifland fpeak the Mandarin language, and have fhewn the moft ardent defire to be inftructed in the Catholic Religion, which is the only good and fatisfactory worfhip. Their zeal proceeded fo far as to induce them to affift me in the laborious charge of propagating the faith, and by the miraculous affiftance of the holy patron of the company of Jefus, I had the fatisfaction of feeing two hundred and fixty Neophites baptifed the firft year, whofe zeal, conftancy, and patience have confirmed my hopes. In the year 1750 my other three brothers repaired to the adjacent iflands, and there is no doubt but that they performed their duty with as much zeal as myfelf. In the year 1754, finding myfelf oppreffed with illnefs, I thought proper to communicate the prefent declaration to the

COUNT DE BENYOWSKY. 3

the chiefs of the ifland, in order that they might give the moft neceffary information to thofe of the Company of Jefus, who might be conducted by Providence to this ifland, to enable them to employ their zeal and ftrength for the good of chriftianity, by promulgating the name of our Saviour among this people, who are fober, and of good manners, and live in the moft abfolute independence, both of China and Japan. Excepting fome merchant veffels of thofe nations, no other have ever been feen here. Neverthelefs I have feen Dutch veffels pafs at a very fmall diftance from this ifland. A. M. D. G. B. V. M. E. S. P. N. I. Done the 18th September, 1754, at the Ifland Ufmay Ligon."

> IGNATIO SALIS, Miffionary to the Indies, of the Society of Jefus, and of the Portuguefe Nation.

After I had perufed this paper, I returned it to the perfon from whom I received it. But I firft kiffed it, which mark of refpect feemed to have conciliated their efteem: they gave us to underftand by figns that they were defirous of returning to inform their countrymen of the news. After their departure, finding myfelf entirely recovered, I went out to fee the fituation of the work, and I had the fatisfaction to find that the veffel was entirely unladen. But my grief was extreme to fee that all our furs were rotten. I gave orders therefore to open all the packages, and expofe the whole to the air, with a view to fave at leaft, part. I charged Mr. Baturin to fuperintend this

B 2 bufinefs,

business, as it related to the only resource on which we could depend, when we should arrive at China. On the approach of night, we appointed a guard and centinels, and the night passed in the most profound tranquility.

At day break I was informed that other inhabitants of the country had presented themselves, to the number of three hundred, without arms, each person having nothing but a parasol in his hand. Two chiefs, who preceded them, approached me, and after having made the sign of the cross, they presented their hands, and then exhibited to me an old Breviary, which was borne upon a carpet by four men. By the inscription I saw that the Breviary had belonged to the Missionary Salis, and in order to join in the respect these islanders shewed to the memory of that Jesuit, I likewise kissed this book. I then gave orders to my companions to bring a large crucifix, which they had taken out of the Church of Bolsha. I directed them to present it to the islanders. It was covered with a veil, and as soon as this was raised, the islanders fell on their knees, and raising their hands towards heaven, cried out Hisos, Hisos, Christos, Christos, and as I saw that they would not rise as long as the crucifix was before them, I caused it to be removed; whereupon the two chiefs arose, and embraced me alternately, and gave me to understand that their friendship was sincere. It was unfortunate that we could not make ourselves understood by words, and we found much difficulty in the use of signs. I succeeded however in explaining, by my signs and gestures, that our vessel was damaged, and that we were in want of habitations and fresh provisions.

Having

Having thus comprehended my requeſt, they left me; and in the courſe of an hour we ſaw ſeveral boats arrive, which brought mats and wood, and others with people on board, who came to build huts for us. Another party of the iſlanders arrived with rice, potatoes, bananas, ſugar-canes, a kind of brandy, with proviſions of fiſh, fleſh, and fruit. Theſe immediately ſet to work to cook for us all. Laſtly, about noon, another party arrived with carpenter's tools, and gave us to underſtand that they were diſpoſed to aſſiſt us, by working on board. I was deſirous however that the company ſhould have ſome reſt, and therefore made ſigns that the work would not begin till two days after.

According to the Report, five ſick: the veſſel aground at the iſland Uſmay Ligon.

Tueſday, Auguſt the 16th: the whole company was buſied in aſſiſting the natives of the country to conſtruct cabins, in which four of the aſſociates might lodge together, or two officers. One hut was built for myſelf alone, at the head of the camp, about which we raiſed a paliſade, flanked with four cannon.

The inconvenience we ſuffered in not being able to make ourſelves underſtood by the iſlanders, induced me to give orders to all the company who could write, to make a kind of Dictionary of Ruſſian words, and enquire their ſignification from the natives in their own language. This appeared to me to be the only practicable means of making ourſelves underſtood.

At two o'clock dinner was ſerved up to the company. It conſiſted of rice, bananas, and potatoes, ſtewed with fleſh; and our new cooks informed us that the cuſtom

of

of the country was to make three meals a day. For drink they gave us a kind of hydromel and arrack.

This day, being defirous of regulating every thing which concerned our intereft, I caufed the work to be renewed on board by fourteen aſſociates, under the command of Mr. Czurin: Mr. Kuzneczow undertook to repair the fails and rigging: Mr. Baturin, took charge of the cargo: Mr. Cruftiew undertook to look to our fubfiftence: the military fervice was put under the command of Mr. Panow, and I undertook to treat with the natives of the country, whofe good and amiable character often excited in me the defire of fharing with them an eafy and happy life. For the ifland was exceedingly fertile; the climate though hot, appeared excellent, and the people were independent. Thefe were powerful motives to a man who was weary of being the fport of fortune: but unfortunately the hour of my repofe was not yet arrived, and it was neceſſary for me to bear the burthen of the charge I had undertaken.

In the evening feveral iflanders came to me, and being feated, they often repeated the word Dzignaro, raifing their hands towards the fky. Mr. Panow was the firft who fufpected that they meant to pronounce Ignatio, and in fact when they attempted to repeat that word, they always faid Dzignaro. The refpect with which they pronounced this name, convinced me that the Miſſionary had fkillfully availed himfelf of their difpofitions to imprefs them with the moft profound reverence for his religion. They left me at laft with much regret. After their departure I collected the different notes of the names of things which had been made in the language of the country, according my orders, and I had the fatisfaction to find, that their number amounted to above a hundred, which could not fail of proving highly ufeful. Mr. Kuzneczow requefted permiffion to make an excurfion over the ifland with fome of the affociates; but I refufed him that fatisfaction, at the fame time obferving, that I was apprehenfive of giving occafion to fome mifunderftanding between our people and the natives.

The night paffed in a ftate of tranquility, and in the morning I was vifited by an iflander of diftinction, whom I then faw for the firft time. He was attended by a number of others, among whom I perceived feveral of our earlier friends; and as all the natives fhewed him the moft profound veneration, I judged it proper likewife to pay a particular attention to him. He was clothed in a robe of fky blue taffeta, with a long cloak of white filk, a black fafh, and wooden flippers, covered with fatin. On his head he wore a kind of hat of a very fine fur. When he came near me he likewife made the fign of the crofs, and took me by the hand. I did the fame, and as I had learned fome words of the language, I faluted him, by pronouncing the word *Tho*. He inclined his head, and fmiled at my embarraffment. But I was greatly furprifed to hear him fpeak to me in very bad Portuguefe, though fufficient to make himfelf underftood. He faid, *Sinor eo fono Tunqunio vay con Padre Dzignaro eftas Iflas Ufma Padre vay morte eo fies a ca Capiton di Genté.* I comprehended that he meant to inform me that he was a native of Tonquin, who came to thofe iflands with Father Ignatio, and that the father being dead, he remained, and was chief of the people. This difcovery of the power of making

myfelf

myself understood gave me the highest pleasure. I seized the immediate occasion to express my joy. He then demanded if I was desirous of seeing the tomb of Dzignaro; and upon my answering in the affirmative, he appointed three old men of distinction to accompany me. But as it was necessary to cross the bay, we embarked in the shallop, with Messrs. Panow, Kuzneczow and Baturin.

Our conductors directed us to the mouth of a river, where the shallop, not being able to enter, we anchored, and the natives called boats, which set us on shore. On our landing we found about fifty persons of both sexes, who kneeled down, and cried *Ilo Dzignaro*, (The Friend of Ignatio.) Our conductors then led us to a garden, where we found an old man, busied in collecting flowers and plants. He introduced us into a very neat and well-built hut, and entertained us with tea, but without sugar. Our conductors then spoke privately with him, who immediately made a sign to us to follow him, and led us to a small hill, which overlooked a very agreeable valley, regularly planted with pulse and sugar canes. When we arrived at the summit we found a small square building, in the interior part of which we saw an altar, and upon it a crucifix, and an image of St. Mary, which, though very ill executed, was distinguished by the crescent beneath her feet, and the crown on her head. I observed the letters upon the crown which are represented in fig. 1, plate 16.

The guardian of the chapel shewed me likewise two urns, in which the ashes of Dzignaro (Father Ignatio) were contained. At going out of the chapel I could clearly distinguish the letters I. H. S. O. H. M. D. G. B.

COUNT DE BENYOWSKY.

B. V. M. O. S. Nque JESU, Anno 1751. I likewife obferved fome verfes, but the writing was fo much decayed that I could not make out a fingle line.

After having vifited the facred monuments of thofe people, I returned home, where I learned, with the greateft fatisfaction, that the damages of the veffel would be eafily repaired, and that our people was employed in making new pumps, the old ones being unfit for fervice. Mr. Czurin having likewife informed me that the main top fail yard was fprung, I gave him orders to fearch in the woods for a piece to replace it, but I was anfwered that the natives had brought feveral pieces exceedingly proper for the purpofe. This day I gave orders for diftributing pieces of filk and cotton to the company, to make fhirts, frocks, and trowfers, in order that they might all have an uniform appearance. Mr. Winbladth, who, notwithftanding my prohibition, had made an excurfion, informed me, that he had feen very handfome habitations and villages, and had obferved large quantities of different fruits, fuch as cocoa nuts, oranges, lemons, pine-apples, bananas, water melons, fweet mellons, grapes, potatoes, rice, maize, millet, peas, and other pulfe; and that in the plantations he had feen bee-hives, fugar-canes, tobacco and cotton. He affured me befides that he had vifited a manufactory of pottery and a diftillery of fpirits; and added, that all the women in the villages were bufied in making ftuffs, either of filk or cotton. I verified this information myfelf the fame day, and my ftay upon this fortunate ifland increafed my ardent defire to form an eftablifhment there.

According to the Report, two fick: the fhip under repair.

Wednesday, August the 17th, we had scarcely finished our repast, when the Tonquin Captain arrived; I informed him of my wishes, and the advantageous idea I had formed of the happiness of this people. He replied, that it depended only on myself, whether I should fix my residence among them, and that if I chose it, he would propose to the nation to give me a tract of land; but in the first place he was desirous of knowing who I was; how we came to the island, &c. I told him the truth, and my narration, though it was impossible he should well understand it, affected him so much, that he wept, and offered me his friendship. It was, doubtless, with a view to repay my confidence, that he likewise related his adventures, which were to the following effect.

He was born at Tonquin, of a free family and studied at Siam in the college of Missionaries. He afterwards, accompanied a Missionary to China, who joining himself with three others, at Nankin, embarked together with himself in a Chinese vessel, called a Sampan, which conveyed them to one of the islands of Usmay. Father Ignatio established himself, at this Island, Usmay Ligon, and the others departed for other islands. He afterwards gave a full account of the means employed by Father Ignatio to convert the islanders to Christianity, and protested that the said Father enjoyed a supreme power in this island, until his death; after which the islanders forced him to marry among them. He observed that they had the greatest veneration for himself; but he declared that it was not in consequence of any particular right attached to his person, as the government of the island depended on an assembly of old men, to which the chiefs of the families of the neighbouring islands were often invited. This form of government surprized me, and I could

could not avoid asking a thousand questions, which led me to a just idea of the constitution and government of this people, of which I propose to give a note at the end of the Journal of my happy residence on this island. Our discourse was interrupted by the arrival of a troop of islanders, whom my friend Nicholas informed of my desire to establish myself amongst them: this declaration was very agreeable to them, for they assured me that they would divide their possessions with us, instruct us in the manner of working and tilling the ground, and would give us their daughters in marriage. But as I saw that the idea of our establishment gave them great satisfaction, and was aware that in order to form a colony it was necessary I should be provided with a set of men, very different from my present companions; I thought it proper to inform them that my establishment could not take place until two years were elapsed, which were necessary for me to return to Europe, and return back again. I found no difficulty in bringing these estimable people to my wish; the open simplicity of their answers shewed their virtuous and innocent dispositions. They assured me that they would pray to God for my happy voyage, and quick return, and that during my stay I might consider them as my brothers.

After this declaration, they demanded, why I did not come among them, nor permit my companions to live with them in a cordial manner. I declared to Nicholas that my only apprehension was that our good intelligence might be interrupted by the inconsistency of my companions, who might displease the islanders by caressing their women. But he set my mind at ease in that respect, by
informing

informing me that they were at liberty to connect themselves with the girls, provided they abstained from the married women, who were known by a veil which covered them. Upon this assurance, I promised that from thenceforth, considering the natives of this island as our brothers, we would visit them. But I pressed M. Nicholas to make my excuses for not having politely informed the ladies before hand, and apologized by freely telling my reasons, and the fears I had entertained. The islanders answered laughing, that their daughters were younger than their wives, and that therefore I had no reason to fear their displeasure on that account.

After this explanation, the islanders retired, no doubt for the purpose of acquainting their families, with the intention that they might receive us with kindness. When they were gone, I assembled the company, communicated my apprehensions to them, and required of each individual a solemn promise to behave with the utmost circumspection to these islanders; and having received their oaths, I declared that they were free to visit the whole island, provided one third of their number always remained at work. This news produced universal joy among them, and they immediately dispersed themselves, but without arms, as I had caused them to leave their arms with me. In the evening a meeting was held, consisting of Mr. Crustiew, Panow, Kuzneczow, Baturin, Winbladth, Meder, Gurefinin and Czurin, where we debated on the means of deriving advantage from the discovery and knowledge we had acquired of this fortunate island. We determined that the disposition of our companions rendered it impossible to leave any of them behind; for I was desirous of leaving a party

COUNT DE BENYOWSKY. 13

in order to difpofe the minds of the natives to receive a colony in future. Being thus difappointed in my hopes, I felt the moft lively regret at not being able to profit by fo favourable an occafion; and after having difmiffed the meeting, I was plunged in a feries of reflections which were exceedingly diftreffing.

At day break I repaired to the neareft village, which was not above a quarter of an hour's walk from our camp; but concealed by a thick wood. Upon my arrival near the enclofure, I was received in a fmall building of wood, from which I could eafily fee all the houfes in the village. It confifted of about eighty houfes, each having a court-yard before, it with a garden and feveral huts, or out-houfes. All the houfes were conftructed of wood, and covered with planks, and formed a fingle, wide, and handfome ftreet, bordered on each fide by very lofty and tufted trees. Upon entering the village I met Nicholas, who conducted me to his houfe, before which all the people were affembled. He afked me if I was difpofed to make choice of a girl, but, as I replied in the negative, he declared that my companions were of a better compofition; and, in fact, I found few of them who were not accompanied by young women, fome of whom were real beauties. My friend Nicholas regaled us with tea, and engaged the iflanders to form matches at wreftling, at which they are very expert, and afterwards the young women danced to the found of feveral ftringed inftruments. Thefe amufements lafted till the repaft was ferved up in the court-yard of the houfe, which was a fquare enclofure, furrounded with trees. Every head of a family caufed difhes, ready dreffed, to be brought from his own houfe, and the whole was conducted in fuch a manner that

every

every one contributed his fhare, without the charge falling upon any individual. The women eat feparately, and the young women waited on both parties.

At the end of our meal, the juice of fugar cane, which we drank, was mixed with a kind of fpirit made from rice. This drink was very ftong and exhilerating. From one fubject to another, our converfation at laft returned to the propofal made to me to choofe one of their young women, which was again urged, and at laft fo ftrongly preffed, that I could not avoid faying that I was willing to make my choice at that time, but fhould referve the accomplifhment of my marriage till I returned. I had fcarcely faid this, before the chiefs arofe, and the whole company difappeared, and left me alone with my friend Nicholas, by whom I was informed that the iflanders were gone to nominate feven young women to be prefented to me, in order that I might choofe a wife from among them. In fact, we had fcarcely time to take a furvey of his court-yard, his garden, and the fmall houfes of his women, (for a plurality of wives is eftablifhed and conftitutional, notwithftanding the religion of Father Ignatio) before we were informed of the arrival of the iflanders.

The old men firft feated themfelves upon mats in the court, forming a circle. Seven women, whofe faces were covered, led each a young woman, clothed from head to foot in white filk, with a blue fafh; their hair flowed loofe on their fhoulders, and was interwoven with flowers. When the feven young women entered the circle, my friend Nicholas led me likewife there, and requefted me to fit down and examine thefe charming objects, in order to determine my choice. During this interval, one of the old men pronounced

pronounced a difcourfe of fome length, which he end' i by prefenting me with a veil, and by the mediation of Nicholas, he gave me to underftand, that I was requefted to cover her with it, on whom my affections were fixed. The choice would have been rather difficult, if it had really been incumbent on me to decide; for there were three among them who might have difputed the preference with the moft perfect work of living nature. But as my embarraffment was only imaginary, I afked my friend whether my choice would not offend the others, and upon his anfwering in the negative, I threw the veil over one of them. The others immediately began to dance round her, and carefs her, and at laft conducted her out of the houfe to the ftreet, where fhe was preceded by mufical inftruments. My friend Nicholas informed me that this ceremony would laft upwards of an hour, becaufe the young woman would be conducted to every houfe, to announce her own marriage, and receive prefents. In the mean time the chiefs were regaled with tea, and fmoked tobacco.

About five o'clock I faw the new married lady return, conducted by her mother, who was about four or five and thirty years of age, and they were accompanied by a refpectable old man, who was grandfather to the young woman. This old man made a fpeech, and embraced me; the mother put her daughter into my hands, and leaving her with me, they difappeared fuddenly, as did likewife the reft of the chiefs. Nicholas then acquainted me that I muft myfelf conduct the young lady to his houfe, in which he affifted me, by leading the way. At the door of this houfe fhe quitted me, and Nicholas attended me back to the camp.

During our walk, he informed me, that the newly married young woman was the daughter of a very devout
chriftian

chriftian mother, who had been conftantly attached to Father Ignatio; and as he had mentioned his grandfather to me without telling the name of his father, I queftioned him pofitively on the fubject. He at firft affected concealment, but at laft confeffed that Seignior Dzignaro was his father, and he had likewife two elder fifters, who were among the feven prefented to me for my choice. He informed me that the young perfon I had chofen was named Tinto Volangta, (or luminous moon) and that I might certainly expect her foon at my own place of refidence. He then left me, after promifing to come again to vifit me in the morning.

As foon as I found myfelf alone, I informed my companions of my adventure, and feveral of them determined to pafs the night with me, in order to avoid certain embarraffments; and to anfwer this purpofe more effectually, I requefted all the female companions of our voyage to be prefent, to amufe thofe who might come from the village. At nine o'clock I was acquainted with the arrival of a body of young women, who came towards our camp finging. Their number amounted to twenty, and they were received and introduced by our women. But as foon as Tinto Volangta entered my hut, the others retired, fo that I found myfelf under the neceffity of having a female companion. It was a fortunate circumftance that one of our lady paffengers was greatly interefted by the young iflander, and gave her much entertainment by finging and mufic; but the reft of our converfation was pantomime.

The break of day furprifed us without fleep, except the Ufmayan lady, who fell afleep about eight o'clock. When fhe awoke, two other young women attended to drefs her, and afterwards ftaid with her. At ten my friend Nicholas arrived

arrived with a numerous company. I went out to meet them, and upon being informed that they came to make a treaty, or oath, I gave immediate orders for affembling our company. The heads of the contract were, that the inhabitants of Ufmay Ligon, fhould acknowledge me as their friend, and that I fhould engage in an attachment to them. That as I was about to leave them, only with the intention of returning to form an eftablifhment among them, they would clear a piece of land on the Southern part of the ifland, and build a village, of two hundred houfes, for the accommodation of myfelf, and thofe who might come with me. And laftly, that on my return to Ufmay, I fhould conform to all the ufages and laws of my friends.

Thefe articles being ratified by the invocation of God, the creator of all things, I thought it incumbent on me to make my new countrymen a prefent. Accordingly I gave them eighty mufquets, twenty barrels of powder, ten barrels of ball, fix hundred Japanefe fabres, fix hundred lances, and twelve hundred different articles of iron work. This prefent was highly valuable to them, for they had not above ten mufquets on the ifland, and thofe had matchlocks. It was a very unfortunate circumftance that I could not leave a detachment on this ifland.

According to the Report one fick: the fhip under repair, careening.

Thurfday, Auguft 18. About two in the evening, the iflanders brought ten oxen, forty hogs, a quantity of rice, millet, and other provifions. On this day likewife, having, by the credit of Nicholas, brought the chiefs to liften to my reafons, I fent Tinto Volangta back to her mother's houfe, whom I loaded with prefents from the Japanefe prize. As to my friend Nicholas, I made him a confiderable prefent of furs, though I had but a fmall quantity remaining, the fea water having damaged almoft all the packages. In the evening I informed the iflanders of my approaching departure, at which they were greatly affected, and expreffed their regret on the occafion. The open and benevolent character of this eftimable people, was fuch as will make me ever regret that I could not fix my abode here, where the vices and wickednefs of Europe are yet unknown, and the government is founded only upon the principles of humanity.

After the departure of the iflanders, I ordered my people to float the veffel, and get the cargo on board. Our work commenced the next day. At nine o'clock, five of the affociates appeared before me, and demanded permiffion to remain upon the ifland. I faw that their refolution was fixed; and having reafon to fear that they might excite a greater number of the company to the fame determination, I reprefented to them that they were wrong in taking fuch a refolution at this time, as they were fure of returning: for I protefted to them that I would ufe every exertion, when we arrived in Europe, to obtain a proper armament to eftablifh a colony on the ifland. At firft they feemed difpofed to quit their purpofe; but one of them, named Laphew, declared that it was only a lofs of time to attempt to diffuade them, as they were determined not to change their mind; and therefore, that if I were difpofed to give them a proof of my friendfhip, I might fhew.it by leaving them a fupply of tools, arms, and ammunition. I promifed this to make them eafy; but I made them fwear that they would not feduce any others of the company.

When

When they were gone, I assembled a Committee, to whom I communicated the desire of the five men. The Committee referred the business to the General Meeting, which was immediately convened, and their decision was, that leave should be given them to remain on the island. Three others joined them, and M. Stephanow was likewise desirous of remaining; but the others refused him, saying, that as they had taken their resolution for no other reason than to live in peace, they would not have an incendiary among them.

In consequence of this resolution of the meeting, I ordered Mr. Crustiew to divide what we could spare, into eight lots, in order that every subsequent controversy between our companions who were to remain behind, might be prevented by a proper division made in our presence. At eleven, we saw three large barks enter the harbour, where they anchored. My friend Nicholas informed me, that they were Japanese, from the coast of China, who were driven in by stress of weather. He requested, that I would invite them to come on shore, which they did, bringing with them a present of tea, porcelain, and some pearls.

August 19. This day we were visited by upwards of one thousand islanders, every one bringing some present. The whole amounted to upwards of one thousand eight hundred ells of cloth, two hundred and five parasols, with a quantity of china vessels, and some ivory figures, ornamented with gold. In the evening, by the mediation of Nicholas, I recommended to the islanders those companions who had determined to remain, and they all protested that they would receive and acknowledge them as friends and brothers, and give them a share of their lands and possessions. In this manner I secured their respective interests. At four o'clock I gave orders for going on board. The value of my cargo was so much reduced, that out of a million and a half of piastres which I expected to receive at China, I had scarcely sufficient to realize twenty or twenty-five thousand piastres. The night was employed in work; and at day-break I had the satisfaction to see all my people on board. I judged it proper to assure myself of the disposition of the islanders, by a formal oath and contract, which was drawn up in the language of Lequeio, and the counterpart in Latin, signed by both parties. I took the Latin part with me, and they preserved the other. Its contents were as follow:—

" A Treaty, concluded between the chiefs and people
" of the islands Lequeio, and the Baron Mauritius Au-
" gustus de Benyowsky, in the name of the company
" under his direction. Contracted and signed on the 19th
" of August, in the year 1771, at the island Usmay Li-
" gon, one of Lequeio."

" In the presence of God, who created the heavens
" and the earth, We, the chiefs and people of the island
" of Usmay Ligon, and the other Lequeio, of the one
" part, and I, the Baron Mauritius de Benyowsky, of
" the other part, do stipulate:"

" That I, Mauritius Augustus de Benyowsky, do oblige
" myself, and do promise, upon my faith as a Christian, to
" return to this island, as soon as possible, with a society
" of virtuous, good, and just men, to dwell upon this
" island, and to adopt the manners, usages, and laws of
" the inhabitants."

" And

COUNT DE BENYOWSKY. 21

" And we, the chiefs and people, call to witnefs that
" God who created the heavens and the earth, that we will,
" at any time hereafter, receive our friend Mauritius, with
" all thofe who fhall be his friends : that we will fhare
" with them our lands, and will affift them in all their
" labours, until their eftablifhments fhall be equal to our
" own ; and, in the mean time, his friends, who remain
" with us, fhall be confidered as the children of our
" families, and treated as brothers."

" Mauritius, in the name of
" the company of Euro-
" peans."

" Nicholas, for the chiefs
" and people of Ufmay,
" and the Lequeio iflands."

After the conclufion of this treaty, I affembled thofe among my companions who were determined to fix their refidence among this worthy people. I gave them inftructions for the regulation of their conduct, and at laft I embraced and quitted them to go on board. A prodigious number of iflanders followed me, who, by their cries and tears, exhibited an affecting fpectacle of goodnefs of heart, and tendernefs of difpofition. We were ready to fet fail at day-break : I therefore begged my friend Nicholas to requeft the iflanders to go on board their boats ; but feveral of the chiefs, faftening their canoes to the veffel, determined to accompany me till my departure. I weighed, at 10 A. M. and failed out of the harbour with out any unfortunate accident.

According

According to the Report, the whole company in good health; the veffel making no water.

Saturday, Auguft the 20th, at fea, under the top-fails; fine weather, but exceffively hot; a frefh breeze, and fmooth water; faw a large quantity of fif.ing birds around us. At half paft one P. M. the iflanders at laft took their leave, and embarked in their canoes, to return to the ifland. About fix we faw a great number of porpoifes; the weather was fine throughout the night. About eleven we difcovered land a head, extending from N. W. to S. E. I therefore came to an anchor in twenty-eight fathom fine fand, and took advantage of this anchorage to fet up the rigging afrefh, as this part of the fervice had been neglected. At day-break we perceived that the whole of the ftanding rigging required fetting up, for which reafon I was forced to continue the work. During this time feveral boats arrived, with which we trafficked, exchanging knives, and fome other trifles, for a quantity of fhells, very neatly wrought.

According to the Report, all well; the fhip making no water.

Latitude in 28° 43'; longitude in 327° 18'. Wind E. N. E. Current from the Northward. Courfe S. S. W.

Sunday, Auguft the 21ft. fine clear weather, and fmooth water. At one P. M. weighed, and made fail, with all the fails fet, and hauled the wind, to double the Southern point of the ifland. At fix we doubled another fmall ifland, which lay to the Northward. About day-break we faw another on the ftarboard beam, to the Southward.

According to the Report all well; the fhip making no water.

Latitude

Latitude in 28° 8'; longitude in 329° 2'. Wind E. N. E. ¼ N. Current from N. to S. Courſe S. E.

Monday, Auguſt the 22d. Fine weather and ſmooth water, but the heat almoſt inſupportable. About noon the wind became variable, and veered to the Southward. It fixed at S. E. I therefore took advantage of the fine weather, and ſet all our ſails, with which I might have made a good progreſs, if the wind had not abated, and came round to the Eaſtward. At nine A. M. ſaw two ſhips ſtanding from S. to N. right towards us; I therefore gave orders to prepare for battle, and appointed a number of the beſt markſmen in the tops. At eleven we were within cannon ſhot, and I then perceived that they were Hollanders, one carrying eighteen guns, and the other twelve.

According to the Report all well, prepared for battle, under the top-ſails. The ſhip making no water.

Latitude 26° 20'; longitude in 327° 2'. Wind E. No current. Courſe S. E. ¼ S.

Tueſday, Auguſt the 23d. One of the two veſſels coming nearly within muſket ſhot of us, fired a ball, and hailed us to come on board, and bring our papers. This behaviour of the Dutch Captain ſurprized me greatly, and ſo much the more as being entirely ignorant of the maritime laws, I knew not what he meant by my papers: for this reaſon I anſwered by four cannon-ſhot, and the muſquetry began to play from the tops, which greatly incommoded him. He waited for his companion, who at laſt came to his aſſiſtance, but was contented to keep out a conſiderable diſtance from us. I then hoiſted the colours of the Republic of Poland, and continued my courſe due S.

They

They were at first disposed to follow me, but having observed that I made preparations for receiving them, by clewing up my courses, they adopted the wisest conduct for them, which was to put about, and continue their course; for I had determined to board one of the two, and make them pay dear for what they had done. This slight combat, the first I ever saw at sea, cost us only a few shot, and the trouble of performing our manœuvres. As to the Hollanders, I know not what their acquisitions were.

According to the Report, all well; the ship making no water.

Latitude in 24° 45′; longitude in 327° 0′. Wind E. No current. Course S.

Wednesday, August the 24th. Weather rather blustering, but without rain, and a rising sea. Being underway, with all sails set, the associates, from the information they had found in Anson's Voyage, requested me to sail to the island of Formosa, in order that they might add the knowledge of this island to their other discoveries. Their proposition was likewise agreeable to myself, I therefore promised to carry their request into execution.

According to the Report, all well; the vessel making no water.

Latitude in 23° 18′; longitude in 327° 0′. Wind E. Current from the Southward. Course S.

Thursday, August the 25th. The weather constantly disposed to squally, with rain at intervals. Conformably to the request of my associates, I changed my course, and stood to the Westward, and W. ¼ S. we had a strong current setting to the Southward.

According

According to the Report, all well; the ship making no water.

Latitude in 23° 22'; longitude in 325° 0'. Wind E. Current from the Southward. Course W. ¼ S.

Friday, August the 26th. About three P. M. a strong breeze arose, which obliged me to hand all the sails but the mizen. At six, a heavy rain came on, and abated the wind, which veered round to the N. E. About three A. M. I was awakened by the news of land. We had barely time to turn the ship's head to the Southward, when we clewed up the mizen, and let go an anchor in eighteen fathom water, the bottom being coral rock. At daybreak we found ourselves near a rock; the island of Formosa being in sight, and appearing to be very high land. I immediately weighed, and doubling the North point of the small island, stood towards the land, and moored at the opening of a bay, in fourteen fathom water, greenish sand. The associates were busied the whole night, in preparing the boats, and clearing their arms, which were distributed with the necessary ammunition. At four A. M. Mr. Kuzneczow, and Mr. Wynbladth, were sent on shore, with the canoe and the shallop, with sixteen men. At eight we heard three musket shot on shore, which I answered with one of my great guns. After this we heard a constant firing. At half-past nine we at last perceived our boats, returning round a point of the land. Three of the detachment were wounded with arrows, and they brought with them five prisoners, two of whom were dangerously wounded.

Here follows the Report of Mr. Kuzneczow.

After having reached shore, in a commodious bay, where I found the soundings every where from eight to five,

five, and three fathoms, I advanced with a detachment of ten affociates, towards a fire, which we difcovered. Mr. Wynbladth remained with the boats under his care. We found two Indians, and a woman, near the fire, whom we gave to underftand, that we were in want of food. One of them immediately went off, and returned in lefs than an hour after, with three other Indians, armed with lances, who made figns to us to follow them. They conducted us to a village, and as we refufed to enter into their huts, they brought us boiled rice, with roafted pork, and a quantity of lemons and oranges. The iflanders appeared quiet, and were not numerous; but as I had obferved a crowd, at the extremity of the village, and feveral armed bodies of men who went out, I imagined that they intended to feek a caufe of quarrel with us; for which reafon I perfuaded my companions to proceed back again, in order to carry the news on board, that we had formed a very convenient anchoring place. Accordingly, after having given the iflanders fome knives, in return for the refrefhment we had taken, we began to return. But we had fcarcely reached the place where we had firft feen the fire lighted, before we heard a cry, and were attacked by a fhower of arrows, which wounded three of my people. I gave orders to fire immediately on the enemy, and the firft difcharge checked their impetuofity, when they faw half a dozen of their party extended on the ground. For my own part, not being defirous of amufing myfelf in that place, I gave orders to carry one of my companions, who could not walk, and effected my retreat. The iflanders were preparing to fall upon us a fecond time, when fortunately for us, the cannon fhot, from on board,

intimidated

intimidated them, and caused them to leave us for a time at liberty. But when we came to the sea shore we were attacked by a great number of the savages. It was a happy circumstance that Mr. Wynbladth was on the spot. We then fell upon them, and after having overthrown at least sixty, we made five prisoners, and collected a quantity of lances and bows, which are now in the boats.

Upon this information, I would have quitted the place, as I was not desirous of expofing myself to a war with the natives; but my associates insisted that I should enter the harbour. I found it impossible to calm their fury, and for that reason, at last consented. We therefore weighed, and with a slight breeze from the Eastward, and the boats a-head, I entered the bay, and anchored at the distance of one hundred fathoms off shore.

According to the Report, three wounded, and five prisoners of war.

Saturday, August the 27th, moored in a bay at the mouth of a river, on the island of Formosa. As soon as I had got the ship moored, I ordered twenty-eight men on shore, under the command of Messrs. Baturin and Cruftiew, who went on board the shallop, and rowed towards the shore. As soon as they landed, they were met by fifty islanders, who held branches of trees in their hands; and as these people came without arms, Mr. Baturin received them kindly. They threw themselves first at the feet of my people, and by their signs gave them to understand, that they intreated forgiveness. This voluntary submission disarmed the rage of my companions, and several of them ran to the shore, and called out, that all was well. Upon these pacific appearances, the associates imagined that they might enjoy themselves in the habitations of the Indians, and declared to Meſſrs. Baturin and Cruſtiew, that they were defirous of going to the village. Their abſurd obſtinacy gave way to no perſuaſions; for in ſpite of the remonſtrances of thoſe gentlemen, twenty-two departed for the village. Being informed of this mutiny, I determined to go on ſhore myſelf, with fifteen other aſſociates, and immediately directed my march towards the village, which was not far off. I had ſcarcely made a few ſteps, before I heard a violent firing and horrible cries. The noiſe increaſed, and at laſt I ſaw my people retreating, and purſued by a number of blacks, who haſtily followed them. When they came near me, they rallied; but no more than ſeven of them were armed, the others being entirely naked, with ſeveral arrows ſticking in their bodies. I gave orders, therefore, for thoſe who had no arms, to retire towards the veſſel, and rallied the others; by whoſe aſſiſtance I ſtopped the crowd of iſlanders, among whom I obſerved ſeveral armed with our muſkets. Unfortunately for them, they knew not how to uſe them; and as they were more advanced than the others, they were quickly deſtroyed by our fire. Only two of them eſcaped, who threw down their muſkets to favour their flight. At the moment the Indians made their retreat, or rather fled, Mr. Kuzneczow arrived with twenty freſh companions, who chaced them out of their village, and at laſt ſet fire to it in ſeveral places. After the total defeat of the iſlanders, the dead were counted; and it was found that they amounted to upwards of two hundred, without reckoning thoſe who were wounded, and had fled.

On our return from this expedition, a party of the affociates difcovered a fmall harbour in the river, in which they found feven boats, and a bark in an unfinifhed ftate. They fet fire to the bark, and brought away the boats, which were loaded with the arms of the iflanders. As foon as this operation was ended, I went on board, and put the chiefs of the mutiny againft Meffrs. Baturin and Cruftiew in irons.

This accident abated the defire of the company to prolong their ftay. They therefore requefted me to feek another anchoring place. Taking advantage of the calm, I weighed, and by the help of the boats towed the veffel out of the found. We had fcarcely doubled the North point, before the current carried us to the Northward. At day break we found ourfelves oppofite a fmall bay, into which I determined to enter; but as the current tended to drive us beyond it, I came to anchor in twenty-fix fathom. About eight, a light breeze fprung up, and I was preparing to fet fail, when I faw two canoes rowing towards us. At ten they came near us, and one of them hailed us, crying out, Signor Houvritto, vai, vai. They made figns to us to follow them, which I did, having all my boats out to affift in cafe of accidents; but we happily entered into a very beautiful harbour, where I anchored near the Southern fhore, with a view to be fheltered from all winds. The depth of water was three fathom, and the veffel was fo near the land, that a man could jump on fhore.

According to the Report, eleven wounded, three prifoners of war, two having died.

N. B.

N. B. I muſt here obſerve, that I found in this ſeaſon, a violent current along the iſland Formoſa, which carried the veſſel* 1¼ leagues per hour; but I obſerved that this current cauſed the veſſel to follow all the ſinuoſities of the ſhore, and kept us always at the ſame diſtance from it.

Sunday, Auguſt the 28th. At anchor in the harbour† on the iſland of Formoſa, fine clear weather, but exceſſively hot. We had ſcarcely time to coil up our running rigging, before a prodigious number of iſlanders, of both ſexes, appeared with poultry, rice, ſugar-canes, hogs, oranges, and other fruits, which they exchanged with us for pins, needles, and other ſmall articles. Though theſe people behaved themſelves with circumſpection, I would not venture to place any confidence in them. For this reaſon, I conſtantly kept a dozen of the aſſociates armed. About three, P. M. a crowd of iſlanders appeared, having at their head a man cloathed in a droll manner, partly in the European, and partly in the Indian faſhion. On his head he wore a laced hat, a large ſword hung by his ſide, his ſtockings were made of cloth, and his ſhoes were no doubt of his own manufacture. This appearance ſurprized me, and I immediately ſent Mr. Kuzneczow to meet him; but as he could not underſtand his language, he brought him on board, where I learned, that he was a Spaniard of Manilla, who had lived ſeven or eight years among theſe iſlanders, and he had acquired the confidence of ſeveral cantons. He made me a very civil offer of his houſe; but as I thought it neceſſary to make a minute enquiry before I truſted him

* To the Northward; as it appears from the preceding text.
† A blank left in the MS by the copyiſt, and neglected to be filled up by the Count.

COUNT DE BENYOWSKY. 31

him, he informed me, that he had fled from Manilla to the ifland Formofa, in a veffel, manned by fix of his flaves; and that he had been forced to this proceeding, in confequence of his having, in a moment of rage, maffacred his wife, and a Dominican, whom he had found in her company. He faid his name was Don Hieronimo Pacheco, formerly Captain of the port of Cavith, at Manilla. This Spaniard affured me, that I might truft the people of that canton, who were the beft people in the world, and thought themfelves under an obligation to me for having ill-treated their enemies: for he informed me that the news of my conduct, with refpect to the*   had already arrived thither.

Upon this good news, I made him a prefent of a complete fuit of cloaths, with fome fhirts, and a good fabre; I promifed, befides, to give him fire arms, and other utenfils, provided he was careful in affifting us, during our ftay; upon which he promifed, and declared that he would not quit me during the whole time I fhould remain on the ifland. In fact, after having fpoken a fhort time to the iflanders, they retired, and he remained with us that night.

In the evening, having received information that our water was in a putrid ftate, I gave orders for taking in frefh water at day-break; in confequence of which I enquired of Don Hieronimo Pacheco, the place where we could obtain the beft water. He informed me that the iflanders would bring me good fpring water; but that there was a brook near an advanced rock, which he fhewed me, in which we might obtain the beft water in the world. But he warned me,

* Blank left in MS.

me, at the same time, that the islanders of that canton were at war with his friends, and that it would, for that reason, be necessary to send a party of armed men thither, to guard the sailors while they filled their casks. Upon this information, I gave instructions to Mr. Panow to go early with twelve associates on the business; and recommended to him, at the same time, to be upon his guard against a surprize. Not content with this precaution, I gave orders for awakening me before their departure; and having called them all before me, I recommended to them a second time to be on their guard. They set off at last at eight A. M. having been detained to set up some casks.

After the departure of the boats, I entered into conversation with the Spaniard, who appeared to be perfectly acquainted with the island. It was from him I learned, that part of the island on the Western side, was subject to the Chinese; but that six parts out of seven were independent, one-third part of which only were savages, among whom we had at present fallen. He assured me, that with very little assistance, he thought it practicable to conquer the island, and drive out the Chinese. His reasoning, and the combination of circumstances which he mentioned, pleased me, and I attended to him with so much the more willingness, as I had conceived the project of carrying his plan into execution. I therefore availed myself of the present opportunity, to propose that he should return into Europe with me. But this he positively refused, and assured me, that he was sufficiently acquainted with Europe, to thank heaven that he was out of it. To this he added, that he was become familiarised with

the

the manner of living in Formosa, and that as he had a good wife, and several children, neither his duty nor his inclination, would suffer him to leave them. Our conversation was interrupted by dinner.

According to the Report, eleven wounded, and three prisoners.

Monday, August the 29th. At anchor in port Maurice. Don Hieronimo remarked, that as the watering place was so near, he was surprized that our people did not return; and he begged me to send the shallop upon discovery. Mr. Kuzneczow immediately went with eight men, and returned about two, P.M. with the canoe and periagua in tow. As soon as I perceived them at a distance, I was surprized to see that some of them were covered with blood, and had arrows sticking in their bodies; and as I did not see either Mr. Panow or Mr. Loginow, I began to fear the worst. When the shallop came on board, Mr. Kuzneczow informed me, that Mr. Panow and Mr. Loginow were mortally wounded, and that John Popow was the first slain. After having received Messrs. Panow and Loginow, in order to give them every assistance, I enquired concerning the fact; and was informed, that Mr. Panow having visited the environs, and discovered no signs of any person being near, had been desirous of bathing, while the associates were at work, filling the casks; and that he himself had invited the others to follow his example. But he had scarcely laid aside his arms and cloaths, when he was attacked by twenty Indians, who shot at him with arrows; that Popow was one of the first who fell dead; and that afterwards Panow and Loginow fell, and all the others were wounded; and that certainly not one of them could have

have escaped, if Volinsky and Andre had not fired at the islanders from the canoe, into which they had retired. They added, that they dared not return on board and abandon Mr. Panow, who from time to time gave signs of life, as well as Mr. Loginow. They were in this situation when the shallop came to their relief.

After this information, I ran to my friend Panow, around whom I found all the company assembled ; but as I was desirous of hearing what he said, without interrupting him, I did not come forward. The following were the words of this invaluable friend, which will ever be present in my memory.

" My brothers," said he to his companions, " inform my friend, our commander, that my only regret at quitting life is, that I shall no longer be able to second and support his labours. Alas ! he is very far from seeing their conclusion. Tell him, that I love him as my life ; and that I should die contented, if I could have seen his merit and virtue recompensed. Intreat him in my name, not to revenge my death; but content himself with informing my brother of this misfortune. Take example, my friends, by me ; if I had followed the advice of our chief and friend, I had still lived. Respect and obey him as a father ; and thou, unhappy friend, Stephanow, lay aside thy haughtiness, and that hatred which is concealed in the bottom of thy heart, against this worthy friend.— Supply my place by thy fidelity to him." At these words I came forward ;—but my God, what a sight ! He seemed to have recovered all his powers. He grasped my hand, wept, and embraced me, but was unable to speak for a long time. At length, he exclaimed, " Alas, dear friend !

friend! I shall soon be no more.—I am myself the cause. —But forgive me.—My last wish is, that heaven may ever give thee friends like me.—Thou art worthy of them, and happy are they who shall know thy worth, as I do: May heaven grant, that this land, which soon shall cover my bones, may be thy patrimony."—The power of death interrupted his words, and deprived me of this dear and most valuable friend.

Loginow had paid the debt of nature a few instants before. I determined to bury them immediately; but as I was desirous of providing, that their bodies might not be disturbed, I begged Don Hieronimo, to speak with his friends, the islanders, and request permission to bury them on their territory. To this they readily consented, and we performed their funerals with the greatest order. I fired twenty-one guns on this occasion, and ordered Andreanow to engrave the following words on a stone.

" Here lies Vasili Panow, a Russian gentleman of illustrious birth and merit, the faithful friend of Mauritius Benyowsky, who was treacherously slain, with two other companions, John Loginow and John Popow, by the inhabitants of this island, on the 29th of August, 1771."

After the burial, Don Hieronimo declared to me, that his friends had determined to avenge the death of my companions; and that, consequently, they would proceed to attack their neighbours. My associates joined in this proposal for vengeance, which had already began by the massacre of our three Indian prisoners. While I was thus urged to come to a determination, the Spaniard informed me, that the canoe we saw rowing towards us, was filled with our enemies. My associates waited for no orders, but rushed on board the boats, and attacked them. Their first discharge flew thirteen, and the others they immediately brought on board, and hung at the yard-arm. I represented to them that this execution was enough, and that it was prudent to terminate our warfare here; but, alas! I preached to the deaf. They persisted in their determination to go in quest of the Indians, and make them feel their vengeance. As I saw I could make no impression on the minds of these enraged men, I was forced to promise to direct their proceedings, that they might not expose their lives to no purpose.

My resolution being once made, I entered seriously into the business. For this reason, I requested the Spaniard to guide my people towards the principal residence of the nation, who has given so bad a reception to us; and as he promised to accompany us, I gave him a good carabine. He requested leave to bring with him a couple of hundred of his Indian friends; in answer to which I represented, that these poor people might become the victims of their good intentions, and be slain by my comrades for want of knowing them. However, he removed my objection, by proposing, that every one of our party should wear a piece of white cloth on his left arm. This precaution appearing to me to be sufficient, I acquiesced in his demand, and he immediately went on shore to make his necessary preparations for the attack which was appointed to be made at day break.

About seven in the evening, I caused the boats to tow our vessel to the river of the massacre, where I anchored. At three, I ordered forty-six companions on shore, commanded by Messieurs Crustiew, Kuzneczow, Baturin, Wyndbladth, i

Wyndbladth, and Stephanow; and we only waited for Don Hieronimo, who arrived at four. They then proceeded inland, and we heard nothing till about three quarters after fix, when the noife of the mufquetry convinced me that the action had began. Soon after I faw a number of iflanders retiring towards a fteep mountain; and then it was that my companions on board directed their pieces at them, and made a dreadful flaughter. Thefe unhappy men, feeing themfelves preffed on one fide by my troops, and on the other by the iflanders, under the conduct of the Spaniard, threw themfelves proftrate upon the ground. I was then forced to declare to my whole party, that I would fire upon them if they continued the maffacre. On this meffage, the parties contented themfelves with making prifoners, the number of whom amounted to fix hundred and forty-three. The killed were reckoned and proved to be eleven hundred and fifty-fix. What furprized me the moft was, that among the wounded and prifoners there were a great number of women armed in the fame manner as the men.

Our expedition being thus ended, without any of our fide having received the flighteft wound, I went on fhore, and the Indians prefented me with the flaves. But as I refufed to keep any of them, the Spaniard chofe fifty, and abandoned the reft to his friends. I contented myfelf with carrying all their arms on board. About ten o'clock, a party of our friends of the iflanders, appeared with near two hundred women, children, and old men, whom they had made prifoners. The whole troop appeared to be overjoyed, and returned towards their habitations: but for my own part, being defirous of leaving a fpot which prefented

nothing

nothing but the defolation of the village, which our party had fet on fire, I retired with my veffel to our firft ftation.

According to the Report, eleven wounded.

Monday, Auguft the 30th. Having this day informed my friend the Spaniard, of my wifh to eftablifh a camp on fhore, he begged I would permit him to make the neceffary preparations. In confequence of my acceding to his requeft, he went on fhore, and about three o'clock he returned with about five hundred iflanders, who began to erect huts for us. Several were finifhed before evening. I therefore went on fhore myfelf with the women, and fuch of our people as were wounded, and a guard of fixteen men. At the clofe of the day, the iflanders fet a guard of forty men on our right flank, in order to fecure us, as they faid, from the attacks of the allies of the nation, with whom we had been at war.

At day-break, Don Hieronimo prefented his family to me, with a great number of his friends, and likewife acquainted me that Huapo, a prince of the country, was coming to exprefs his gratitude for my having avenged his fubjects upon the two nations who were their enemies. He informed me, that Huapo lived in a town about thirty or thirty-two leagues diftant inland; that the central parts of his dominions were well civilized, as was alfo the whole Weftern part of the ifland; the Eaftern coaft only being poffeffed by a favage people, among whom, however, he excepted the territory belonging to Huapo, which was inhabited by a gentle and induftrious race. He added, that the Prince Huapo could mufter twenty, or five and twenty
thoufand

COUNT DE BENYOWSKY.

thoufand armed men, notwithftanding which he was often difturbed in his capital, either by the Chinefe party, or their allies.

After this information, he infinuated that it would be eafy to conclude a treaty with this prince, to form eftablifh- ments in his country, the productions of which confifted in gold, cryftal, cinnabar, rice, fugar, cinnamon, filk, and par- ticularly the moft beautiful kinds of wood, might form advantageous branches of commerce; in exchange for which they would receive a quantity of hardware, iron, and Euro- pean cloth, to the profit of two hundred per cent. to the fellers. Such was our converfation, when it was inter- rupted by the arrival of the Bamini, or General. The Spaniard immediately haftened to meet him, and I caufed my companions to honour him with three difcharges of their mufquetry. When he had arrived near my barracks, he caufed a tent to be put up, the ground underneath being covered with a rich carpet, upon which he feated himfelf, and invited me to do the fame. The Spaniard ftood up to attend us, and ferve as my interpreter.

After the firft civilities, he demanded who I was; whence I came; what caufe had determined me to land on the ifland of Formofa? &c. I replied to his queftions in fhort, that I was a General of a kingdom, who, having been made prifoner of war, had effected my efcape with a party of my people to return to my own country; that having found the ifland of Formofa on my way, I anchored on the coaft to procure water; but that the cruelty exercifed by the two nations towards my companions, had demanded ven- geance, which I had fatisfied, and was preparing to return to my country.

He

He replied by requesting me to defer my departure till the arrival of Huapo, who having heard such wonders of me, had determined to come in person to visit me; in consequence of which, he had been dispatched with a party of troops to defend me against my enemies. To this compliment I replied, that I was truly sensible of the good disposition of the prince; that I should be infinitely flattered by the honour of seeing him; and still more in rendering him every service in my power. That the precaution of sending his troops to defend me, was superfluous, as no force could have any effect upon me. To this declaration I added the most flattering compliments to the Bamini, to whom I immediately made a present of a beautiful sabre, which, however, he politely refused, by observing, that he could not accept it without the knowledge of his master. After this conversation, he regaled me with tea and tobacco, at the same time that at intervals, he caused betel and the areca nut to be presented to me, with a small quantity of lime, all which together I chewed, and found most execrable.

The habits of this General consisted of a long red pautalon*, Chinese half boots, a white shirt, with a vest of black, and a red surplice, or outer garment, which had some buttons of coral, set in gold. His head was covered with a bonnet of straw, exceedingly pointed, and the upper extremity was ornamented with horse hair, dyed red. His arms consisted of a sabre, a lance, and a bow, with a quiver, containing twenty-five arrows. The troops who attended him were entirely naked, except a piece of blue

---

* The pautalon is a close garment fitted to the body, and all of one piece from head to foot. T.

blue cloth round their middle, and their arms were lances and bows.

According to the Report, seven wounded.

Wednesday, August the 31st. This day all our huts being finished, I landed all my people, and having raised two epaulements, I placed four pieces of cannon upon them, two on each flank of my camp. No more than eight men remained on board, as a guard.

Our repast was not of long duration. The Formosian General eat with astonishing rapidity, without speaking a word; and after he had devoured a quantity of rice, with some pieces of roast meat, he rose, and began to chew his betel, and smoke tobacco. As I was desirous of making my court to him, I followed his example, though my palate suffered for it. After dinner we walked round my camp. When we came near a battery, Bamini requested me to order some cannon shot to be fired. I immediately gave orders to fix a butt at five hundred paces distance, and pointed the pieces myself. At the second fire, the boat which the islanders had exposed as a butt, was broken in pieces; at which the Formosian General testified the greatest surprize. To increase his astonishment, I gave orders to my companions to take their arms, and fire at a plank at eighty paces distance. Very few of their shot missed; and as the plank was shot through, this exercise gave him great satisfaction, and induced him to spare no flattering expressions on the occasion.

About five in the evening, Bamini received a courier, who announced the approaching arrival of the Huapo. The General therefore left me, and went to prepare a camp.

camp. I embraced this opportunity to give orders for some fire-works; and at the same time give the Prince the diverſion of ſeeing our military exerciſe. The iſlanders, in the mean time, had become ſo familiar with us, as to leave their daughters freely in our camp; and it is remarkable, that there was no inſtance of any pilfering committed by them, though our people were exceedingly negligent. I employed the night in making ſeveral different fuſees, and a large ſerpent for the fire-works.

At day-break, Don Hieronimo waited on me, to acquaint me with the arrival of the Prince, and adviſed me to ſend two of my officers to meet him, inſtead of going myſelf. As he offered to ſerve as their interpreter, I immediately ſent Meſſrs. Cruſtiew and Kuzneczow, with ſix of our aſſociates armed, to attend them. After their departure, I aſcended an hill to ſee their camp prepared. I perceived that the arrangement was made after a certain order; the tent of the Prince being in the centre, and the others round about it. About eight o'clock, I ſaw the troops march in, and at laſt the Prince arrived.

Their order was as follows: Firſt came ſix horſemen, with a kind of ſtandard. Theſe were followed by a troop of infantry with pikes. After theſe came thirty or forty horſemen, and another body of infantry with bows. A troop armed with clubs and hatchets came next; and laſt of all came the Prince, attended by twelve or fifteen officers, mounted on ſmall, but beautiful horſes. The reſt of the troops came after without any regular order. On their arrival at the camp, every one lodged where he could, and there was no guard ſet.

About

About eleven o'clock, Don Hieronimo returned to invite me, in the name of the Prince, to come and see him; and he brought several horses, though the distance was very short. I immediately mounted, and soon arrived at the Prince's tent. His appearance struck me at first sight. He was between thirty and thirty-five years of age, about five feet three inches high, of a strong and vigorous make, with a lively eye and majestic carriage. Upon being introduced to him, I found Mr. Crustiew already in great familiarity with him; who said to me in Russian, this youth would do our business, if we proposed to remain at Formosa; and his good disposition would permit him to assure me, that I might be King of the island whenever I pleased. He had scarcely spoken, when the Prince addressed me by our interpreter, assuring me, that I was welcome on the island; and that he had heard, with the greatest satisfaction, of the manner we had treated his enemies, for which he thought it proper to make his grateful acknowledgements. To this he added, that he had no doubt but that I was the person whose coming was announced by the Prophets, who had foretold that a stranger should arrive with strong men, who should deliver the Formosans from the Chinese yoke: in consequence of which he had determined to pay me a visit, and make me an offer of all his power and forces to support and obey me. This commencement changed my system, and the Spaniard insensibly led me to play a new part, by assuring the Huapo that I was a great Prince, who had visited Formosa, with the intention of satisfying myself concerning the position of the Chinese, and to fulfil the wishes of the inhabitants of the island, by delivering them from the power of that treacherous people.

Upon this information, I thanked the Prince for his good intentions, and affured him that I fhould always make it a part of my glory to contribute to the happinefs of a nation who were fo fortunate as to be governed by a Prince of fuch wifdom and penetration as himfelf. But that upon the prefent occafion, having came only for the purpofe of contracting alliances with the natives of the ifland, and more efpecially with the Huapo, I fhould explain myfelf more at large on another occafion; as thefe affairs and interefts required to be treated of in fecret. The Prince appeared to be fatisfied with this reply, and invited me to dine with him. Meffrs. Cruftiew and Kuzneczow were likewife of the party, as well as the Spaniard, whom the Prince took into favour, and caufed him to be immediately clothed after the fafhion of the country; at the fame time that he gave him a belt and a fabre, as marks of diftinction.

After dinner, the Prince propofed to vifit my camp, and while our horfes were getting ready, Mr. Cruftiew went before, to prepare the men to render due honour to the Prince, who was attended by near fifty officers on horfeback, and his whole body of troops following him at the diftance of about three hundred paces. When we came in fight of our camp, the cannonade began, and the aftonifhed Sovereign was in great danger of fharing the fate of his officers, moft of whom were thrown by the frifks and leaps of their horfes, who were not accuftomed to the noife, and could not be made to advance. We therefore difmounted, and arrived at the camp, where the affociates faluted the Prince with three difcharges of mufquetry, and the ceremony ended with twenty guns from the fhip.

ship. This honourable and noisy reception gave him infinite pleasure, and as a mark of friendship, he put his hand in mine, and in this manner we proceeded to my tent, followed only by his General and three other officers. He soon resumed his discourse, by giving a detail of the reasons, which made him desirous of driving the Chinese out of the island; and he left me no reason to doubt, that vanity induced him to declare war upon them. His inclination, in this respect, would certainly have been highly advantageous to me, if I had proposed to remain in the country; but as my determination was to return as speedily as possible into Europe, I thought it would be very unsafe to engage in enterprizes, which, even on the most happy event, would not make my return the less necessary. But, on the other hand, being well convinced, that by an alliance with this Prince, I should be enabled to propose the establishment of a colony on the island to some European power, I resolved to do every thing in my power to preserve his favourable disposition towards me.

About four in the evening, the Prince expressed a desire to see the vessel: I accordingly ordered thirty of my companions to go on board immediately; and afterwards sent Mr. Crustiew to attend him, with directions to amuse him as long as possible, that I might have time to prepare my fireworks. All was ready at half past seven, when I conducted the Prince to a place where he might see the whole fire, which began after the discharge of three great guns. He expressed his admiration at this exhibition, but informed me that the Chinese made the same. When the fireworks were ended, the Prince retired, after giving me his belt and sabre, as a token that he would share with
me

me his power over his army, which amounted to eight thousand men, of whom only two hundred and fixty were horsemen.

As foon as the Prince was gone, I affembled a Committee, in which I declared Mr. Stephanow our equal, and capable of being admitted to our confidence; and I gave orders to Mr. Cruftiew, to acknowledge him as fuch before the whole company. At the fame time I gave directions for preparing the prefents for the Prince Huapo, which confifted of two pieces of cannon I had brought as ballaft, thirty good mufkets, fix barrels of gunpowder, two hundred iron balls, and fifty pounds of match. At day-break, I detached Meffrs. Cruftiew, Wyndbladth, and Kuzneczow, to inform the Prince of the prefents; to which I added thirty common Japanefe fabres, one fabre very elegantly wrought for himfelf, and twenty others for his principal officers.

About eight o'clock, Don Hieronimo came to announce a vifit on the part of the Prince, who came attended only by his confidential officers, as well to receive the prefents, as to treat with me on objects of the greateft importance. About ten he arrived, and as I had the whole intermediate time to converfe with, and make enquiries of the good Spaniard, I had my anfwers in readinefs. In the firft place, the Prince caufed a very magnificent tent to be erected near mine, in which very rich carpets were laid; and here it was that he received me. He began the converfation, by thanking me for the prefents which he had accepted on my part, and then proceeded to make the following demands:

1. Whether I could leave part of my people behind to remain with him till my return?

2. Whether

2. Whether I could bring back a number of troops armed with muskets, and skilled in the management of cannon; and what would be the expence of maintaining one thousand men?

3. Whether I could procure for him vessels armed with cannon, and captains to command them?

4. Whether I would accept the concession he would make me of the province of Havangsin; which, with its cities, towns, and inhabitants, he would cede to me in propriety, on condition that I should support him with Europeans, until he should have driven the Chinese out of his dominions, at which period he would yield up to me his whole kingdom?

5. And lastly, whether I would assist him in an expedition he was going to make against one of his neighbours, on condition that he should allow me a certain sum, with other advantages?

6. That after having received my answer, he should propose to me to enter into a permanent treaty of friendship with him?

These questions appeared to me, to be the work of Don Hieronimo; though he would never acknowledge that they sprung from his brain.—My answer was as follows:

1. That having a very long voyage to make, I could not leave any of my people behind me.

2. That it was in my power to bring armed troops and cannon along with me; but that the transport of one thousand men, would cost one thousand five hundred pounds of gold; and the maintainance of such a body of troops, would cost yearly, five hundred pounds of gold.

3. That

3. That I could procure armed veſſels, ſuch as he demanded; but that each veſſel of twenty guns, would coſt fifty pounds of gold.

4. That I ſhould accept the commiſſion of the province of Havangſin, ſuch as he was deſirous of beſtowing it; on condition that I ſhould ſupport him againſt the Chineſe, until they were driven out of his dominions; and that he ſhould veſt the property of his kingdom in me.

5. That though the ſeaſon preſſed my departure, yet, with a view to teſtify my attachment to the Prince Huapo, I ſhould be ready to aſſiſt him in his military operations, without demanding any recompence, except what he ſhould voluntarily pleaſe to beſtow upon my companions.

6. That I was ready to conclude a treaty of friendſhip with him, and hoped, that, provided he acted with as much ſincerity as myſelf, I ſhould ſoon ſee him ſovereign of the whole iſland of Formoſa, and in a ſituation to avenge himſelf and family on the Emperor of China, for the perſecutions they had formerly ſuffered from that potentate.

The Prince having liſtened with the greateſt attention to my replies, cauſed them to be written upon a paper, on which I perceived that his demands were likewiſe written. He then cauſed the queſtion to be put to me, whether my reſolution was invariable; and upon my anſwering in the affirmative, he propoſed to make the ceremony of the oath; to which I conſented with all my heart. During the time the preparations were making, I embraced the opportunity of preſenting him with a ſabre, and a pair of choice piſtols. I did the ſame to his
Generaliſſimo,

Generaliſſimo, and begged he would diſtribute the others to the moſt diſtinguiſhed officers of the army.

Soon afterwards the Prince informed me that all was in readineſs, and went out with me. We approached a ſmall fire, upon which we threw ſeveral pieces of wood. A cenſor was then given to me, and another to him. Theſe were filled with lighted wood, upon which we threw incenſe; and turning towards the Eaſt, we made ſeveral fumigations. After the ceremony, the General read the queſtions, and my anſwers; and whenever he pauſed, we turned towards the Eaſt, and repeated the fumigation. At the end of the reading, the Prince pronounced imprecations and maledictions upon him who ſhould break the treaty of friendſhip between us; and Don Hieronimo directed me to do the ſame, and afterwards interpreted my words. After this we threw our fire upon the ground, and thruſt our ſabres in the ground up to the hilts. The aſſiſtants immediately brought a quantity of large ſtones, with which they covered our arms, and the Prince then embraced me, and declared that he acknowledged me as his brother.

On our return to his tent, he cauſed a complete habit, made according to the faſhion of the country, to be brought, with which I was cloathed; and in this manner we ſet out for the camp of the Prince, where we were received with every demonſtration of joy. On our arrival at his tent, dinner was ſerved up in a more plentiful manner than uſual; and as the Prince had requeſted the company of my officers, I cauſed them all to attend, except Mr. Baturin, who commanded in my abſence. During the whole time of our meal, our ears were ſtunned

with a very noisy kind of music, and the continued beating of drums. At our rising from table, I was not a little surprized to see the two pieces of cannon planted at the entrance of the camp. But Mr. Wyndbladth informed me, that my associates had paid the Prince the compliment of placing them there; at which he was exceedingly well satisfied. At four o'clock, all the principal officers being assembled, with the Bamini at their head, the Prince spoke to them for a long time; and after having ended his discourse, he dismissed them. Half an hour afterwards, the Prince and myself, accompanied by the Spaniard, mounted our horses, and passed through the camp; where I was saluted by all the officers. The manner of salutation consisted in each officer touching with his left hand, the stirrup of him whom he salutes. When we had made several turns in the camp, we returned to the Prince's tent, who urged me to come to a determination to accompany him in his enterprize; and, as I had resolved to assist him, I thought it proper to make some enquiries into the subject. The information I received was as follows: The Prince Hapuasingo, Sovereign of a neighbouring territory, who was allied and tributary to the Chinese, had demanded, in consequence of a private quarrel of individuals, that Huapo should put several of his own subjects to death; and as Huapo did not chuse to comply with his wishes, he made war upon him, in which Huapo was not successful, but was constrained at last to pay a considerable fine to Hapuasingo: and though he had fulfilled the treaty, yet the Chinese Governor demanded a further reimbursement, on pretence of the expences he had been at in bringing his troops into the field; and upon this plea
the

the Chinese, with the assistance of Hapuasingo, had usurped one of his finest and most fertile provinces. That, considering the present as a favourable moment to avenge himself on his neighbour, and the Chinese, he hoped, by my assistance, to bring his wishes to a happy termination. He informed me, moreover, that the army of Hapuasingo did not consist of above five or six thousand men; and that the number of Chinese who could come to his assistance, were about one thousand, of which no more than fifty were armed with muskets. That the distance of Hapuasingo's capital was not more than a day and a half's march from the place we then were at; and that the roads were very good.

Upon this information, I promised my ally to maintain his quarrel, and required no more than one day to get ready, and sixty horses for my companions and their equipage. My promise transported the Prince with the greatest joy, and induced him to declare Don Hieronimo his General of cavalry. I thanked him for this mark of confidence; but as I had need of him near me to serve as an interpreter, I begged the Prince to cause him to be declared in the mean time a principal officer, bearing the Prince's orders and mine, which were necessary to be implicitly obeyed. The Prince promised that every thing should be done according to my desire; and then I quitted him, to return to my camp with the Spaniard. Immediately on my return, I assembled my intimate friends, to whom I explained my interests and intention, which was supported by the assurance of our being able to establish a colony hereafter on this island, under the guarantee and friendship of the Prince Huapo. But as it was of the utmost importance that the company should consent, I directed my friends to excite them to make a request to me to carry his project into execution. At day-break, the effect of this stratagem exceeded my expectation. When I came out of my tent, or rather barrack, I saw two deputies, who, in the name of the company, requested me to permit a certain number of them to assist the good Prince Huapo in his war against the Chinese. On this message I assembled the company, to whom I represented, that I thought it improper to comply with their demand, because it was an absurdity for us to interfere on such slight grounds in this quarrel, so much as to send some of our number to assist in the enterprize. That an undertaking of this kind might effectually destroy all our hopes respecting the island, as it would be sufficient for this purpose, that the Prince Huapo might be beaten. My speech altered the countenance of my companions; but I soon revived their spirits, by declaring, that I was no less sensible than themselves, of the importance of the services we might render to Huapo; but as I was convinced that our whole reputation in the place depended on this measure, I begged them to chuse forty resolute men of their number, with whom I would myself go upon this expedition. On this declaration they demanded to cast lots, and assured me, that they unanimously approved of my determination. I therefore left the care of regulating the lots to Mr. Crustiew, and nominated the officers myself, as follow:

The Left.	*The Center.*	*The Right.*
Mr. Kuzneczow,	Myself,	Mr. Wyndbladth,
Mr. Bocsarew,	Mr. Stephanow,	Mr. Baturin,
13 Associates.	Mr. Sibaew,	13 Associates.
—	16 Associates.	—
15	—	15
	18	

After

COUNT DE BENYOWSKY. 53

After having declared and fixed this order, I caused ammunition to be diftributed, and ordered four patereros, which belonged to the fhallop, to be got ready, with fixty rounds of ball, and twenty of rubbifh for each; and with a view that thefe pieces might be more effectually ferviceable, I caufed piquets to be fhod with iron to drive into the ground, and provided each with a focket at top to fix the piece. This commiffion was very ingenioufly performed by Mr. Baturin. About ten we received fixty horfes; but as eight more were wanting to tranfport our patereros and ammunition, I difpatched Don Hieronimo, who brought them. This day we dined all together; and after having placed the command, in my abfence, in the hands of Mr. Cruftiew, and Meffrs. Gurcfinin, Meder, and Czurin under him, I took my leave of them.

Thurfday, September the 1ft, 1771*. On the ifland of Formofa, marching to affift the Prince Huapo in his war. At four, P. M. I entered the camp of the Prince, who immediately ftruck his tents, and prepared to follow me, after having appointed one hundred and twenty horfemen, and four hundred infantry to clear the way. We did not halt till eleven o'clock, near a brook called Halavith. At four in the morning we renewed our march; and at feven Don Hieronimo, as we were defcending a mountain, made

---

* Here is an inadvertence of the Count, with regard to time. Under the date of Auguft the 31ft, are included the adventures of three whole days, as appears by the fucceffion of the hours. It feems probable, that during his ftay on fhore, he kept minutes of the principal events, and afterwards divided them into day's tranfactions by memory; and that the prefent date fhould be September the 3d; a fuppofition, which, by including the three following days in one, agrees very well with the Prince's affertion, (page 51.) that Hapualingo's capital was diftant only a journey of one day and a half. T.

me take notice of a small town belonging to Huapo; but as we left it near a league distant on the right, I could not judge of its extent with any precision. Its environs, however, seemed to be well cultivated. At nine we halted to refresh our horses, whom they fed with rice; and, after having pitched our camp on the border of a wood, we remained there till four in the afternoon, to avoid marching in the noon-day heat, which was extreme.

Friday, September the 2d. At four in the afternoon, we resumed our march, and continued our progress till ten at night; at which time we stopped in a valley, where we received twenty oxen loaded with rice, a quantity of fruit, and several casks of a kind of brandy. At three in the morning we set out again, and continued till nine, when we came to a village with a pond of water near it, in which we caught some excellent fish. As I found this village abandoned by its inhabitants, I imagined it belonged to the enemy; and the information I received from the Spaniard, confirmed this opinion. From this, I had no doubt, but that Hapuasingo was apprized of our invasion; and for that reason I should have been glad to have conversed with the Prince. And as he only followed me at the distance of a march, I thought it proper to wait for him.

Saturday, September the 3d. Encamped near a deserted village. The Prince Huapo did not appear till near five o'clock. I took the liberty to remonstrate with him for his slowness; which he excused, by representing, that his troops being loaded with provisions, could not march so quickly. At three in the morning we resumed our march; and at half-past four, being in the van with Don Hieronimo, we observed thirty or forty horsemen before us. I immediately

diately advanced with six associates, and the Spaniard. They paid no attention to us till they supposed us to be in their reach; and then, turning about, they came on full gallop, with their lances in their hands. Their courage was, however, not a little disconcerted, by the first report of our fire arms, which dismounted two of them, whom we made prisoners. From them we learned, by the examination of Don Hieronimo, that we should soon see the main army advancing towards us; and that we were then at no greater distance from the capital than a six hours march.

The rest of my troops having joined me, we continued our march without seeing any thing remarkable, except some villages on our right and left, and a prodigious quantity of cattle. As we were now very near the enemy, I pitched my camp to advantage, and fixed my patereros for its defence. About noon we perceived a troop of about an hundred horse, who approached to examine us at leisure; which I permitted, with the intention of familiarizing them with us.

Sunday, September the 4th. At two o'clock we observed another body of upwards of fifty horsemen on our right; and at last, a great number of troops, amounting at least to ten or twelve thousand men, but very few cavalry. As I made no movement, these troops began to prepare for the attack; and at the same time I put my men in readiness to keep up a continued fire. I was desirous of working the patereros myself; and for that reason had them brought near the center. About half past three, a party of about twenty horse approached to insult an outpost which I had set. As soon as they came within reach, I fired a few shot at them, which had no other effect than

that

that of intimidating them. They soon, however, recovered from their apprehensions, and disposed their whole troop to attack me; but their reception was so warm, that near two hundred were slain. This loss, instead of checking their impetuosity, appeared to increase their fury. They came on a second time; and, after very considerable loss, were forced at last to retreat. I pursued them for two hours, when the approach of night obliged me to halt.

The Prince did not come up with us till eleven, and a council was held, wherein it was determined to attack the enemy in our turn. At two I disposed our troops in order, and placed a division of my comrades on each wing, and myself, with my own division, occupied the center. At three we marched towards the enemy; and when we had arrived very near them, we waited only for the break of day to commence the attack. At three quarters after four the attack began; but the noise of our patereros and muskets was sufficient to put them to flight. This loss was so much the more considerable, as they had no thought of providing for a retreat. The greatest number retired into the town. The spirit of the troops of Huapo likewise carried them before us, in which situation the enemy, no longer intimidated by our fire arms, turned upon them, and began a dreadful slaughter, which however ceased at our approach, as soon as we could make use of our arms.

While the battle began in the city, Don Hieronimo proposed to send fifty horse to the other side of the town, to prevent Hapuasingo from escaping. I immediately gave orders for twenty of my associates, under Messrs. Stephanow and Baturin, to perform this office; and they were so fortunate as to make Hapuasingo prisoner, with four of his

women,

COUNT DE BENYOWSKY. 57

women, with whom he was endeavouring to make his escape. This capture decided the whole quarrel; for he promised to Don Hieronimo to comply with all the demands of Huapo, on condition the lives of himself and family should be spared. When he came before me, I declared that he was my prisoner; and that so far from being desirous of putting him to death, I should wish to cultivate his friendship, on condition of his giving every satisfaction to Huapo, who was justly irritated. About eleven, all the noise of war having subsided, I caused enquiry to be made after Huapo, in order to put Hapuasingo into his hands: but as this Prince was desirous of being a spectator, instead of an actor, he did not return till about noon; at which time I delivered Hapuasingo to him, on condition that he should not suffer any personal injury: and then I thought proper to encamp on the other side of the town.

Monday, September the 5th. In camp, near the Town of Xiaguamay, on the island of Formosa. At three, I received a visit from Huapo, accompanied with Bamini, who overwhelmed me with protestations of friendship; and, as I understood that all the operations of war were ended, I declared to the Prince my resolution to return, and set sail, as early as possible. This information was very unpleasant to him; but as he was convinced that he should not succeed in attempting to dissuade me from my purpose, he contented himself with entreating me to return as soon as possible, which I solemnly promised to do. This day we regulated the order of my departure; and the manner in which the province was to supply me with provisions, pursuant to the order of the Prince. In the evening, Don Hieronimo requested me to leave one of my companions

VOL. II.   I   behind

behind to affift him in his functions. On his preffing entreaty, I perfuaded young Loginow, whofe brother had been flain, to fix his refidence here till my return, in order to learn the language of the country, and affift our future operations.

The next morning I received the Prince's prefents, confifting in fome fine pearls, eight quintals of filver, and twelve pounds of gold. He apologized for the fmallnefs of the prefent, on account of his diftance from home, and becaufe my precipitate departure prevented his making it more confiderable. But with regard to myfelf, he fent me a box, containing one hundred pieces of gold, weighing in the whole thirteen pounds and a quarter; and gave orders to Bamini to accompany us with one hundred and twenty horfemen, to provide for our fubfiftence. Don Hieronimo likewife attended me as interpreter; and I gave orders for our departure at four in the evening.

Tuefday, September the 6th. After renewing our oaths and engagements with the Prince Huapo, we took our leave at three; and I had the fatisfaction to fee, that he did not part with us without tears. At four we began our march; and at the moment that my troop filed off, I made the Prince a prefent of my patereros, with the greateft part of the ammunition we had brought; at the fame time, that I requefted the favour that he would appoint our companion Loginow, who ftaid behind, his General of artillery. This he promifed in his prefence. Our march was very eafy and pleafant; for we were mounted on good horfes, and went by the moft direct road; and we were plentifully fupplied with provifion of all kinds, at the places where we halted.

Wednefday,

Wednefday, September the 7th. We continued our march through a pleafant and well cultivated country, watered with fine rivers, and very populous, as we could judge by the fmall diftance from one village to another. Whenever we refted, we were furrounded by a multitude of people, who brought prefents. Their good will was, however, chargeable to us by the returns we made. This day I made an offer to Bamini, of part of the gold and filver I had received of the Prince; but he pofitively refufed to accept it, faying, that he was contented in poffeffing my friendfhip, which he begged I would preferve till my return.

Thurfday, September the 8th. At three, P. M. we at length arrived at our camp very much fatigued, and exhaufted with the exceffive heat we had fuffered, as there had been no rain during the whole of our excurfion. General Bamini, after having given the neceffary orders to the chief inhabitants of the country refpecting our fubfiftence, took leave of me. He embraced all my affociates one after the other; and at the inftant of his departure, he put into my hands a collar of pearls on the part of the Prince, and a rich tent, with a carpet of fuperior workmanfhip.

After the departure of Bamini, I received the congratulations of my companions, and faw with the greateft fatisfaction, that Mr. Cruftiew had difpofed of every thing in the beft manner. In the evening, being defirous of giving my companions a mark of liberality, I diftributed among them the whole of the filver and gold by weight; and I put the pearls and the box of gold, which had been privately given me, into the hands of my intimate friends, the officers and women. When the affociates were informed, that I had kept nothing for myself, they proposed each to give me a half share of their possessions; but I refused, and begged them to preserve the whole, and to reserve their generous disposition for some future occasion, if I should find it necessary to apply to them for assistance; in which case I should not scruple to have recourse to them for a loan.

This conduct on my part seemed to elevate their minds, and gave me a perfect empire over them. And at this moment I was convinced, that though a man of genius may avail himself of his superiority over common minds, yet, an act of generosity at a proper time, is worth a thousand speeches, however eloquent.

After the company had separated, none remained but my intimate friends, who endeavoured to persuade me to fix my residence at Formosa, in the province which the Prince Huapo had ceded to me. They represented, that the associates being this day witnesses of the mildness of my command, and guided by the most profound respect towards me, would be sufficient to form a colony; and that we might besides send, by the way of China, at some future time, certain emissaries into Europe, to engage some sovereign power in our interests; or, at all events, to raise recruits. Their opinions were so well supported, that at last I could make no other objection, than my own peculiar interests; namely, that I had a wife who loved and was attached to me by the bond of marriage, and who probably at that instant had a child, as she was with child at the time of my departure. But, in order to conceal my own private sentiments, though I communicated as much to them as I thought necessary, I did not fail to represent, that

that a person on the spot could do more than a thousand written messages; and that, therefore, upon my return in Europe, I might reasonably expect to obtain the favour of some court, as we could assure them the greatest advantages; such as that of forming an establishment in the Aleuthes islands, to carry on the rich commerce of furs; to open the trade of Japan; to form an establishment on the islands Lequeio; and lastly, to establish an European colony on the island of Formosa. I expressed my firm assurance, that these propositions would insure our happy success; and that in case the European courts should abandon us, we should always have it in our power to carry our project into execution, by the fitting out of private vessels. This reasoning at last determined them, and they requested permission to explain it to the whole company; for they assured me, that every individual was resolved to demand my consent, not to quit the island of Formosa.

After having gained this essential point, I retired to rest, which was very necessary to me; and did not awake till ten the next morning. When I arose, I received the deputies of the company, who, having been informed by Mr. Crustiew of my intention, had paid respect to it, though they had already made a different determination themselves; for which reason they confined their request to that of desiring that I would not quit the island until the 12th of the month, in order that they might have time to recover themselves from the fatigues and difficulties they had undergone. I granted their request with so much the more readiness, as in reality the fatigue of our march had been excessive, and the good conduct of my companions was such as led me to comply with every request they might make. I therefore

fore promised to remain on the island until the 12th; and my consent was followed by expressions of the most lively gratitude on their part. This day the whole company dined together.

Friday, September the 9th. After dinner, I gave orders for putting an end to all work, that all the associates might follow their recreations, except a guard of six on board, and four on shore. The officers likewise seized this opportunity to make some excursions into the country; and, for my part, I employed myself in drawing up some notes respecting the project of forming a colony on the island. These were as follow:

Some notions and details respecting the island of Formosa; and the plan of forming an European colony there.

The island of Formosa is called by the Chinese, Touaiouai; and by the natives Paccahimba. It is one of the finest and richest islands of the known world. The soil, in an infinity of places, produces two harvests of rice and other grain, with a great variety of trees, fruits, plants, animals, and birds. Cattle, sheep, goats, and poultry, are very abundant here. This island is intersected by great rivers, lakes, and waters, abounding with fish. It has many commodious harbours, bays, and sounds on its coasts. Its mountains produce gold, silver, cinnabar, white and brown copper; and likewise pit coal.

The island of Formosa is divided into eight principalities, three of which, situated on the Western side, are governed by the Chinese, and peopled by the same nation. Every year an Ambassador arrives from China, to receive tribute from these three provinces, which is raised by a poll tax; and the Emperor of China keeps five hundred vessels

vessels for the purpose of annually exporting this tribute, which consists of a large quantity of rice, wheat, millet, salt, beans, raw silk, cotton, gold, silver and mercury. The Governors of these three provinces continually extend their possessions, either by alliance or intrigue, in such a manner, that they have obtained several towns and districts from their neighbours.

The inhabitants of the island are civilized, except those who live on the Eastern coasts. They are of an effeminate disposition, without any marks of courage; given to indolence, and are indebted to the goodness of the climate for their preservation, as the soil supports them with very little labour. If we except the three Chinese provinces, the mines on the island are no where worked. They are contented to wash the sand to extract gold out of it; and if they find pearls in the shells, it is by mere accident. The common people of Formosa are cloathed only in blue cotton cloth; the towns are always built in the plains; and the villages are upon the mountains. The houses of people of condition among them are extensive and beautiful, but plain. Those of the people are mere huts; and they are not permitted to build better. Most of them are covered with straw and reeds, and are divided or separated from each other by rows of pallisadoes; their moveables are nothing more than what necessity has rendered indispensible. In the houses of men of rank, there are advanced rooms, in which they eat, receive strangers, and divert themselves. The apartments of the women are always separate, and apart from the house. Though they are built within the court, no one is permitted to approach them. In this country there are no inns for travellers;
but

but thofe who are on a journey fit themfelves down near the firft houfe they come to, and the mafter of the houfe foon after receives them, and entertains them with rice and fome flefh meat, with tobacco and tea.

The only commerce of the inhabitants of Formofa is with fome Japanefe barks, who touch here, and with the Chinefe.

In each province there are five or fix towns, which have eftablifhments for inftructing youth in reading and writing. Their characters of writing, and for the expreffion of numbers, are as difficult as thofe of the Chinefe. Their pronunciation is fometimes quick and elevated, and at other times flow and grave. They obtain their books from China. There are forcerers or diviners here, who have a great influence over the people. Their religion confifts in adoring one God, and in the performance of good offices to their neighbours. The provinces which are not conquered, are governed by Princes or Kings, who have an abfolute power over their fubjects. None of thefe laft, without any exception of the great men, has any property in the lands. They receive the advantages of their lands, fubject to the good pleafure of the Prince, as well as the gains they derive from the multitude of their flaves. Some of the principal people have as many as one, or even two thoufand. The princes always compofe their councils of their principal military officers, and always keep their troops on foot, divided into four, five, and fix divifions, which remain conftantly on the frontiers. The body guard of the Sovereigns confifts of no more than five or fix hundred young men, born of the principal families among their fubjects. The ancient foldiers are employed in the command of towns or villages;

villages, for there is no village in Formosa which is not commanded by a soldier, and each commander is obliged to present annually to his superior, a list of the people under his jurisdiction. Formosa being surrounded by the sea, these princes constantly maintain a certain number of vessels, each of which has two masts and twenty-four oars; they do not use cannon, but make great use of artificial fire works.

A plan for forming a colony on the island Formosa.

Previous to entering into the project of establishing a colony, it will be necessary to mention a few maxims.

1. Before any attempt is made to found a colony, it must be previously considered, whether its establishment be intended to be made upon a military or mercantile footing; and whether it be properest to cultivate the commerce of exchange, of œconomy, or of industry?

2. In the formation of a colony, it is necessary to conciliate the benevolence, the confidence, and the attachment of the natives of the country. When a superiority is acquired over their minds, their own proper impulses will render the colonists masters of the country; and in this case it will be easy to establish the constitution intended to be adopted, or to set on foot that kind of commerce which is proposed. The constitution may likewise be maintained with very little force, and the country defended against the attempts of foreigners.

3. It is necessary that the basis of the colony be military, animated by glory; for in that case it may conquer, but will never be conquered.

4. The salubrity of the place of establishment must be ascertained, and no labour neglected that may tend to procure this advantage so necessary to humanity,

5. It is required to make sure of the possession of good harbours, fertile grounds, and the course of the principal rivers, to comprehend all the branches of commerce; to carry cultivation to its utmost extent; and to facilitate by these two branches the different departments of industry.

6. In an infant colony it is proper to avoid fortifications of the first order, and to establish the chief place in the inner part of the country; where, consequently, it will be out of the reach of any sudden stroke. In this manner, when a colony is master of the country, the first attack of an enemy, and the capture of a post, established near the sea coast, will not decide the possession.

7. The multiplicity of councils, and the number of people employed, must be reduced to the smallest number, which can be dispensed with in the management of the affairs of the colony.

8. Luxury must be banished; but it will be proper to establish external marks of grandeur, according to the different ranks of citizens who form the colony; as by this means emulation will be encouraged.

9. Industry must be encouraged and recompensed by gradual transition from one class of citizens to another, and by procuring to the colonists the sale of their commodities. The money which is thus disperfed among the colonists in the purchase of productions, always returns to government in the course of exchanges.

10. Restraint

10. Restraint of conscience must be banished and prohibited for ever. Happy is he who shall establish toleration, and the belief of one only God.

11. A code of laws ought to be established in favour of slavery; in which, means should be appointed to enable this unfortunate order of men to arrive, by the force of labour and industry, to the rank of free citizens.

12. Population being the only true foundation of national force, it will be necessary that government should encourage it by sacrifices, and preserve it by law. It will succeed by punishing libertinism severely, and by granting privileges and gratifications to fathers and mothers, who shall have presented a number of children, the issue of their marriages.

It is therefore on these principles that I should wish to establish a colony on the island of Formosa, supposing that an European power should accept my offers.

1. I should demand, that this power should confine itself to the Suzerainity; and, on this principle, it should possess no other advantages but such as are derived from subsidies, and the commerce of its European subjects.

2. Conformably to this plan, I should require three armed vessels; one of four hundred and fifty tons, another of two hundred and fifty tons, and another of one hundred and fifty tons, with provisions for eighteen months.

3. And likewise permission to raise a body of workmen, of different kinds, to the number of twelve hundred men, with the necessary officers whom I should chuse.

4. That I should be furnished with a necessary quantity of arms, ammunition, and the value of one million two

hundred thousand livres, in articles of trade, which I should point out.

5. That for the space of three years, permission should be granted me to raise recruits to the number of four hundred men yearly, and the transport of two hundred foundling children of both sexes annually.

6. That permission should be granted to all the subjects of the sovereign power to trade with the new colony.

7. That permission should be granted me to establish warehouses and factories in its colonies.

These articles being granted, I would stipulate,

1. That the new colony should furnish a certain sum of money annually, to the power who had protected it, as a grateful acknowledgement.

2. That the colony should assist its protector in every war, by furnishing a stipulated number of soldiers and seamen.

3. That no merchandize, or objects of European luxury, should be admitted into the new colony, except the product or manufacture of the dominions of its protector.

4. That the whole sum advanced in fitting out armed vessels, with the ammunition and objects of commerce, on account of the new colony, should be entered into a regular charge; that the interest should be paid during the three first years, and the capital reimbursed during the fourth.

These stipulations being thus fixed, I would repair to port Maurice, where, conformably to the treaty entered into with the Prince Huapo, I would disembark; and, after having established a military post, I would repair to the capital of the province which has been ceded to me.

Saturday,

Saturday, September the 10th. The affociates came to work of themfelves, and began to load the veffel. This day Don Hieronimo entered into an oath with me before the whole company; in which he engaged to fupport the favourable difpofition of the Prince towards me. I made him a prefent of feveral Latin books, and fome arms.

Sunday, September the 11th. I gave orders for our embarkment, and the natives of the country affifted us with the utmoft readinefs, with every thing in their power. This day Mr. Stephanow afked leave to go on fhore, which I durft not confent to, as I had reafon to fear the wickednefs of his character, which certainly might have deftroyed all our credit and intereft on this ifland. But as I was not defirous that the refufal fhould come from me, I promifed to explain his wifh to the company; and promifed, that the moment they gave their confent, I would make no objection. I gave orders for the immediate calling together of the company on board, in the morning, to decide on this affair; but Stephanow was fcarcely gone, before I affembled a committee, to whom I communicated his intention. Every individual, urged by the fame motives as myfelf, oppofed his purpofe; and feveral among them undertook to induce the whole company to refufe him. I employed this night in writing out inftructions for Don Hieronimo, and at day-break I went on board, accompanied by him. After I had taken a formal leave of the iflanders, at ten I put a letter for the Prince Huapo, into the hands of Don Hieronimo, with inftructions for Mr. Loginow, who at laft took leave of us, and returned on fhore. Immediately after his departure, the company affembled, and deliberated upon the
propofition

proposition of Mr. Stephanow. Their determination was, that it was impossible to suffer any other person to go on shore; and more especially Mr. Stephanow, who had given so many proofs of his evil intentions. This unhappy man, urged by despair and rage, attempted to throw himself overboard; and by his outrageous deportment, obliged me, at length, to order him into confinement. In the mean time, we weighed anchor, and set sail under the two top-sails, with the boats a-head, as well as five or six of the country boats, who were ready to come to our assistance, as the road was difficult.

According to the Report, all the company in good health, the vessel making no water.

Monday, September the 12th. A light breeze at E. S. E. with fair clear weather. When we had got to the mouth of the harbour, it fell calm; which obliged me to tow the vessel out by the boats, where I anchored in sixteen fathom water. At sun-set the wind sprung up at S. E. and I set sail, and stood to the Northward, in order to double the Northernmost extremity of the island of Formosa. In the night the wind slackened, and we saw many fires on shore. At eight, A. M. we discovered two islands a-head, with a channel between them of sufficient extent, to induce me to sail through it. At eleven, saw a large vessel at the distance of three leagues to the Northward, and prepared to chace her; but finding she outsailed us, I gave up the attempt.

According to the Report, all in good health. The ship making no water.

Latitude in 24° 15′ N. Longitude in 324° 08′. Wind S. E. Current from S. to N. Course N. N. E.

Tuesday,

COUNT DE BENYOWSKY. 71

Tuesday, September the 13th. Fine weather, inclining to squally. This day Mr. Stephanow was released from confinement; and I declared to the company, my resolution to direct our course to Macao. In the night the weather was moderate, and we continued our course very agreeably.

According to the Report, all in good health.
Latitude in 25° 15' N. Longitude in 323° 56'. Wind S. E. ¼ E. Current from S. to N. Course N. ¼ E.

Wednesday, September the 14th. Squally weather. Saw a quantity of water snakes. In the night, continual rain, with thunder and lightning. Sounded several times, but got no ground.

According to the Report, all well.
Latitude in 24 41' N. Longitude 322° 00'. Wind S. E. Current from N. to S. Course S. W. ¼ W.

Thursday, September the 15th. Close cloudy weather throughout, with heavy rain. At three, A. M. sounded, and got ground at thirty fathoms, fine sand, and broken shells; and we observed a very strong current from N. to S. At day-break, saw a quantity of fishing boats around us. At nine, the coast of China was in sight, and I determined to go into some harbour. At ten, several fishing vessels being near us, offered to sell us some fish; and upon our expressing our willingness, several canoes immediately came along side, from whom we bought all their fish for twelve piastres. Two Chinese among these fishermen, spoke a little Portugueze; and were at last persuaded to pilot us into Macao. They demanded for this service one hundred piastres; but in the mean time, requested leave to go on shore for their cloaths; to which
I con-

I confented, on condition, that one only fhould go on fhore, while the other remained on board. This agreement being made, they conducted us to an anchoring place; where we came too in eighteen fathom, fine fand and mud.

Friday, September the 16th. The pilot having returned on board, made me to underftand his direction to weigh, and make fail along the coaft, in order to put in at Tanafoa; and by way of explaining the reafon, he faid, Mandarin hopchin malas, Mandarin tanajou bon bon malto bon; all which I made fhift to comprehend wonderfully well. I therefore made fail without delay, and ftood along fhore. At day-break, the pilot fhewed me the bay of Tanafoa, into which we entered, and anchored in five fathom water, oppofite a caftle, which I faluted with three guns, and received the fame number in return. The pilot immediately went on fhore, and did not return till ten o'clock, when he appeared, together with a Mandarin, and an interpreter. He demanded who I was; to what nation the fhip belonged; where I came from, and whither I was bound? To this I replied, that I was an European, and one of the nobles of Hungary; that the veffel had belonged to the Ruffians, but having taken it from them, who were my enemies, it now belonged to myfelf; that I came from Kamchatka; was on my return to Europe, and propofed to put in at Macao. The Mandarin wrote my anfwers with a hair pencil, and faid, he was furprized to fee Hungarians arrive at China. He afterwards afked, what I was in want of; and being told that I wanted frefh provifions, he confented that a party of my companions fhould go on fhore shore with the interpreters. I therefore availed myself of this permission, to send Messrs. Winbladth and Kuzneczow on shore, accompanied with six of our companions, to carry my presents to the Governor. They consisted in a beaver's skin, and two sables.

Saturday, September the 17th. At anchor at Tanafoa, before the town. At five, P. M. my officers returned, and brought word, that the Mandarin had accepted my presents with pleasure; and had sent me in return, a service of porcelain, with two chests of tea, six cows, and twelve hogs, with a quantity of poultry, and a kind of arrack. The associates brought an hundred different kinds of sweetmeats, and some toys, very nicely wrought. The interpreter acquainted me, that the Mandarin was desirous of purchasing some furs, but secretly; I therefore sent one hundred and fifty beavers, and three hundred sables; in return for which, he sent six thousand eight hundred piastres, in three casks. Here I had additional cause to regret the loss of my furs. My companions likewise opened a trade with the inhabitants, and sold every scrap of bear's skin they could collect. In the night several Chinese vessels anchored near us, and my companions went on board them. They assured me, that every boat had several cabins, which were filled with girls, who sold their favours. A. M. Set up the rigging, and cleaned the ship thoroughly. My companions were incommoded by the quantity of fruit they eat on shore, and six of them were taken with illness.

Sunday, September the 18th. My pilot took notice that the wind was favourable, and that we ought to take advantage of it. I therefore set sail, and after standing off ſhore, I directed my courſe to the Southward, which was contrary to the wiſh of my pilot, who was abſolutely averſe to loſing ſight of the ſhore. The quantity of fiſhing boats we ſaw were innumerable. Towards the evening they all made for the ſhore; and as I was importuned by my pilot, I conſented to do the ſame. At day-break we ſaw many water ſnakes around us, ſome of which I cauſed to be taken, and the pilot eat them. At nine it fell calm, and at noon our latitude was by obſervation, 22° 32′. Eighteen of our people were this day ſick, which I attributed to the ſpirituous liquor they had drank.

Monday, September the 19th. The pilots enquired whether my veſſel drew more than ſix feet of water; and when I informed them that ſhe drew upwards of eight, they begged me to come to anchor; becauſe at the fourth hour of the tide, the depth of water at this place was eight or ten feet. The under current here was contrary to that at the ſurface. I therefore anchored, in compliance with their wiſhes, and I determined to note this obſervation in my journal, in order that more ſkilful navigators might, at ſome future time, aſcertain the fact. At ſix, P. M. weighed with a light breeze at Eaſt, and the tide in our favour. This night one of the women who was attached to Mr. Cſurin, was brought to bed. The Chineſe boats which ſurrounded us the whole night, made a conſiderable noiſe with their oars. At day-break we ſaw a fleet, at the head of which was a veſſel of prodigious magnitude, almoſt entirely gilt, and hung round with numberleſs ſtreamers. My pilots informed me that

it

COUNT DE BENYOWSKY.

it was the Canton fleet, which carried the revenues to Pekin. We counted one hundred and eighty-six veffels. This day our fick amounted to no more than eight.

Tuefday, September the 20th. This day I was attacked by a violent fever, for which the pilots advifed me to eat an orange, roafted in its juice, with fugar, and a good deal of ginger. They prepared this remedy for me, and it produced a ftrong perfpiration, which diffipated my complaint. Meffrs. Winbladth, Baturin, Gurefinin, and Kuzneczow, with twelve others, were affected in the fame manner. At eight, P. M. Mr. Sibaew acquainted me, that Mr. Stephanow, taking advantage of my indifpofition, had formed a party; but as he could not yet fay what their intentions were, he promifed to watch their motions. Sibaew had fcarcely finifhed his difcourfe, before I heard a noife on board. I went out of my cabin, where I found Mr. Cruftiew engaged in a quarrel with Stephanow. I gave orders to feize the latter; and after receiving the information, that this wretch had propofed to the company, to fign an act of complaint againft me, to be delivered to the Governor of Macao on our arrival, I ordered him to be put in irons. This day we had twenty-two fick.

Wednefday, September the 21ft. About fix, P. M. anchored among the iflands, called Ladrones, where we remained all night. At five, A. M. weighed, and at ten the pilots fhewed me an ifland, which they called Omy; and at laft made me underftand, that Omy is the Chinefe name for Macao. At half paft eleven we faw the fort, and the Portugueze colours difplayed. At noon, being oppofite the fort, I faluted it with twelve guns.

L 2　　　　　　　　Thurfday,

Thursday, September the 22d. At half past one, P. M. we were fairly entering the harbour, where we saw several vessels at anchor. At two, in passing the pass,* I was hailed to come to anchor; but as I did not think it necessary to lose time in superfluous ceremonies, I entered the harbour, and anchored at last, near a frigate of forty guns, in four fathoms water. As soon as I had brought too, I saluted the Admiral's colours with twenty-four guns, and he answered with twelve.

I went on shore immediately after, and passing near the Commodore, I paid him a visit. On my arrival at the Governor's, I was introduced into the hall, which I found full of priests and monks; among whom I perceived several negroes of the Canary islands. After some time, the Governor, M. de Saldagna, arrived, and received me with the greatest politeness. When I had acquainted him with my misfortunes and my deliverance, he gave me permission to hire houses in the town, to accommodate my people, till I could find a favourable opportunity of conveying them to Europe. Several persons of the magistracy, who were present, expressed some suspicions of me; for which reason, to prevent debates, I thought proper to put my vessel as a deposit, in the hands of the Governor; reserving only for each of my companions, the necessary arms, such as guns, pistols, and swords, which I likewise deposited in the castle. After this convention, the Governor charged M. Hifs, a gentleman of French extraction, but settled at Macao for some years, to assist me in my affairs, and serve as interpreter. At six, P. M. the guard having come on board, I caused all my people to

---

* *Passant la passe*—I do not understand this. T

to go on shore. For the first day, my companions lodged in a public house, and the excess and avidity with which they devoured the bread and fresh provisions, which they were now supplied with, cost thirteen of them their lives. These died suddenly, and twenty-four others were seized with dangerous illness.

September the 23d. M. Hifs having found two convenient houses, I hired them, and went to reside in them with my companions. This day I dined with the Governor, in company with a number of priests, who from that moment aspired to the glory of converting my associates to the Roman religion. On my return home, I found all my people commodiously lodged, and an apartment completely fitted up for myself; the Governor having supplied the furniture out of his own house. I employed this day in making visits to the Bishop of Mitelopolis, the Procureur of the town, the different convents, and principal inhabitants. I likewise gave orders to clothe my companions uniformly, in red and white, as well as the officers; and the Portugueze ladies undertook to provide the apparel for our female fellow travellers. When the accounts were made up, these charges were estimated at eight thousand piastres, and the monthly expence for lodging and provisions, amounted to six thousand two hundred piastres.

On the 24th, I received visits from the Governor, and the principal men of the town, as well as from the Bishop, accompanied with the different religious orders. These all together, accompanied me to the Hoppo, or Chinese Governor, who regaled us with tea and sweetmeats. This day three more of my associates died, and their conversion was published throughout the town. In the evening, a Dominican priest, and friend of the Governor, named Zunitta, came to me, and offered every assistance in his power; and as I thought I might dispose of my furs by his assistance, I proposed the business to him, and he consented to take them. I therefore put into his hands four hundred and eighty beavers skins, five hundred sables, and one hundred and eighty dozen ermines; and he agreed to pay me for each beaver fifty piastres, for each sable six piastres, and for every dozen of ermines eight piastres; which produced the sum of twenty-eight thousand four hundred and forty piastres: the whole, and only remains of so considerable a fortune, as I had brought from Kamchatka! a scanty pittance, scarcely enough to pay the expences of putting into Macao.

This day, likewise, I gave orders to release Mr. Stephanow from his confinement, having received a formal apology on his part. The town made me, on the same day, a present of one thousand piastres in gold, with forty-two pieces of blue cloth, and twelve pieces of black satin. Their present was accompanied with a request, that I would deposit a copy of my journal in their archives. I promised the deputies, that I would give them an historical extract, as I could not act so much to the prejudice of my own interests, as to deprive myself of the merit of my manuscripts. This day I dined with the Bishop of Mitelopolis, Mr. le Bon, of French extraction; and I agreed with him that I would claim the protection of the French flag, for my passage to Europe, in which he promised me his advice and assistance.

On the 25th, Mifs Aphanafia paid the debt of nature. Her premature death affected me greatly, and more efpecially as it deprived me of the fatisfaction of repaying her attachment, by her marriage with the young Popow, fon of the Archimandrite, to whom I had given the furname of my family. This day I difpatched Mr. Cruftiew with letters to the Directors of the French Company, containing my reclamation of the protection of the colours of his Moft Chriftian Majefty. He returned on the 29th, and brought me a very favourable anfwer, and the afiurance of my paffage, which news was very acceptable to me.

At Macao, October the 3d, 1771. A certain Mr. Gohr, Captain in the fervice of the Englifh Company, came to fee me, and made me offer of fervices on the part of the Directors, and a free paffage to Europe, provided I would bind myfelf to entruft my manufcripts to the Company, and engage to enter into their fervice, and make no communication of the difcoveries I had made. This propofition, fo evidently interefted, difgufted me; but I was contented to anfwer, that I was very fenfible of the obliging offer he had made; but that, as I had accepted thofe of the French Directors, it was not in my power to change my determination: that with refpect to my entering into the fervice of the Company, it did not appear to me to be fo eafy; becaufe it was not only neceffary that I fhould be affured of a fuperior ftation, but that in the mean time all my people fhould be provided for; and that our common lot, and the execution of feveral projects fhould be fecured. My anfwer furprized Mr. Gohr, who took his leave in an affected manner. The moment after his departure, I learned that Mr. Stephanow had accompanied him; and
from

from thence I inferred, that I should still find new causes of discontent on his part, which accordingly happened, as will appear in the sequel.

On the 4th of October, I received a letter from Mr. L'Heureux, Director * for the Dutch Company. He sent me a present of cloth, wine, beer, brandy, salt provisions, and two thousand piastres. His letter and presents were accompanied with the offer of a passage for me to Batavia, and the assurance that I should be received into the Company's service. But, as he made the same proposal as the English, I refused the acceptance of his presents, except the liquors.

On the 6th, Mr. Jackson, an English merchant established at Macoa, arrived with Mr. Beyz. They renewed the propositions made by Mr. Gohr, and shewed me full powers, signed by the English Council at Canton, to regulate the conditions of my engagement, and to offer a present of fifteen thousand guineas. The first *sine qua non* was, that the Company, in consideration of my consigning my manuscripts, and entering into their service, should grant me a pension of four thousand pounds sterling, reversible to my children; and that they should settle on each officer a pension of one hundred pounds, and each associate thirty pounds; and that they should give me every assistance in forming establishments beyond China. On this first condition the Plenipotentiaries acknowledged, that they had not sufficient authority to conclude with me, and retired, after begging that I would well consider their offers. This evening the Governor informed me, that the four English

* Or Supercargo.

gentlemen

gentlemen had been with him, and that he thought several of my affociates were gained by the Englifh. In fact, thefe gentlemen, piqued at their want of fuccefs, raifed embarrafments among my people, in which Mr. Stephanow was of wonderful fervice to them.

On the 12th, I received a letter from Mr. de Robien, Director of the French Company at Canton, wherein he informed me that two of the Company's fhips, the Dauphin and the Laverdi, were ready to receive me and all my people on board. The fame day Mr. Kuzneczow informed me, that he had difcovered a plot, at the head of which was Stephanow, who had engaged to deliver my journals and papers to the Englifh, for the fum of five thoufand pounds fterling; and to prove the fact, he fhewed me a letter of Mr. Jackfon, wherein that merchant afferted, that Meffrs. Gohr, Hume, and Beg, were ready to pay the fum on the delivery of all my papers. On this information, I took all my papers out of my cheft, and put them into the hands of the Archbifhop of Mitelopolis, unperceived by any of my companions.

On the 15th, the affociates met by my order. I informed them, that I was affured that a number among them were difcontented with me; for which reafon I thought proper to declare to them, that all thofe who were defirous of feeking their fortune elfewhere, were at liberty to quit me; and that as they had all received a retribution at my hands at the ifland of Formofa, I thought myfelf acquitted from them. I had fcarcely made a finifh, before Mr. Stephanow loaded me with invectives, and charged me with an intention of depriving the company of their fhare of the advantages I was about to receive,

receive, from the knowledge I had acquired during the voyage; and that the moderation I had shewn at Formosa, in delivering my share of the presents of Prince Huapo, was merely a scheme to deprive them of greater advantages. He then excited the companions to throw off my authority, by assuring them that he would secure them a large fortune the instant they should determine to put my papers in his hands, and follow his party. The infamous plot of this wretch was nothing extraordinary; but when I understood that he was supported by Mr. Wyndbladth, my ancient Major, the companion of my exile, and my friend, I was incapable of setting bounds to my indignation, and could not avoid declaring, that their proceedings were highly disgraceful; and to confound them, I displayed their secret projects to the company, and justified my words by shewing Mr. Jackson's letter, which convinced them that Messrs. Stephanow and Wyndbladth, under pretence of serving the company, were desirous of securing the five thousand pounds to their own use. They were highly irritated, and threatened them; but Stephanow preserved a party of eleven, with whom he went to my lodgings; and while I remained in conversation with my friends, he seized my box, in which he supposed my papers were deposited. As soon as I heard of this outrage, I went to his chamber, followed by twenty associates; and as he refused to open the door, I broke it down. On my entrance he fired a pistol at me, which missed. In consequence of this attempt, I gave orders for seizing and keeping him in strict confinement; and as it was necessary likewise to secure Mr. Wyndbladth, I went to his chamber; but he had retired into the garden, armed with a pair of pistols and a sabre.

fabre. I determined to shut him in, being convinced that he could not get over the walls on account of their great height. This whole affair passed without the least alarm without, as the doors of the house were shut.

On the 16th, Mr. Wyndbladth, fatigued by a continual rain, and perhaps urged by hunger, requested forgiveness, and surrendered himself to two companions I had appointed to watch him. Having thus made sure of these two turbulent men, I thought it proper they should be separated from the company; and they were therefore conducted to the castle by permission of the Governor. The officers of our company, being desirous of avenging themselves on the English emissaries, played them a trick, the whole effect of which fell upon a Jewish agent, who was severely flogged. Upon this wretch there were found minutes of proposals which he made to the companions, as follow:

1. That the English would pay to each associate one thousand piastres, in case they would serve the company, and put my papers in his hands.

2. That in case the associates refused to take the English party, the company would arrest them by force, in the name of the Empress of Russia, to deliver them up.

4. That the company would answer for obtaining the Empress's pardon for them, if they would determine to make a voyage to Japan, and the Aleuthes Islands.

Such proceedings cannot be attributed to men of sense. It was in my opinion a forgery, concerted between Mr. Stephanow and the Jew, to excite the associates against me.

On the 22d, I was attacked by a violent fever, and the Governor had the goodness to offer me an apartment in his house.

84   MEMOIRS AND TRAVELS OF

houſe. I accepted his offer with the more pleaſure, as the noiſe of my companions was inſupportable. I therefore entruſted the command this day to Mr. Cruſtiew, and retired to the Governor's, where my illneſs continued till the 18th of November. During this period, four of my aſſociates and three of their women died. The following is a liſt of thoſe who died at Macao:

Miſs Aphanaſia du Nilow,
Meſſ. Maxim Cſurin,
　Aſaph Baturin,
　Philip Zablikow,
　Nicolas Perevalow,
　John Perevalow,
　The Wife of Perevalow,
　Andrew Maſchinſkoy,
　George Panow,
　Gregory Novozilow,
　Stephen Kazakow,
　Alexander Ziran,

Meſſ. George Nolinkin,
　George Voronow,
　Alexis Juſka,
　Cath. Kuzmika,
　Alexis Zacharka,
　Boleſlaus Sipſkoy,
　Laurence Chodin,
　Prince Zadſkoy,
　Nicolas Zarſkoy,
　Caſimir Levantiew,
　James Lubimoy.

The great number of deaths in ſo ſhort a time, gave me a very unfavourable opinion of the climate of China, at leaſt of the Southern Provinces of the empire.

On the 25th of November, the Governor, ſeeing my health eſtabliſhed, and being determined to lodge me in future among my companions, informed me that during my illneſs he had had great debates with the Chineſe on my account, becauſe the Engliſh Directors had informed them, that I was a pirate, and deſerter from the Ruſſians; and that upon this information, the Governor or Viceroy of Canton,

COUNT DE BENYOWSKY.   85

Canton, had required the Governor to deliver me up, or, at all events to make me depart immediately; and that he had obtained a delay till my recovery. For this reason he advised me to pretend that my illness still continued, until the time the French vessels should be ready to sail. From his embarrassment, I perceived he was apprehensive that he might find my affair troublesome to himself. I therefore begged him to remain neuter, and undertook to terminate the business with the Chinese myself.

On the 26th, I secretly dispatched Mr. Hiss and Mr. Crustiew to Canton, with a memorial for the Viceroy, and a letter for Mr. Robien, in order that he might present it at the audience of the Chinese chief.

My deputies did not return till the 3d of December; when they brought me a chopp, or permission to wait upon the Viceroy at Canton. This imperial officer sent a superb vessel, with sixty-four oars for me, and caused a letter to be written to me, importing, that he was informed of the falsity of the insinuations against me, and hoped to convince me of the justice, which the Chinese knew how to render to heroes like me. This disposition was very flattering; but my satisfaction was of short duration, for on the 5th, which was fixed for my departure, the Mandarin, Hoppo of Macao, let me know, that if I did not intend to travel as far as Pekin, it was of no use to go to Canton, as the Viceroy had nothing to communicate. This sudden change surprized every one, and especially the Bishop of Mitelopolis, who was strongly interested in my favour. I was in doubt with myself this day, whether I should go to Pekin. I was greatly affected; for I should have been exceedingly gratified with

the

the view of the capital, and interior parts of the Chinese empire; and a favourable opportunity now presented itself: but to have embraced it, would have required me to abandon my project, and defer my return to Europe. It was not till after much deliberation, that I at last determined to give up my intention of going to Canton.

On the 6th of December, my Japanese traveller appeared again, having suffered an illness of ten weeks. His recovery was very agreeable to me, as his person interested me strongly. This day, upon examining my chests, I found that the collections I had made of various kinds, in the course of my voyages, had disappeared; and I at last heard, to my extreme grief, that Stephanow and Wyndbladth had sold the whole to the English Jew. I immediately sent after him; but the rascal had retired, after his correction, to Canton. Mr. Sibaew assured me, that the Jew had bought the whole for one thousand five hundred piastres; whereas the pearls alone which I had, were worth five times that sum.

On the 7th, the Bishop of Mitelopolis informed me, that he was informed by the Secretary of the Hoppo, (a Christian in secret) that the declaration of his master was false, and that the Viceroy was angry at not seeing me. He attributed this conduct to the intrigues of Mr. Jackson, and endeavoured to persuade me to write another memorial to the Viceroy; but as I thought this step of no advantage to my interests, I refused to comply with his advice, being contented with being permitted to remain undisturbed at Macao.

On the 10th, I assembled all my companions, and proposed to them to embark on board the French ships, in order

order to return to Europe. They confented, and fubmitted entirely to my orders. This day, having received the apology and entreaties of Mr. Wyndbladth, I releafed him from confinement; but as I could not place the fame confidence in Mr. Stephanow, I paid him four thoufand piaftres, with leave to go where he pleafed. He immediately took part with the Hollanders, whofe director, M. L'Heureux, expecting to derive fome information from him concerning our voyage, received him, and fent him to Batavia.

On the 20th, I gave orders to make every preparation for our departure, having this day received the conventions, figned between me and the Captain, M. de St. Hilaire, in the fervice of the French Eaft-India Company. Thefe conventions were ratified by M. Robis,* Director of the Company; in which I engaged to pay the fum of one hundred and fifteen thoufand livres Tournois, for the paffage of myfelf, and all my people, to L'Orient.

On the 26th, having received information that it was neceffary I fhould be provided with a chopp, or order of the Viceroy, to permit me to enter the river Tigu, I fent Mr. Hifs, as my commiffioner for that purpofe, to the Viceroy.

January the 1ft, 1772. M. Hifs returned with the order, which coft me four hundred and fifty piaftres for three boats, which had been permitted to carry myfelf and people to the mouth of the Tigu.

On the 2d, I fold my veffel to a Portugueze merchant, for the fum of four thoufand five hundred piaftres, ready

* Robien is the name of the Director mentioned page 81, where it is written in the M S. in the Count's hand-writing. T.

money, and as much on credit. The Governor reserved to himself the whole of the stores.

From the 5th to the 12th, I was employed in liquidating my accounts; and after having settled every thing, I found myself totally destitute. On the 13th, I took my leave of the Governor, and chiefs of the town; and in the evening I embarked on board three sampans, with all my people, to go on board the French vessels, which were appointed to receive us at the time of their leaving the harbour of Canton.

On the 14th, we quitted Macao, where the Governor saluted me with twenty-one guns, from the principal fortress; and, after a tedious passage, we arrived at last at the mouth of the Tigu; where we were very civilly received by a Mandarin, though he at first refused to permit us to go on shore. The sight of a purse of piastres, however, abated his severity; which was so much altered by this circumstance, that he offered permission for us to take lodgings in the fort. His complaisance was very acceptable, for the ships did not arrive till the 22d; and in the mean time, I was at liberty to ride out on horseback, accompanied by some Tartars.

On the 22d, we at last saw the two ships; the first of which was the Dauphin, of sixty-four guns, commanded by the Chevalier de St. Hilaire, on board which I embarked, with half my people; and the second was the Laverdi, of fifty guns, which received the other half. After our embarkation we sailed for the isle of France.

On the 27th, we passed the English bank, on which we had soundings at thirty-six fathoms, sand and broken shells.

On the 4th of February we crossed the equator.

On the 6th, in the Straits, we joined a Spanish armed frigate, named the Pallas; and on the 16th of March, we arrived safely at the isle of France. My arrival here was so much the more agreeable, as I was perfectly tired of the many questions the French proposed to me, respecting my discoveries during my former voyage. This voyage gave me an ample knowledge of the predominant character of a nation, to which I shall probably attach myself in future. As soon as we came to anchor, and the Governor, the Chevalier de Roche, was informed that I was on board, he sent a boat belonging to the government, to bring me on shore. On my entrance into the town, I was received with military honours, and had the pleasure to be very amicably received by the Governor, who offered to accommodate me in his own house. I accepted this friendly offer with great satisfaction; more especially as I hoped, that his experience would be of service to me, in directing my conduct, with regard to the French Court and Ministry. After a day's repose, the Governor invited me to accompany him in his excursions upon the island; and these little journies made me acquainted with some of the interests of the French government, though I could never agree to call this establishment a colony. For the isle of France can never be made any thing more than a military post.

The arrival of Lieutenant Kreguelin, was a great relief to me. For this navigator having returned from a voyage to the Southern lands, gave employment to all the politicians

ticians and idle talkers of the ifland; who before his appearance, had no other object but myfelf. I became acquainted with this officer; but from what I had myfelf feen in the North, I could not believe that he had difcovered fuch agreeable countries, as he afferted to exift on his Southern continent.

On the 1ft of April, the Captain acquainted me, that he intended to depart on the 4th, and I got ready my little accommodations, by the generous affiftance of the Governor, who lent me a fum of money. On the 4th, having taken my leave, I embarked; and the Governor, with all the officers, paid me a vifit on board. In the evening we fet fail.

On the 12th, we anchored at the Ifland of Madagafcar, where I went on fhore at Fort Dauphin. Some particulars of information I had received from the Governor of the ifle of France, induced me to wifh for more ample information, refpecting this fine and extenfive ifland; but unfortunately for this purpofe, I could not prolong my ftay, but went on board again on the 14th.

On the 27th, we doubled the Cape of Good Hope.

On the 28th, we fpoke two French veffels, outward bound to India.

On the 24th of May, we faw two Englifh veffels in the latitude of St. Helaira; and on the 18th of July, we happily arrived at the Ifle de Croix. As foon as we had come too, I fent an officer to the Lieutenant du Roy, at Port Louis, who permitted me and all my people to lodge there.

On the 19th, I went on shore, and was very politely received by the Commandant; who agreed to send a courier to the Minister with my packets, which I addressed to the Duc D'Aiguillon.

On the 2d of August, I received an invitation from the Duc D'Aiguillon, which was brought by a messenger of state.

On the 8th of August, I arrived in Champagne, where the Minister then was, who received me with cordiality and distinction, and proposed to me to enter into the service of his master, with the offer of a regiment of infantry; which I accepted, on condition that his Majesty would be pleased to employ me in forming establishments beyond the Cape. In France, likewise, I had the happiness to find my uncle, the Count de Benyow, Commandant of the castle and town of Bar, Commander of the Royal Order of St. Lazare, and Chevalier de St. Louis. The assistance of this worthy relation, and the benevolence of his Majesty, put me in a condition to send an express into Hungary, to enquire after my spouse and child. She arrived at the end of the year; but she had the misfortune to see her son expire, at the instant of the arrival of my courier. An event which was the more affecting, as I was then in a situation to provide for him very advantageously in France. In the course of the month of December, the Duke d'Aiguillon proposed to me from his Majesty, to form an establishment on the island of Madagascar, upon the same footing as I had proposed upon the island Formosa; and I at last complied with the desire of this Minister, to whom I shall be ever bound in gratitude, as well as perfonal esteem and attachment.*

* Here ends the second volume, according to the division of the Count, who has in this place annexed his abridged signature.

A MEMOIR

A
MEMOIR

CONCERNING THE

EXPEDITION to MADAGASCAR, for the Formation of a Royal Eſtabliſhment on that Iſland; the Execution and chief Command of which, were intruſted by his MAJESTY*, to the COUNT DE BENYOWSKY, proprietary Colonel of a Corps of Volunteers, in 1772.

PRELIMINARIES.

AS the ſucceſs of every remote enterprize which is intended to form an eſtabliſhment of Europeans, dependant always on preciſe orders and inſtructions, as well as preparations and well-founded operations, made in conſequence of a knowledge of the country, and proportioned to the advantages which are propoſed to be obtained, I think it neceſſary to give an account of the circumſtances which preceded my arrival on this iſland. Circumſtances which prove, that notwithſtanding the very ſcanty means which have been afforded me, I have ſucceeded in forming treaties of friendſhip and alliance with the greater part of

* The King of France.

the inhabitants of this extenfive ifland; and, confequently, that if I had not been, as I may fay, totally abandoned by the Minifter, which was the fource of the miferies, difeafes, and mortality, to which myfelf and my people were expofed; the ifland of Madagafcar, at this day in alliance with France, would have formed a power, capable of fupporting her colonies of the ifles of France and Bourbon, and defending her eftablifhments in India, as well as fecuring new branches of commerce to that kingdom, which would have carried immenfe fums into the royal treafury.

In order to exhibit in the moft perfpicuous manner, the different obftacles which I have experienced fince my arrival in this ifland, and to develope thofe events which by fudden revolutions have procured me favourable advantages in forming this eftablifhment, I fhall give an account of the original difpofitions of the Minifter, upon which it was ordered that I fhould regulate my operations.

Here follows the account:

'On the 15th of September, 1772, Mr. De Boynes, Secretary of State for the Marine department, communicated to me the intentions of his Majefty, to make a confiderable enterprize on the ifland of Madagafcar, and that his Majefty had determined to entruft this expedition to my care. In confequence of which, he informed me of thefe determinations, that I might take the moft fpeedy and proper meafures to carry this important and honourable enterprize into execution.

After having thanked this Minifter for the confidence he honoured me with, I obferved, that having no knowledge of Madagafcar, and being abfolutely ignorant of the nature of the enterprize which his Majesty was desirous of entrusting me with, I could not myself regulate the measures necessary for such an expedition; the success of which would depend on orders and means, in conformity to which I should regulate my operations with the greatest exactness.

The Minister, after having assured me that nothing which might be necessary to secure the success of my mission should be wanting, added, that the intention of his Majesty was to form an establishment at Madagascar, in favour of which, at some future time, a much more extensive plan might be carried into execution, by gaining the confidence of the King, Princes, and chiefs of the country, and engaging them to put their island under the protection of his Majesty. Upon this I represented, that in order to execute an enterprize of this nature, and of such great importance, in so remote a country, the intemperate climate of which, together with the jealousy of the inhabitants, had so often deranged the projects, and rendered former attempts abortive, the operations would require well-combined dimensions, considerable forces, and continued supplies, to prevent any thing from being left to chance. The Minister approved my representations, and promised to provide for every thing; reserving to himself the regulation of the different details, which my mission might require, and which he proposed to concert with me at the end of the month.

Some days after the Minister, having sent for me to his hotel, informed me, that the intentions of his Majesty were to entrust me with the command of a military corps of twelve hundred men; and that during the time I should be employed

employed in raising them, he would take care to give the most precise orders, that nothing might be wanting to expedite the considerable enterprize to which I was invited. I reprefented to the Minifter, that the number of one thoufand two hundred men appeared to me to be too confiderable for an enterprize, where nothing more was intended than to gain the confidence of the natives of the country; and I requefted, that the troop deftined to accompany me to Madagafcar, might not amount to more than three hundred men. To this propofal the Minifter agreed.

On the 20th of January, 1773, the recruits being raifed, I informed the Minifter, and requefted his orders, and the communication of his inftructions, refpecting the enterprize in which his Majefty defigned to employ me. He replied, that he had not yet been able to work upon it; and that he had put it into the hands of the firft Commis. I waited upon the latter, whom I found bufied in drawing up the plan; but his work not being finifhed, I could not receive any precife information from him.

At the beginning of February, the Minifter having fent for me again, declared that the plan drawn out by his Commis, was not to his mind; and that he left me at liberty to draw it out myfelf. He ordered me likewife to add the neceffary demands for the execution of my miffion, and faid, that the intentions of his Majefty were to form at Madagafcar a fimple eftablifhment, by favour of which the fubfiftence of the iflands of France and Bourbon might be fecured, or new branches of trade might be opened, and men fupported, who might be ferviceable in India in the next war which might happen. He concluded, by exhort-

ing

ing me to omit nothing in this plan of all the demands neceffary for its execution. From thefe particulars of information, which I learned from the mouth of the Minifter, concerning my commiffion, I continued to confer with Mr. Audat, the firft Commis, who had no knowledge of Madagafcar, but from the contradictory relations of merchants, which were more fuited to confufe the fubject, than to give the flighteft information relative to my expedition. He communicated to me feveral accounts of Madagafcar, and a map of the ifland; from which, as well as from the particular account of Mr. Johannis, Captain of a veffel, who had made feveral voyages to Madagafcar, I founded the plan which follows:

A PLAN WHICH WAS PRESENTED TO THE MINISTER FOR SECURING THE PERFORMANCE OF MY OPERATIONS AT MADAGASCAR.

ARTICLE I.

The Minifter will pleafe to give orders for my paffage, with my corps of volunteers for the ifle of France, with one year's provifion of meat, drink, and pay.

ARTICLE II.

He will pleafe to give orders to the chiefs of the Ifle of France to furnifh me with two veffels of the burden of one hundred and twenty, or one hundred and fifty tons each; which will ferve to tranfport the troops and neceffary provifions for the eftablifhment at Madagafcar. One of thefe these veffels fhould remain fubject to my orders, to be employed in the coafting fervice of the ifland, and the other to return to France, in order to inform the Minifter of the pofition and fuccefs of the enterprize, with other circumftances neceffary to be communicated.

ARTICLE III.

The Minifter will pleafe to give orders to the chiefs of the ifle of France, to fupply me with merchandize to the value of two hundred thoufand livres, with a fupply of artillery and warlike ftores, together with utenfils for the hofpitals, and workmen, with their inftruments and tools for the conftruction of the neceffary habitations of his Majefty's people.

ARTICLE IV.

To avoid the ravages which the unwholefomenefs of the climate of Madagafcar might occafion, during the time of erecting proper buildings on the fpot, the Minifter will pleafe to order the chiefs of the ifle of France to fupply me with four buildings framed in wood; one to ferve as a general ftorehoufe; the fecond as an hofpital; the third as a barrack; and the fourth for my own habitation.

ARTICLE V.

The Minifter will pleafe to join to my miffion, perfons attached to the adminiftration, to regulate and conduct the affairs of finances and accounts; and who, at the fame time,

time, may take charge of the commercial bufinefs, while my attention is directed to the forming of the eftablifhment.

ARTICLE VI.

The Minifter will pleafe to order the chiefs of the ifle of France to affift me, in cafe of need, with men, provifions, ammunition, articles of trade, and money for the pay of my troops.

ARTICLE VII.

The Minifter will pleafe to fend out to me the firft year, one hundred and twenty recruits, to keep up the eftablifhment, until I can receive his final inftructions.

After having prefented to the Minifter this plan, reduced into feven articles, I protefted to him that I fhould fucceed in gaining the confidence of the natives of the country, and in forming the intended eftablifhment, if my demands were exactly complied with; but that, as operations of this nature indifpenfibly required a particular and ftudied knowledge of the place, I fhould have the honour to addrefs to him a more extended and better combined plan, with circumftantial details and topographic charts of the country, and information refpecting the manners, laws, and governments of the iflands; and, laftly, a regular ftatement of the demands proper to be complied with, to fecure the execution of fo vaft a project.

The Minister, after having read my propositions, approved them so far as to assure me, that he would give an account of them to his Majesty, and that I might depend on the whole being executed to my utmost satisfaction. The particular conferences which I had, during the course of the month of February, with Mr. De Boynes, and the Duke D'Aiguillon confirmed me more and more in the persuasion, that nothing would be wanting for my expedition.

On the 19th of March, being sent for by the Minister, I received a letter, which contained the intentions of his Majesty, concerning the formation of the establishment of Madagascar, with the copy of another, addressed to the chiefs of the isle of France; and he recommended to me at the same time, to repair without delay, with all my men, to port L'Orient, where I should receive his orders for my passage to the isle of France.

I then saw that my mission was in some respect abandoned to the discretion of the chiefs of that island; and that the slightest want of disposition, or misunderstanding on their part, would be capable not only of injuring my operations, but even of entirely frustrating them. I made my representations to the Minister, at the same time requesting him to change the contents of the letter addressed to them; and to cause me to be supplied from France with the most indispensible supplies. His answer was, that there was no more time to make any change in these dispositions; that he was assured of the good disposition and zeal of the chiefs of the isle of France, who certainly would not suffer me to be in want of any assistance; and, lastly, that being upon the spot, I might do every thing which I judged of advantage

to

to the service. He added, that he would besides provide by new orders for the particular supplies, which the safety of the establishment required.

Notwithstanding this decisive answer, I ventured to make new representations on the inconvenience which might result from such an arrangement; but the Minister persisted in his first answer; and added, that the intentions of his Majesty being, that I should repair as speedily as possible to the isle of France, I could not hasten my departure too much. I therefore left him, with my mind filled with the evils and sufferings to which myself and my troops would be exposed. It was with a view to prevent these that I addressed myself to the Duke D'Aiguillon; to whom I communicated the orders and dispositions of the Minister, respecting my mission, and the just fears which they produced of my want of success. But the Duke comforted me with the promise that he would confer with Mr. De Boynes, that the face of affairs would certainly change, and that I might make myself easy.

The following day Mr. Audat, first Commis of the marine, came to me, and informed me, that the Minister being busied with important and pressing affairs, could not confer at that moment with me, concerning my mission, but that he had sent him to assure me, that every thing should be done to my utmost satisfaction; that he had determined to change the letter addressed to the chiefs of the isle of France, and even to augment the demands I had made; that I might depart immediately for that island, as I should soon be joined by succours dispatched immediately from France; and that, in the mean time, the chiefs of the isle of France would supply me
conformably

conformably to the orders tranfmitted to them with the fupplies I might want before the arrival of thofe which I fhould receive immediately at Madagafcar, and which would in future place me in a fituation to do without fupplies from that ifland; and, laftly, that with regard to the letter addreffed to the chiefs of the ifland, the moft effential articles had been changed, in order to let them know that I was left mafter of my operations, and that they were no otherwife concerned in my miffion than in fupplying me with the indifpenfible affiftance I might want.

This overture of the firft Commis, fatisfied me fo much the more, as I conceived the pleafing hope of acquitting myfelf with honour, in the important commiffion, which it had pleafed his Majefty to entruft me with.

On the 22d of March, I took my audience of leave; and had the fatisfaction to hear a confirmation of the news from the mouth of the Minifter; who put the letters and inftructions which are annexed to the prefent volume, into my hands, and added the following words, " I fhall provide for all your demands, and you will have reafon to be contented with me." Being thus difpatched by the Minifter, I departed for L'Orient; where I embarked on board the veffel La Marquife de Marbeuf.

On the 22d of September, I landed on the ifle of France, where I found a detachment of my corps, who had arrived before me; the reft had remained at L'Orient to wait for fhips. On my arrival in this colony, Mr. De Ternay, the Governor, was abfent, and did not return till the month of October; and as Mr. Maillart had refufed to confer alone with me on the affairs of my miffion, sion, before the return of the Governor, I waited till that time; and then demanded four days to regulate affairs with them, concerning my departure to Madagascar. In answer to this, these gentlemen replied, that their objects being separate, they would not confer with me, but each individually. I therefore waited on Mr. De Ternay, on the 22d of the month; of whom, after having communicated my orders, I demanded the furniture and assistance necessary to my operations. But he replied, that no particular order had been addressed to him relative to my mission; that the general letter of the Minister, regarded Mr. Maillart more than himself, since the furniture and assistance I stood in need of, depended on the treasury funds, which he did not concern himself with; that he would do his duty, in whatever related to the formation of my corps, and would put into my hands his Majesty's packet the Postillion, which had been forwarded by the Court, for the service of my mission; and, lastly, that all the rest related to the intendant.

After this interview, I waited on Mr. Maillart, to whom I likewise communicated the orders of the Minister; and gave him a statement of my demands of furniture and assistance, necessary to the execution of my mission, of which I gave a detail of the circumstances; at the same time urging such reasons, as appeared to me the most persuasive, to induce him to concur in every thing which might depend on him, and might promote the good of the service, on this occasion. But what was my surprize to hear him say, that he was very much astonished, that the Court had undertaken such an expedition, so prejudicial to the isle of France; all whose merchants would

would be ruined, if the establishment should succeed at Madagascar; where, by their concurrence, they carried on an advantageous commerce, which could not be legally prohibited by a simple letter of the Minister; but that, nevertheless, he would see what could be done, until he received the most positive orders of the Court: but that he could not avoid informing the Court, that the project was impracticable; because the Madagascar people having for one hundred and fifty years past, repelled all the attempts of France, they would not submit at this moment, when they were united under a solid government, formed by themselves.

Such an answer, from the second in command of the colony, confirmed still more the fears I had conceived at Versailles, that I was to be abandoned to the mercy of a jealous party; who, as several reports evinced, did not scruple to declare publickly, against the establishment at Madagascar, and who had already began to strike the first strokes; which, as will hereafter be seen, have placed the establishment in the most unhappy situation.

On the 28th of October, Mr. De Maisonville, whom the Minister had nominated to the place of sub-commissary and store-keeper under me, having refused to go to Madagascar, Mr. Maillart nominated in his place, the Sieur Vahis, a ship's clerk, of known bad character; whose public impositions rendered him unworthy of a post, which required an equal share of probity and capacity. I made my representations on this subject to Mr. Maillart, assuring him, that I never would have any connection with a disgraced man; and that he must immediately make choice of a person, more worthy of such a situation.

COUNT DE BENYOWSKY.

situation. He contented himself with answering, that the Sieur Vahis was good enough for Madagascar; where he had no wish to expose people of any value, as it was sending them to certain destruction. The indignation which such a reply deserved, led me to take the most prudent step. I turned my back upon him.

On the 24th of the same month, I conferred again, and more amply, with Mr. De Ternay, respecting my mission; and gave him an affecting sketch of the unhappy position in which my corps was about to be placed, and the sufferings to which we should be exposed, if he persisted in refusing the assistance I demanded. But I could do nothing with this Governor, who publickly asserted, that the establishment at Madagascar could not succeed, because the Minister had been so indiscreet, as not to consult the chiefs of the isle of France, on the means necessary to be employed.

Mr. Maillart, on the other hand, continually repeated, that the Minister ought to have confided this expedition solely to the chiefs of the isle of France; because, being personally interested, they would have provided for all the assistance which might have been required; instead of which, the orders of the Minister concerning the supplies to be made to the establishment, being ambiguous, they durst not proceed upon them.

I perceived, therefore, that no other steps remained for me to take, than that of hastening my departure for Madagascar, at the risque of being exposed to the last misery, and to be abandoned in the most cruel manner, until the arrival of the supplies directly from France, which I expected from the Minister. This determination, though violent,

violent, was most suitable to my engagements, and my sense of honour. I therefore overlooked all the inconveniencies, and gave orders for the departure of the packet, the Postillion, with a detachment of thirty men; and instructions for making enquiries respecting the place, manners, and power of the inhabitants; in order that I might be better enabled to expedite my operations, in obedience to the orders his Majesty had honoured me with.

On the 7th of December, the Sieur Saunier, Lieutenant of a frigate, and Commander of the Postillion, set sail, and departed the same day with my detachment, on his way to Madagascar. From the road he wrote me a letter, in which he informed me, that Mr. Maillart, notwithstanding the requisition I had made for the good of the service, and the repeated promises he had made to comply with them, had given no orders, but for objects of small consequence; and those not sufficient for the ordinary presents to the chiefs. He added, that he had refused him a supply of brandy, for the subsistance of the detachment; and that he should be obliged to deliver that article out of his own stores.

Justly astonished at what I heard, I waited upon Mr. Maillart, for an explanation of these circumstances; but his answer was, that the Court had left him master of his own operations, in whatever related to Madagascar, and that it would be of no use for me to apply to him in future, upon that subject.

In several conversations I had with Mr. De Ternay, for the seven following days, I begged him to persuade Mr. Maillart to comply with his duty, in respect to my mission; and, jointly, to let the merchants who frequented
the

COUNT DE BENYOWSKY.

the coaft of Madagafcar know, that they were to fufpend their commerce, till new orders were received from the Minifter; in order that I might take cognizance of abufes, and put the trade upon a footing more fuitable to the advantage of the public, and of the fettlement in particular. He acquiefced in my demand; but upon hearing that he had merely written, but not publifhed his order, I redoubled my complaints; and had the mortification to receive for anfwer from Mr. Maillart, that he thought it very extraordinary, I fhould infift on an object, which was foreign to my department, as it related to a commerce, which being authorized, could not be prohibited, and ftill lefs abolifhed, by a fimple letter of the Minifter.

On the 22d, the armament of my corps not being yet arrived from France, and having been obliged to exercife them with arms which had been borrowed, I requefted arms of Mr. De Ternay, Lieutenant of the arfenal of the ifle of France; and after feveral contefts, I obtained them, and armed my troops in a proper manner, in confequence of the care I took to get the greateft part of the arms repaired.

On the 25th, being informed that a private fhip was on the point of fetting fail for Madagafcar, and being defirous of feizing this opportunity, of forwarding my orders to Mr. Saunier and D'Efteruby, I fent for the Sieur Vahis, who ftill performed the functions of ftore-keeper, and enquired of him concerning the ftate of the fitting out of my expedition. To this he anfwered, that he was accountable only to Mr. Maillart, and not at all to me; and that he was not bound to attend to the fmalleft advice I might give him. This unexpected anſwer from a man, who by the nature of the ſervice was ſubjected to my orders, induced me to complain to Mr. Maillart; who coolly anſwered, that the Sieur Vahis acted according to his inſtructions, and that I muſt expect nothing more.

On the 28th, I again waited on Mr. De Ternay, to engage him to renew his conference with Mr. Maillart, upon the ſupplies required for my expedition. But he anſwered, that the Miniſter having addreſſed his orders directly to Mr. Maillart, it was he alone who was charged with their execution. I therefore waited upon this Intendant, accompanied with my Major, and a Captain of the corps; and made the moſt preſſing repreſentations to him, by obſerving, that my demands were founded on his Majeſty's orders, ſignified by the Miniſter; and that he could not, without failing in his duty, refuſe me ſuch things as my operations indiſpenſably required. But his anſwer was ſuch as I had no reaſon to expect from a man in place. He indulged himſelf in the moſt indecent obſervations on my miſſion; and had the confidence to ſay, that if Mr. De Ternay would follow his advice, he would put a ſtop to my expedition, becauſe the Court had not reflected on this project, formed by a mere adventurer; and that even if the Miniſter ſhould give him the moſt poſitive orders, he would rather throw up his employment, than have any concern in a ſcheme ſo badly projected. This indecent anſwer obliged me to quit him without anſwering a word; and I availed myſelf of the departure of a ſhip for France, to inform the Miniſter of all that had paſſed between the chiefs of the iſle of France and myſelf.

At the beginning of the month of December, the rest of my people having arrived at the isle of France in the Laverdi, and being desirous of hastening my departure for Madagascar, I demanded of the chiefs of the isle of France vessels for my transport; at the same time that I delivered to them a list of the most indispensable things, such as tools, medicines, and particularly twelve casks of vinegar, and three filtering stones. I insisted more strongly on these last articles, because I was fully informed of the bad qualities of the waters of Madagascar, which were either muddy, or charged with metallic matter; and that filtering stones and vinegar were the only means of rendering them less noxious, as had been proved with great success, in different European garrisons.

On the 11th of December, Mr. Maillart invited me to a conference, either at his house, or at that of Mr. De Ternay. I gave the preference to the former, where Mr. Maillart, in the presence of Mr. De Ternay, and Mr. De Bellecombe, ancient Commandant at Bourbon, made excuses for his former behaviour, requested my friendship, and assured me, that the veil that had hitherto covered his eyes with regard to my mission, was now removed; and that he now knew, that the Minister had particular reasons for employing me in the establishment at Madagascar; the labour of which he was ready to share with me, as far as it depended on the supplies to be furnished by him. He begged I would forget all that had passed, and grant him my friendship. My answer had no need to be studied. The Intendant appeared to be sensible of the impropriety of his conduct, and protested, that he was ready to exert himself, in promoting the success of my enterprize.

enterprize. I therefore assured him, that my esteem and friendship would always go together; and that from that moment, he was in possession of both. This protestation, on my part, was the more sincere, as I could form no idea, that a man in possession of a confidential employment, could be guilty of such a degree of imposition and hypocrisy; but the sequel will shew, that the Intendant had no such scruples.

On the 17th, Mr. De Ternay supplied me with artillery and military stores, which I was in want of for my departure; and I seriously set about exercising part of my men with the artillery, which they managed to my great satisfaction. Mr. Maillart, on his part, took the treasury chest out of the hands of the Sieur Vahis, and entrusted it to the Sieur Senaut, whom I was not acquainted with. These chiefs, some days afterwards, let me know, that they designed the vessel Le des Forges for my transport, which was every day expected from Bourbon; but Mr. Maillart observed, that he could send only a very small part of the articles of trade by that vessel; that the storehouses were absolutely without vinegar, and that he did not know what had become of the filtering stones: but that he would not fail to forward these by the first ship, even if he were obliged to buy them of the merchants. On the last day of the same month, I begged Mr. De Ternay to make a review of my corps, with that commissary. I caused my men to be supplied with clothes, as those which had been sent me had proved exceedingly defective.

January the 1st, 1774. Having received a packet from Madagascar, by which I learned, that the supplies delivered

COUNT DE BENYOWSKY.

delivered by the Poftillion were fo fmall, that my detachment had fcarcely three months eatables, and that my prefence was highly neceflary, becaufe fome of the chiefs had already began to commit hoftilities; I addreffed myfelf to Meff. De Ternay and Maillart, entreating them to furnifh me with a veffel as early as poffible, to carry me to my place of deftination. But as thofe gentlemen replied, that they could not procure me one in the courfe of the month, all thofe which were at their difpofal being employed in the fervice of the colony, I determined to freight a veffel myfelf, to carry fuccours and a reinforcement of men to my detachment. But I was prevented from doing this, by the promife of Mr. De Ternay, who affured me, that I fhould have the veffel I demanded before the expiration of January. I therefore prepared my corps for their departure; but upon the report, that fixty-three men were in the hofpital, I determined to leave them under the orders of Mr. Maring, my Lieutenant Colonel, under the conduct of Captain de Sanglier, until their perfect recovery, when they were to be tranfported to Madagafcar without delay. I learned, at the fame time, that part of my troops were feduced by the other regiments; that fome of my volunteers had already deferted, and that the difadvantageous obfervations on our expedition had been urged with fuch malice and fuccefs, that part of my officers had pretended ficknefs, with a view to delay their departure for Madagafcar. I underftood, likewife, that the chiefs of the ifle of France had fent emiffaries to Madagafcar to the King Hyavi, and other chiefs, to warn them that I was come to deprive them of their liberty, and that I had no other

intention

intention than to impose the yoke of slavery upon the whole island.

In this unhappy situation, being apprehensive that his Majesty's service might greatly suffer from so horrible a prejudice, I harangued my troops, and particularly my officers, who, conquered by the force of reasoning and their own sentiments of honour, returned to their duty, and chearfully disposed themselves to follow me. I then published my departure for Madagascar, and caused it to be proclaimed, that all volunteers, particularly workmen, who might be disposed to accompany me, should come and propose their conditions. This produced a considerable number of applications; but not knowing whether they were free, and being desirous of avoiding the slightest offence, I addressed myself to Mess. De Ternay and Maillart. The first replied, that he could not give permission to any one to leave the island; and Mr. Maillart said, and publickly repeated the assertion, that he would openly oppose any person's departure who might chuse to follow me to Madagascar, because it would be sending them to the butchery. For he said, he had received information, that several bodies of armed islanders waited for me, in readiness to attack my forces. This Intendant carried affairs to such an height, as to endeavour to seduce one of my chief officers, and to prevail on him to send him a full account of my operations at all opportunities. Thus it was that this chief exerted himself in carrying the Minister's orders into effect.

On the 22d, I profited by the departure of his Majesty's flute La Triquaire to send my packets to the Court. The following days I was busied in embarking the effects of my troop;

troop; and Mr. Maillart having affured me, that he would take care to deliver all the articles he had orders to furnifh for Madagafcar, I became eafy. My vifits being made and returned, I gave an entertainment on the 2d of February on the occafion of the birth of my fon, at the Great River; after which I commanded my troops to repair to the harbour with colours flying. They immediately went on board, and I had the long-expected pleafure of fetting fail for Madagafcar at fix in the evening.

On the 5th, the North winds obliged us to anchor at Bourbon, whence we departed on the 7th, and at laft we arrived at the bay of Antongil, where we anchored on the 14th of the fame month.

As the facts which I have related have no other connection with what follows, than by the various unhappy confequences they have produced, which originated in the want of difpofition, or as I may fay, original jealoufies of the chiefs of the ifle of France, they may be confidered only as preliminary to the hiftory of the eftablifhment I have formed at Madagafcar.

A

FULL ACCOUNT of PARTICULARS

RELATING TO THE

ROYAL ESTABLISHMENT at MADAGASCAR,

Entrusted to M. the COUNT DE BENYOWSKY: from his Arrival on the Island on the 14th of February, 1774.

AS soon as the Des Forges had come to anchor, I sent the small boat on shore, to bring the earliest news of the situation of my detachment, and the disposition of the islanders. The shore was lined with chiefs, who expressed the greatest satisfaction at seeing me; a circumstance which gave me no small pleasure. But these agreeable ideas were much diminished, upon entering the palisade which enclosed my men, and which, for want of effects to pay the blacks, they had been obliged to construct themselves. This hard work, at their first landing in an extremely hot country, had exhausted and reduced them to the most deplorable state. The commanding officer and surgeon were both ill, without assistance or medicines, and under the necessity of keeping a continual guard day and night against the natives, who had made

COUNT DE BENYOWSKY.

an irruption upon my feeble detachment with a number of armed men: and notwithstanding their weakness, they had defended themselves with such firmness, that they took seven prisoners from a chief named Raoul; but whom, by a stroke of policy, they had thought proper to send back without any ransom. All these circumstances, which I had learned by the accounts of Mr. Saunier and the Sieur de la Boulaye, volunteers in my corps, had almost entirely exhausted the detachment.

My first care was to use every exertion to give them all the assistance their unhappy situation required. They had no storehouse, barracks, nor hospital, nor even a lodging to receive me under cover from the open air. These different buildings could not be constructed in a short time, except by the islanders themselves. I therefore thought it proper to neglect no means of inducing them to enter into the interests of the establishment; and to gain their confidence, I caused the greatest number of them to meet together, to whom I distributed presents, and had the satisfaction to purchase several of the huts of the country, which served to lodge my officers and troops, until the indispensable buildings could be got forward. A hut was erected in haste, to serve for my lodging, and the work went on with such spirit, that I was able to disembark the troops I had brought with me the following day. They came on shore with all the pomp and in the best order possible, with a view to inspire the islanders with respect.

While these things were performing to the best of my wishes, I turned my thoughts to the discharge of the cargo. For this purpose, I demanded of Mr. de Saint Felix,

Felix, commander of the Des Forges, the invoice of the effects he had in his charge. But great was my astonishment to see that, notwithstanding the protestations and brilliant promises of Mr. Maillart, the vessel contained little or no liquor, nor articles of trade, and that the greatest part of the ship's cargo consisted of coals, an article then of the smallest importance. In this critical situation I was forced to purchase the wine, brandy, merchandize, and medicines the Captain offered to sell me; and upon his refusing to take a letter of exchange upon the King, as I could by no means dispense with the goods, I gave him a bill on my own account for the sum of fourteen thousand five hundred livres.

The day after, February the 17th, having demanded workmen to assist in the works, Mr. de Saint Felix refused them, alledging an order of the chiefs of the isle of France; but as he did not shew me this order after I had summoned him so to do, I made use of the authority his Majesty had been pleased to entrust me with.

February the 19th, I sent advice to all the chiefs of the province of Antimaroa to repair on the 1st of March to Louisbourg, that I might inform them of the intentions of his Majesty respecting the establishment I was to form at Madagascar, and to engage them as much as possible in our interest. At the same time I gave orders to mount the artillery, and to secure ourselves from surprize. Upwards of two hundred natives were voluntarily employed in carrying earth to raise the ground above the level of the river, and to begin to fill the neighbouring swamp.

On the 23d, his Majesty's frigate L'Oiseau, commanded by a Lieutenant, and his Majesty's vessel Le Rolland, commanded by by Mr. Kerguelin, having anchored in the road, with two hundred of their people sick, I gave them every assistance in my power; and more particularly an abundant supply of refreshments, by means of which their health was speedily restored.

On the 25th of the same month, his Majesty's packet Le Dauphin, commanded by Mr. Feron, an attendant on the expedition of Mr. Kerguelin, anchored likewise in the road.

March the 1st, 1774. Having received information, that all the chiefs of the province of Antimaroa were on their way to Louisbourg, where I had appointed to hold a conference, I gave new orders, to guard against any surprize; and the following day I received them without our enclosure, accompanied with some of my officers, and a detachment of thirty men. These chiefs were twenty-eight in number, and were escorted by about two thousand armed blacks, who formed a circle, at the entrance of which I seated myself; and informed them by my interpreter, that the intentions of the King of France being to favour and take under his protection the inhabitants of Madagascar, in which he was actuated by a knowledge of their attachment to the French nation, he had resolved to form an establishment, to defend them against their enemies; and to keep warehouses, at which they would at all times find, at cheap rates, such merchandizes as they might want; namely, cloth, liquors, powder, balls, gun flints, &c. which should be furnished to them in exchange for the productions of their country, and in particular rice, which they could not cultivate too largely; and that in return for the advantages his Majesty was disposed to heap on them, I required only the three following conditions:

The firſt was, that they ſhould enter into a treaty of friendſhip and alliance with me, and grant me land to fix my eſtabliſhments; and that they ſhould permit the iſlanders to ſell lands to ſuch of the French nation as ſhould be diſpoſed to ſettle among them.

The ſecond was, that they ſhould allow me to eſtabliſh in the inland part of the country, near the ſource of the river of Tingballe, hoſpitals and ſtore-houſes upon a proper ſpot of ground.

And laſtly, in the third place, that they ſhould engage to defend the property of the eſtabliſhment.

My interpreter had ſcarcely ended, before they all ſet up ſhouts of joy; and ſaid, they could not doubt the good intentions of the King, as he had ſent ſhips and troops to them, in preference to the other provinces, to ſupport them againſt their enemies; that they acknowledged him from thenceforth as their friend, and ſhould conſent to cede to me the land upon which I had began to form my eſtabliſhment, provided I entered into an oath not to conſtruct fortreſſes. With reſpect to the land I required up the country, they ſaid they would conſider of it; but that they required an oath, by which I ſhould acknowledge that I had no right over them, and would confine myſelf to the ſimple title of their friend, in which quality I ſhould aſſiſt them againſt their enemies.

Having acceded to the propoſitions, we celebrated the oath to ratify our union. This ceremony, which they call Cabarre, was ſeconded by an entertainment, in which they drank a caſk of brandy I diſtributed among them.

My friends then returned to their own villages, where they celebrated new feftivals, in teftimony of their joy at having gained the friendfhip of the King of France.

On the 3d, I difpatched the Poftillion, commanded by the Sieur Saunier, and attached to my expedition, with orders to repair to Foul Point, and diflodge the individuals who were endeavouring to prejudice the natives againft my eftablifhment; and to affure Hyavi, the King and Grand Chief of the province, of my friendfhip, as well as to make prefents to him, and to engage him to demand my affiftance againft the Fariavas, with whom he was at war. This appeared to me the moft certain method of obtaining permiffion to eftablifh a poft at Foul Point.

On the 9th, his Majefty's packet Le Dauphin, failed for the ifle of France, after receiving from me a fupply of brandy and rice, of which fhe was in the greateft want.

On the information of my people, that the blacks in fpite of their oaths, infulted the fentinels in the night, and the Sieur Senan, ftore-keeper, having at the fame time made complaint, that the magazines had been robbed, I gave notice to the chiefs, that if any natives fhould approach the pofts in the night, without anfwering the fentinel, as had been agreed, I fhould be forced to fire upon them. They only replied to my interpreters, that if I killed one black, they would in return kill ten whites. The fame evening a black armed with his fagaye, having with others come near a fentinel, placed before a magazine, and inftead of anfwering having thrown a fagaye at him, the fentinels fired upon them, flew one, and wounded two others. This action, though juft, appeared to the natives a juft caufe of complaint and retaliation; which I took

care

care to prevent, by removing them to the diſtance of our out-poſts. To ſucceed in this without expoſing my people I propoſed to four chiefs, to ſell me their villages, which ſurrounded Louiſbourg. They conſented, and evacuated them as ſoon as they were paid; and I gave immediate orders for demoliſhing them. In this manner I became maſter of the whole point of land, and my people were leſs expoſed to opportunities of debauchery.

On the 11th inſtant, I ſent on board his Majeſty's ſhips Le Rolland and L'Oiſeau thirty oxen. The blacks, though they had retired, and were ſatisfied by the payment for their villages, did not abandon their deſign of ruining the eſtabliſhment. I was informed by a free negreſs, that they had agreed to poiſon us all, beginning with myſelf, by means of the proviſions they might ſell us. In conſequence of this, I forbad the purchaſing any thing from the natives, until they had themſelves firſt eaten of it. This proof coſt one of them his life; for by taſting ſome fruit he offered to ſale, he ſuddenly fell down lifeleſs. His accomplices being informed of this tragical event, which diſcloſed their plot, fled up the river, where they laboured to ſtop the paſſage by felling trees acroſs it. They likewiſe fired upon a detachment I ſent to reconnoitre them.

The following day, a chief named Siloulout, under pretence of coming to render homage, requeſted an interview near a wood. This extraordinary demand, together with his refuſal to come to the Government, leading me to ſuſpect ſome treachery, I ſent out to watch his movements, and ſoon learned, that in conſequence of an

COUNT DE BENYOWSKY.

oath he had entered into with the Saphirobay, to assassinate me, he waited for my coming with about three hundred armed blacks; and that a much more considerable number were concealed in the wood. To frustrate this base attempt, I sent out two field pieces, preceded by fifty volunteers, commanded by two officers, who marched up to the enemy with such spirit, that this great multitude of blacks were struck with fear. Some retreated into the marshes, and the rest went on board their boats, whence they made the most violent discharge of their pieces, but without effect. This obliged me to point my field pieces at them. The first ball overset one of their largest boats, and killed several men. Two days after this event, I was informed by a female negro spy, that the chiefs Saphirobay and Siloulout, had formed with Raoul the project of a league with the neighbouring provinces, to destroy the establishment effectually. In order to avoid the effects of so dangerous a conspiracy, I gave orders to my Major to march at eleven at night, with a detachment of sixty volunteers, and proceed in the boats of Le Rolland and L'Oiseau, direct to the enemies camp, which was about three leagues distant. The troops landed at three in the morning, and immediately attacked them, and drove them into the wood; after which they reduced their village to ashes, and destroyed their works. This stroke restored the tranquillity of the establishment; and I went myself with my Major and Engineer, to examine an elevated island named D'Aiguillon, which is only one league distant from Louisbourg. Here I gave orders for constructing an oven, an hospital, and a redout for defending a botanical garden at the foot of the mountain of Difcovery.

On the 21ft, his Majefty's two veffels, Le Rolland and Le Des Forges, fet fail; the firft for France, and the latter for the Ifle of France. Mr. Kerguelin left behind him twelve men attacked with the fcurvy.

On the 24th, fix neighbouring provinces, who were overjoyed at the cataftrophe of the chiefs Raoul, Siloulout, and their other mortal enemies, deputed envoys to me, to propofe an oath of friendfhip, and to make prefents; in return for which, as well as to attach them to our interefts, I caufed brandy to be diftributed among them in proportion to their number, which was confiderable.

On the 26th, Saphirobay fent prefents, and requefted peace. I informed them, that after the attempts they had made againft the eftablifhment, it was pardon and not peace which they ought to require; and that I would not pardon them, fo long as they acknowledged as their chief Raoul, whofe infamous behaviour had been manifefted in attempts againft the fettlement; and laftly, that they fhould begin by clearing the river, and leaving us the free liberty of navigating it. They retired with promifes to comply with my demands; but the following day we had evident proof to the contrary, for the river was covered with trees loaded with fruit. I gave orders to examine what it was, and immediately found, that the Saphirobay had covered the river with tanguin, which is the ftrongeft poifon they are acquainted with, and with which they intended to poifon the river, which was the only water we ufed. I was therefore obliged for the preservation of my troops, to cause the river to be cleared, and to send a party of natives, engaged and commanded by a party of volunteers, to encamp and cut down and burn all the trees of this kind, which were in the neighbourhood of the river. This precaution, though expensive, was of the last necessity, to deliver us from certain destruction.

On the 30th, I repaired to Manambia, where I discovered an ore of copper on a mountain. I gave advice of this discovery to the Minister, having first prohibited any one from touching it.

April the 1st, 1774. Several chiefs of Angontzi came to offer their friendship, with a promise of conforming to all the articles which had been proposed in the former Cabars; and at the same time requesting as a favour, that a trade might be established in their country. This induced me to send a Commis with four volunteers, and a quantity of merchandize.

In the night, between the 1st and 2d, having visited the posts myself, I perceived that seven volunteers, with their arms and baggage, were missing. These circumstances led me to suspect that they had deserted, and the accounts I received the following day convinced me of the truth of my suspicions. In this juncture I could make no use of my troops, on account of their imperfect knowledge of the place. I therefore sent a number of Blacks after the deserters, commanded by the officers of my own corps. This precaution was the more necessary, as I had already received information, that more than fifty other volunteers, with two officers among their number, had agreed to follow the seven deserters. To prevent this second evil,

evil, I put the whole troop under arms, and after having reviewed them, and caused them to ground their arms, I commanded them to the right about, and marched them off without their arms, which were all carried into my apartment. I immediately caused the criminals to be seized and bound; and the seven deserters having been brought back that evening, were questioned at a council of war, in which one of the conspirators was condemned to run the gauntlet, and thirty-three volunteers were condemned to the works. Their design appeared to be that of forming a league with the islanders for the destruction of the establishment, and favour their subsequent escape in some private vessel.

On the 6th, his Majesty's packet the Postillion, which I had forwarded on the 3d of March for Foul Point, returned, and gave me an account, that the chief Hiavi, notwithstanding all that had been said by private merchants against the establishment, was earnestly desirous of my friendship, and begged me to establish a post near him. He assured me, that he was ready to construct a palisade according to my demands, and that he would contribute every thing in his power, or in the power of the chiefs, under his orders, to the good of the establishment. The chiefs of St. Mary came the following day to request and stipulate a treaty of peace and friendship, and to enter into mutual oaths. They, at the same time, begged me to establish a post on their island, and begged I would forget the massacre they had formerly committed against the French; to which, they said, they were driven by the cruelty and tyranny of the French themselves. I was convinced of the truth of their account, and therefore promised to forget all that had passed.

passed. We therefore entered into mutual oaths, and I engaged to send a person to open a trade of brandy and effects, for whose safety the chiefs should answer upon their own lives.

On the 9th, the interrogatories, confrontations, and circumstances, relative to the plot which had given employment to a council of war on the 5th of the same month, afforded occasion for a second council, in which the principal mover was condemned to run the gauntlet, another was flogged, and those who were less criminal were condemned to punishments adequate to their deserts.

On the 10th, his Majesty's packet the Postillion being in want of careening, and having no provision of pitch and tar, they were supplied by a gum of the country, named by the islanders ditti moenti, which appeared to be of excellent use in those kinds of work.

On the 17th, I dispatched his Majesty's vessel the Grand Bourbon with a detachment of a Captain, one Lieutenant, two Serjeants, a Drum, and eighteen Soldiers, to Foul Point, with presents for Hiavi, the chief of that province, who had deputed his brother to me to enter into an oath of friendship in his name.

On the 20th, the Saphirobay, who, in order to regain my favour, had driven Siloulout out of their territories and degraded their chief Raoul, came to the number of twenty-two great chiefs and more than two thousand unarmed islanders; and after several testimonials of the most lively repentance, and a renewal of their oaths, I presented them with brandy and presents, which they received with marks of the greatest satisfaction and reiterated promises, that they would immediately bring their commodities,

modities, the price of which had been regulated in the Cabars. The following day the chief Raoul came to demand pardon, and permission to establish himself in his country; which I granted, on condition that he should not assume the title of prince.

On the 23d, judging it to be of the greatest importance to make myself acquainted with the internal part of the country, where, from the account of the islanders, there were very fine plains and rivers favourable to communication; I sent the Sieur Saunier, Lieutenant of a frigate, up the river of Tingballe, to make enquiries. He returned from his expedition on the 26th, and informed me, that the river was navigable ten leagues from its mouth, and ran to the North West into the country; that before it arrives at its source it is divided into two branches, each navigable for about ten leagues. He added, that this river was bordered with very fine plains in good cultivation, and mountains covered with the most beautiful timber, which might be easily and at a little expence brought down to the settlement by water. I was greatly pleased with this discovery, as I already knew that the rivers opened three very advantageous places of trade, one to the West of the island of Bombatok, the other to the North of Cape D'Ambre, and the third to the East of Angontzi, of which all the rivers of communication discharge themselves into that of Tingballe. I therefore proposed to extend the establishment and cultivation into these different provinces, as soon as I should have received more important assistance than those which I had hitherto obtained from the isle of France.

On the 27th, the Grand Bourbon was obliged to return into the harbour, and take provifions for the detachment at Foul Point.

The chiefs of the Southern provinces came with prefents to enter into the oath of friendfhip, and begged me to fend one of my officers to dwell among them, and eftablifh a trade. I fent an interpreter, with orders to make himfelf acquainted with thefe feveral provinces, fome of which are more than one hundred leagues diftant from the chief place; and in the mean time I fufpended my further orders.

On the 28th, in the evening, being informed of the death of Mr. Senan, ftorekeeper of the eftablifhment, I gave inftructions to my Major to affix feals on his cheft and all the magazines, and place fentinels upon them. My juft fears of his bad conduct were confirmed the following evening, when we came to take an inventory of the general ftores, and every part of the adminiftration which had been intrufted to him. The whole was in fuch bad order, that all his regifters, as well of entries as deliveries, were entirely blank.

On the 29th, to haften the advantageous communication, which I propofed to eftablifh by land as far as the Weftern coaft; a communication abfolutely neceffary to open a trade with the coaft of Africa, and particularly with the province of Bombatok, which is extremely abundant in cattle and cotton; I fent Mr. Mayeur, an interpreter, with a Serjeant and one hundred and fifty Blacks, which were furnifhed by the allied chiefs, with inftructions to make different eftablifhments in his march; the firft at the fource of the river Tingballe, at the entry of a wood,

wood, and the other at the coming out; to conftruct a fort oppofite Angonave, the firft village of the Seclaves, dependant on Bombatok; to difcover and clear the fhorteft road towards the Weftern coaft; to enter into treaties of friendfhip with the chiefs of the interior part of the country; to convince them of the real advantages they might obtain from their commerce with the Whites; to difcover the moft favourable branches of trade; to obferve their forces, their inclinations, manners, and the climate of the country; to eftablifh pofts of reft for fuch efcorts as might hereafter tranfport merchandize, and where they may depofit their effects; and laftly, to forget nothing which might contribute to the good of the eftablifhment, and to give me advice of every thing they fhould do in the execution of their commiffion. But more efpecially, to exert themfelves to clear the roads which were moft eafy to be paffed through woods and over mountains. The Sieur Mayeur having received thefe inftructions and the neceffary provifions, began his march with all his people.

On the 30th, his Majefty's Corvette le Neceffaire, commanded by the Sieur Cordé, arrived with the Chevalier de Sanglier, Captain in my troop, with twenty volunteers, fome clerks or writers, and certain individuals, who propofed to eftablifh themfelves on the ifland.

The pofition in which we then found ourfelves, was fo much the more deplorable, as feveral of my officers were either abfent with detachments, or fick; the magazines were ill provided, and ftill worfe adminiftered; the hofpitals furnifhed with very few medicines, and we had no furgeon able to affift the volunteers, who were enervated by the indifpenfable works and the heat of the climate. I

had

had been obliged to employ them in the fortifications and in filling up the marshes. The military service of the night, which our proper safety required, succeeded to the fatigues of the day. Every moment I waited with impatience for the performance of Mr. Maillart's promises, but we were forgotten, or rather forsaken.

The first days of the month of May were so critical, and my troops were so worn out with disease, that for want of a surgeon I was myself obliged to give them that assistance which my own feelings and attachment to the service could not but impel me to administer. But I was soon reduced myself to the same unhappy situation; I withstood the attacks of the fever for a whole week, and the intolerable head-ach with which it was attended. But at last, being unable any longer to resist, I gave orders for carrying me to the island D'Aiguillon for air, and to rest myself a little after my fatigue. His Majesty's vessel the Grand Bourbon set sail on the 1st, to carry my troops to their destination. For this purpose I intrusted the command of my corps to Mr. Marin, Lieutenant Colonel, and that of the place to Mr. Marigni, my Major, and departed with my family. The change of air gave me some relief, and put me in a situation to look after my family, which was likewise attacked by the fever. For want of a surgeon I myself bled my spouse with a trembling hand, and fortunately the effect was answerable to my wishes, and restored her to health.

On the 14th, the Grand Bourbon returned a second time, on pretence of wanting water, though Mr. Marigni, gave me an account of a visit that he made on board the vessel, which shewed that she was provided with water for more than two months. I was then convinced, by the manœuvres of the officer who commanded the veffel, that he had particular reafons for his conduct, founded on inftructions from the ifle of France: but my health not permitting me to take the neceffary informations refpecting it, I determined to diffemble; and having learned, at the fame time, that the Lieutenant Colonel and Major of my corps were continually difagreeing, I embarked with my family, and returned to the main land, where my firft care was to inform the chiefs not to come armed; and I gave orders to my Major to watch more than ever againft a furprize.

On the 18th, his Majefty's veffel the Grand Bourbon fet fail for the third time.

My convalefcence having required fome care on my part, I deferred my operations till the firft of June. I found great affiftance in the care of Mr. Defmafures, Mafter of the Bouquinville, who, in the height of my illnefs, entered the port. Our fituation affected him fo much, that he offered his fervices to Mr. De Marigni, who accepted them with the greateft pleafure; but I learned, with the utmoft grief, that notwithftanding the attention of the Surgeon Major, there died, during my illnefs, Mr. Marin, Lieutenant Colonel of my corps, and fifteen volunteers. This confiderable lofs, and the well-founded apprehenfions of its encreafing, obliged me to affemble my officers, to whom I propofed to fend into the country, to enquire after a more healthy fpot, to which we would immediately tranfport ourfelves. This propofition was unanimoufly approved; and in confequence of their decifion, Mr. De Marigni departed the next morning, with a detachment, on the river of Tingballe, in fearch of an elevated fpot.

This

This day the chiefs of the neighbouring provinces came to teftify their joy at the eftablifhment of my health, and celebrated a public rejoicing, in which mufket fhot were not fpared.

On the 8th, Mr. Marigni returned from his excurfion, and informed me, that he had obferved feveral fine plains up the river, at three or four leagues diftance from the eftablifhment; but that this diftance having appeared to him too near the marfhes on the fea-fide, he continued to afcend the river as far as nine leagues, or thereabouts, from its mouth, where he ftopped at a place named by the iflanders the Plain of Health; which appeared to him the moft proper to tranfport the eftablifhment, becaufe it was extenfive and well fheltered, and was commanded by a mountain of the moft advantageous kind for conftructing a fort, which might fire over the river and a great extent of ground. This difcovery was very agreeable to me, and I immediately fent a fmall detachment, commanded by an officer, to encamp and make trial of the air; and upon the good report they made, I fent the Sieur Corbi with a fufficient number of workmen to conftruct, as fpeedily as poffible, habitations for us, and an hofpital for the convalefcents.

On the 9th, the third appearance of the Grand Bourbon, with my detachment, having fully convinced me of the motives which actuated the Captain of that veffel, who, during three months, had not thought proper to leave the road, I difembarked the troops which were on board that veffel, and gave orders to Mr. Saunier, commander of the Poftillion, to hold himfelf in readinefs to fail for Foul Point.

On the 12th, upon the report of Mr. Pruneau, employed in the administration and performing the office of store-keeper, that several different thefts had been committed in the King's store-houses, I caused the most accurate enquiries to be made; but as they were fruitless, and I had violent suspicion of the clerks themselves, I charged one of my Majors to superintend their conduct.

On the 22d, having received news from the Sieur Meyeur, that he had succeeded in opening a way to the Westward as far as the province Antanguin, and that the chiefs of that province would not permit him to proceed. I immediately sent the Sieur Corbi with a detachment of sixteen volunteers, commanded by a Serjeant, and twenty-four free Blacks likewise armed, to assist and second him in his operations.

On the 23d, the village of Sianie having taken fire, which was not above a musket shot distant from our establishment, and whose effects we could not avoid but by pulling down twenty of our houses, I judged it of the greatest importance to cause that chief to fix his dwelling on the other side of the river, and I obtained his consent, by purchasing those huts which the fire had spared.

On the 28th, his Majesty's vessels the Grand Bourbon and the Postillion, being on the point of setting sail, the first for the isle of France, and the second for Foul Point; and having demanded provisions for their people, I caused all the remaining salt provisions and brandy which were in the magazines; and had been supplied from the isle of France, to be delivered to them; and upon the representations of Mr. De Marigni, that it was indispensibly necessary to send back some volunteers, I gave orders to that effect;

effect; and at the same time I thought it proper to send back one of my officers, with letters addressed jointly to Messrs. De Ternay and Maillart, containing a statement of demands of things, which the establishment could not dispense with; and among others, filtering stones, medicines, surgeons, and some blacks, accustomed to the service of the hospitals, together with persons capable of overlooking the preservation of his Majesty's store-houses, and also flour and liquors. At the same time I demanded of those gentlemen, articles of trade; and assured them, that if I received those articles, I should soon be in a situation to procure them nine hundred thousand pounds of white rice, and three thousand oxen; and that it was of the greatest importance to the service, that they should send me two galliots for the exportation and importation of rice and merchandize from the chief to the out-settlements, as well as to carry my detachments, which had hitherto been obliged to repair to the place of their destination by land, across marshes, which had greatly contributed to their destruction. To these demands, I added that of a reimbursement of the sum of ninety-six thousand one hundred and sixty-six livres, which I had myself advanced to the treasury of Madagascar, upon the requisition of the officers of the administration; which sum had been employed in purchasing various kinds of merchandize, with eatables, drink, and medicines, of which the general magazine was entirely destitute: and, lastly, I observed to Mr. De Ternay, that the deplorable situation of my troops scarcely permitted them to perform the ordinary services; for which reason I requested him to order me a supply of men, and to permit the officer, whom

I sent

I sent directly for that purpose to the isle of France, to raise soldiers, workmen, and engage with such inhabitants as might be willing to come with them.

July, 1774. The Grand Bourbon set sail, and I saw her depart with the hope, that my pressing representations would impel the gentlemen in the administration of the isle of France, to take those measures which were indispensibly necessary, in so urgent and grievous a situation as ours; and that I should in a short time see the supplies arrive, which had been so often promised. But a determination had been made to abandon the establishment, as will be shortly seen.

The same day I sent his Majesty's brig the Postillion to Foul Point; and gave precise orders to the Sieur Seunier, commander of this vessel, to bring all the private vessels he might find in the harbours of St. Mary and Foul Point, and to make the most accurate enquiries into the conduct of individuals.

Our state of extreme weakness inspired several chiefs, who were debauched by the Saclaves, with the design to break their oath of friendship and attachment. But I was happily advised of this by the other chiefs, who were greatly attached to my person; and notwithstanding the weak state of my people, they behaved with so much firmness, as to break the measures of these treacherous chiefs, whom during the night they forced in a camp they had established in a wood, and completely routed them.

Mr. De Marigni, my Major, whose former services had merited the Cross of St. Louis, and who had always seconded me in my operations, was at this time attacked with

with the disorder of the country. His illness became every day worse; and I had the more reason to be apprehensive for the safety of this brave officer, as he had exhausted himself by continual exertions. My son likewise was attacked. While I was thus oppressed with the mortifying reflections, into which their unhappy situation threw me, I received information, that two workmen, the one a carpenter, and the other an armourer, had deserted; and that they had been seen in the boat of the Grand Bourbon, before she set sail. I immediately sent to search that vessel, but they were so well concealed, that it was impossible to find them. Justly irritated by the vile proceeding of the Captain of this vessel, who though in his Majesty's service, had dared to deprive this infant establishment of such necessary workmen, (as I was by his means without an armourer, and incapable of carrying on the works) I immediately gave advice to the chiefs of the isle of France, and determined to inform the Minister of this proceeding by the earliest opportunity.

My health, which had been unsettled for a long time, now began for some days to experience the most dreadful attacks. My only son Charles Maurice Louis Augustus, Baron de Benyowsky, died of the country disorder on the 11th of this month, at seven in the morning, to my extreme regret; and on the 12th, Mr. De Marigni, my Major, for whose life I had been so greatly apprehensive, died at ten in the morning. He was equally lamented by myself, and all the officers of my corps. My fever became every day more violent, and forced me at last, to repair to the Plain of Health. The palisade of Louisbourg being constructed of flight wood, and being too extensive to be
guarded

guarded by the few remaining hands, I had built a fort, which I named Fort Louis. It was constructed of the best wood of the country, with a triple palisade, strengthened without by a sloping of turf, and having a very solid banquette, which favoured the fire of our murdering pieces. It was besides fortified by advanced works. I left the command of this fort to Mr. De Vienne, First Lieutenant, with fifty-six men, and subaltern officers, and directed my course towards the Plain of Health, with thirty convalescents; where I arrived on the 20th of the month, and established a market for the purchase of rice, cattle, and wood; all which took place according to my desire. In a few days I began to recover, as did likewise several of the volunteers, though lodged in huts, made after the manner of the country, and not sufficiently close to keep out the rain.

On the 23d, I heard by report, that the brigantine Le Bouquinville had set sail. I had purchased of this vessel, for the urgent necessities of the colony, effects amounting to upwards of forty thousand livres, for which I gave my bill to the Captain on the Treasury of the isle of France. During the rest of the month I was employed in causing habitations to be constructed and the ground to be cleared.

August the 5th, 1784, the Seclaves sent deputies to request the establishment of a trade among them; but they refused permission to build fortresses. This request of theirs being contrary to my views, I refused to comply with it.

On the 13th, his Majesty's brig the Postillion returned into the harbour, and the Sieur Saunier, the commander, gave me an account, that on passing near St. Mary, he had found the Sieur Savournin trading contrary to the repeated

peated prohibitions which had been communicated to him; and having at laft thought proper to fpeak in degrading terms of the fettlement and its origin, he had feized him in the King's name, and brought him to the bay; that he had likewife found the Sieur Oliver making preparations to trade at Foul Point; but that this laft had followed him to give an account of his operations, and to juftify himfelf by pleading his ignorance of the prohibition.

The common letter of the chiefs of the ifle of France informed me, that having been made acquainted with the preffing wants of the eftablifhment at Madagafcar, they had freighted the private veffel La Flore, to convey ftores to us. The general good, therefore, required, that this veffel fhould repair immediately to the chief fettlement to unload, and receive in exchange, as the chiefs of the ifle of France likewife noticed, a quantity of rice of equal value to the effects fhe might bring. I was informed on the contrary, from Meffrs. Savournin and Fayufe, Captains, that they had not two tons on board for his Majefty's ftores in that ifland; that the veffel was not freighted on account of his Majefty; and that on the contrary, a written bargain had been concluded with Mr. Maillart, that they fhould go to Fort Dauphin, and remain there to take in fupplies for the ifle of France; and in confequence, that he could not take in rice, notwithftanding my fummons for him to take in his loading.

Juftly furprized at the proceedings of the adminiftrators of the ifle of France, who by this conduct gave me reafon to believe, that they were laying a fnare for me, I forbad the Sieur Savournin, in his Majefty's name, to trade to the Southward, upon which he propofed to pay annually to the King, the sum of one hundred thousand livres, for the exclusive right of trading from the point of the bay to Foul Point. This proposition having appeared to me to be advantageous, and for the good of the service, I executed an act agreeably to these conditions.

On the 15th, the natives of Navan, headed by the robber Siloulout, came in the night to the number of about two hundred men, with the intention of robbing the rice grounds; but having been surprized by the sentinel they fled. The following day I sent an interpreter to them, to advise them to live in peace with us; and not to repeat any such attempts, if they wished to avoid exposing themselves to my just vengeance. They answered my interpreter with their muskets, and three of the workmen who accompanied him were slain, and six wounded. Upon receiving this account, I sent a detachment of thirty-six volunteers, commanded by proper officers, with orders to attack them in the night, and put all the blacks of Navan to the sword. But the chiefs attached to my party, not thinking it proper that I should employ whites, took charge of the expedition, which they set about with seven hundred men, well armed. To support them, I ordered Captain De Sanglier to follow them with a detachment. During these transactions, the Sieur Oliver, who had fully justified himself, and whom I had forbidden to trade in any of the offices of the establishment, perceiving that his voyage would be very chargeable, if he was forced to carry his cargo back to the isle of France, and being likewise acquainted with our pressing necessities, occasioned by the want of supplies, proposed to sell his vessel to the King, with thirty-four blacks, and some effects, which I gave

COUNT DE BENYOWSKY. 139

gave orders for the purchase of, upon the valuations which were made by the store-keepers, and others employed in this service, namely :

The vessel	30,000 livres.
The slaves	10,200
The effects	1,600
	41,800

On the 21st, the Sieur Savournin, and the Surgeon-Major, having informed me, that there were several men on board the vessel attacked with a contagious disorder, I gave orders for them to be conveyed to the isle D'Aiguillon, to perform quarantine. This illness proved to be the small-pox.

On the 23d, the Chevalier Sanglier, Captain commanding the detachment I had sent against the blacks of Navan, returned to Louisbourg, and informed me, that the boat which carried his troops having been overset, had retarded his operations; but that notwithstanding this accident, the troops of the allied chiefs had succeeded in forcing their principal village, according to my orders, though it was well defended by forts, palisades, and deep ditches; and that the nest of these robbers had become the prey of the flames.

The following day, several chiefs of various provinces, declared in their Cabar, that they would on this account, consider the Navans as traitors and perjured men; in consequence of which, they declared them slaves. The latter, on hearing this news, took refuge in the Northern parts of the island.

On the 2d of September, perceiving that my situation became daily more critical, and being continually harrassed by the intrigues of the chiefs of the isle of France, who sent emissaries to Madagascar to prejudice the natives against me; and having every reason to fear, that our weak situation might encourage them in the design they had long taken up of exterminating us, I thought it of the greatest consequence to obtain from our allies a supply of men to defend us in case of need. I therefore stipulated them, that they should constantly keep up a force of one thousand two hundred armed men.

This nation have a custom equally cruel and strange, which they have observed from time immemorial. Any child who is born with natural defects, or even on certain days, which they consider as unlucky, is sacrificed at its birth. Most commonly they drown them; and I had an opportunity of being a witness to this cruel custom, in descending the river in my way to the plain at Louisbourg. It happened fortunately, that on the day of my departure I had an opportunity of saving the lives of three of these unfortunate children, which they were carrying with the intention of drowning. I caused them to be conveyed to Fort Louis; and having given directions for summoning a grand Cabar, I caused all the chiefs to enter into an oath, that they would not in future practise any such act of cruelty. I considered this as the happiest day of my life, from the abolition of this execrable custom, which was the effect either of religion, or some more detestable prejudice.

On the 4th, I was advised by one of the chiefs of Antambon, that the chiefs Mahertom, Raboet, Campan, and Saphirobay, had entered into a combination to affinate me. I immediately sent an interpreter to thefe chiefs, to enquire into their intentions. Mahertom denied that he had entered into the confpiracy, but Raboet, having avowed that he was the eighth perfon who took the oath, the blacks could with difficulty reftrain themfelves from rufhing on him, and putting him to death.

On the 5th, Fort Auguftus, which I had caufed to be conftructed on the mountain of the plain I before fpoke of, being finifhed, I fent fixteen men to guard it, until further orders from the Court; and I diftributed among them fix pieces of ground in the environs, for the commencement of a vigorous cultivation.

On the 7th, upon the report of the commanding officer, that very confiderable thefts had been made out of the royal magazines, of which the ftorekeeper had not given any account, I caufed the latter to be arrefted, and proceeded to interrogate two perfons of the name of Picard and Julien, who had been accufed of felling the ftores to the natives. The refult of this proceeding evinced, that thefe two men, who by the negligence of the ftorekeeper had almoft the entire management of the effects, had appropriated a confiderable part to their own ufe. They were thereupon fent off, namely, Julien to France in the Poftillion, and Picard to the ifle of France, with information of the proceedings againft them; and the effects which were found in the hands of thefe two criminals were returned to the ftorekeeper.

On the 8th, the Saclaves came to fell two hundred and fifty oxen, which I was very ready to purchafe, as I was convinced of the great advantage of carrying on a reciprocal commerce between the fettlement and that rich province.

On the 12th, Deputies arrived from Hiavi, grand chief of Foul Point, with one hundred and twenty armed men, who informed me, that the object of their coming was to fupport me againft the Saphirobay, who had entered into a fecret alliance with the blacks of the Southern part of the ifland. They informed me, that their fmall party would be reinforced by a much more confiderable number. The Saphirobay being informed of this proceeding, prepared to abandon their country; but when my interpreters informed them, that their pardon depended only on their repentance, and the confirmation of the oath which I had required of them, to difcontinue the horrible cuftom of deftroying their new born infants, in the cafes before-mentioned, they all repaired to Louifbourg on the 13th, with their wives, who, being convinced by my reafoning, entered with the greateft fatisfaction into the oath of never facrificing their infants in future, as they had formerly been accuftomed to do. Such an interefting engagement was naturally fucceeded by a grand entertainment; and I thought it becoming the honour of the nation to contribute to it, for which reafon I gave orders for the diftribution of brandy and other prefents.

On the 14th, feveral chiefs of St. Mary, and other allied provinces, fent deputies, with near fix hundred men, to warn me, that the Saphirobai were troublefome and

treacherous

treacherous people; and that, notwithstanding their repeated oaths, they continued to engage the Southern provinces in their party to exterminate us; and that they came with their forces to support me against them. The position in which I found myself after this advertisement, led me to the following reflections: I was but too well acquainted with the treacherous disposition of the Saphirobai; and their punishment would be merely an act of justice: but in making war upon them, I exposed my men, who are of such value in this country; besides which, in destroying this nation, I should put an end to the cultivation of the ground; and the indisposition of the isle of France, or rather of its chiefs, gave me the greatest reason to fear, that we should not long receive from them even the most indispensible supplies. It would therefore be evidently a great disadvantage to the establishment, to drive away a people, who being furnished with the most essential articles of subsistence and trade, were the only support upon which I could depend. From these reflections I thought it of the greatest advantage to gain the Southern provinces by presents, to restrain the Saphirobai by flattering promises; and to engage the Sambarives to come and take possession of the lands of the Saphirobai, in case the latter should force me by their treachery, to drive them out of their province.

On the 15th, I convened a general assembly, where the oaths of fidelity were renewed; and it was at the same time agreed, that every chief who hereafter should hold a secret meeting, should be driven from his village, his lands should be confiscated to the establishment, and his family reduced to slavery. That all those who should not assist

assist the establishment in case of an attack, should lose their lands, and that the Saphirobai should pay twenty oxen as a satisfaction, which was immediately done.

At the end of the Cabar, all the women of several provinces appeared, who were desirous of renewing, and causing the chiefs to renew the oath, that they should never destroy their children, upon any pretence whatsoever, and they strongly intreated me to send for my spouse, who on account of her ill health, had been obliged to go to the isle of France for the change; in order, as they said, to deposit in her hands an oath, which in the nature of things, regarded women more particularly, since it tended to the preservation of their immediate offspring. They assured me, that their demands being conformable to their laws, they hoped soon to see my spouse. This request appeared to me so natural, and so conformable to the views which I had proposed of gaining their confidence, that I began to think very seriously of sending for Madame Benyowsky, even at the risk of her health.

On the 19th, I sent the interpreter Descotti, to the Sambarives, to engage that great province to attach themselves entirely to us; and I returned to the plain, where nothing remarkable had happened since my departure.

On the 20th, a private vessel, named the Belle Artier, commanded by the Sieur Auger, arrived in the harbour, with an order from Mr. Maillart, for three hundred thousand pounds of white rice, for the subsistance of the isle of France; but having learned from the Captain, that this rice was on his own account, and that he had purchased it of Mr. Maillart, at the rate of sixteen livres the hundred weight, with the intention of carrying it for sale to the

Cape

COUNT DE BENYOWSKY. 145

Cape of Good Hope. I refused to deliver it to him, as I could sell it for twenty-two on the spot; and as the Sieur Auger begged me to give him the value in slaves, I agreed very willingly, because by that means, I should clear myself of my slaves, of whom I had a number in a situation where they could easily desert.

By the same vessel I received a letter from Messrs. De Ternay and Maillart, in which I saw with the greatest pleasure, that those gentlemen had sent to Madagascar a store-keeper, and people to be employed in the administration, together with the Sieur Des Assisses, to perform the office of supercargo; and that the latter was coming in the vessel La Belle Poule, which was expected to arrive very soon at Louisbourg with stores. I therefore gave orders for making an inventory, in the presence of the Sieur Aumon, store-keeper, and his people, of all the effects in the King's magazines, and directed that they should be put into his hands.

The day after the arrival of these new officers, I was informed, that, not content with the common women, the young men had entered into all the huts of the blacks, and attempted, sword in hand, to force the husbands to abandon their wives to them. The complaints which at the same time were brought by the chiefs of the Saphirobai, having justified this report, I sent a guard to search for these people, who arrested them, and they were thrown into prison.

But as our new surgeons were among them, and these were absolutely necessary for the service of the hospitals, I was obliged to set them at liberty, as well as the clerks of the administration, who had fallen into the same imprudent

VOL. II. U

dent behaviour; and from whose misconduct I had great reason to fear, that some abuses would take place in the store-houses, particularly in the account of receipts and disbursements. But as Mr. Maillart in his last letter, had conjured me to place entire confidence in the persons he had nominated, I agreed to his demand, though I could not but be convinced, that the choice he had before made at first of a supercargo, had been attended with considerable loss of the King's stores.

On the 24th, I put my packets for the Court into the hands of the Sieur Saunier, Commander of his Majesty's brig the Postillion, with my instructions, and twenty-five blacks, addressed to the Sieur Percheron, agent of the islands of France and Bourbon, to be remitted to the Sieur Auger at the Cape, in payment of the three hundred thousand pounds of rice,* and he set sail for France the next day.

On the 28th, in consequence of the packets I received from the Sieur La Boulaye, officer in my corps, whom I had sent to the isle of France to raise men, which were wanting in the establishment; by which I understood, that he had succeeded after many difficulties, in engaging several workmen, and that he waited only for a favourable opportunity of forwarding them to Madagascar. I judged it of the greatest importance to hasten their passage; for which purpose I dispatched his Majesty's vessel La Coureur, commanded by the Sieur Desmousseaux, officer of the blue, in whose hands I put dispatches for

* After the word rice (ris) in the M S. follow the words, *Je le cherchai en meme temps des esclaves portes No. 16,* which I have not attempted to translate. W. N.

Meffrs. De Ternay and Maillart; in which I informed the latter of the behaviour of the clerks he had sent, and strongly preffed Mr. De Ternay for a supply of men to reinforce my troops, in order that I might be able to carry my establishments into the country of the Seclaves.

On the 30th, a private brig, La Flore, commanded by the Sieur Fayeufe, failed out of the harbour with one hundred and sixty million pounds of rice, which he had received in exchange for sea salt, which was placed in his Majesty's store-house.

On the 1st of October, 1774, the interpreter whom I had sent to Manahar, sent information, that he had succeeded very well in the mission I had intrusted to his care; that the Sambarives had nothing more at heart than to secure our friendship; that they were ready to quit their mountains to come and inhabit the lands of the Saphirobai, where they could supply the establishment with four thousand men in time of war. But that as the interpreter had not spoken to them but in his own name, pursuant to my orders, they were then about to send several of their chiefs as deputies to me, to conclude this affair, of such great importance to themselves, since it secured them my friendship, and placed them under my safeguard. I was greatly pleased with this good news, as I found myself by that means in a situation to support a war against the Saphirobai, which was almost inevitable; and I immediately established a post with that friendly nation, to secure their attachment.

On the 2d, I repaired to the plain, where I knew that Meffrs. Mayeur and Corbi, whom I had sent upon discoveries to the Westward, were to make their rendezvous.

As I ascended the river, I received great satisfaction in seeing several places lined with inhabitants, who made repeated discharges of their musquets, and cried out in their language, Long live our father.

On my arrival at the plain, I learned from the Sieurs Corbi and Mayeur, that in passing through the interior parts of the island, which was extremely rich in oxen, cotton, ebony, and gum guttæ, they had found all the inhabitants very much disposed to join my interests; but that the knowledge they had of the small number of my forces, did not permit them to turn their backs on the Arabians, who had long frequented their coast, and had acquired a certain empire over them, as well by the quantity of merchandize they brought, as by the forces they could oppose against them. But that they waited, in order to unite with me, only for the moment in which they could face the Arabs.

Upon this report, I should have been desirous of making a new expedition into the country, more especially as these two officers added, that the road of communication required only a common share of labour, to make it practicable by land: But the want of assistance on the part of the isle of France, obliged me to suspend this important operation. The Sieurs Mayeur and Corbi, had purchased eight hundred oxen, in the two or three days journey they had made.

On the 7th, in consequence of the arrival of his Majesty's frigate the Belle Poule, commanded by the Chevalier Grenier, I left the plain and returned to Louisbourg. On my arrival at Mahetompe, I learned from Mr. Sanglier, Commandant in my absence, that Mr. Des Assises, the supercargo,

COUNT DE BENYOWSKY. 149

supercargo, had arrived in the Belle Poule, with the assistants. I immediately repaired to Louisbourg, to receive him in his quality of supercargo, and the Sieur Aumont, as storekeeper.

The packets of Messrs. De Ternay and Maillart informed me, that the Sieur Des Assises had received from the treasury of the island, a sum more than sufficient to answer the appointments of my corps for a year. I therefore required pay for my troop for six months; but instead of satisfying my demand, he replied, that he had not only received no sum at the isle of France, but on the contrary had advanced out of his own pocket, sums for the purchase of the most necessary articles for the establishment. I therefore again adopted the expedient of applying to the purse of my friends to replenish the treasury, upon the demand of the supercargo and treasurer, with a sum which might pay the troops for the six months which were due.

Some days after his arrival, the Sieur Des Assises convened several chiefs unknown to me, to whom he delivered a cask of brandy, and assured them that he was come to support them against me, in case I should do them any injury; and that they might from thenceforth consider him as their protector, because he was come to Madagascar for that purpose, and to superintend my conduct. This criminal proceeding in a person subordinate to me, was doubtless deserving of exemplary punishment; but, as the transaction related to myself personally, I was content with reprimanding him in a very serious manner, on his absurd conduct. He appeared to be affected with my remonstrances. But a few days afterwards, I had reason to be

convinced

convinced that he was, in more than one respect, the creature of Mr. Maillart.

The continual chagrin and disquiet which I suffered, destroyed my health, and reduced me to such an extremity, that the surgeons despaired of my life. In the height of my illness, the Sieur Des Assises requested my officers to meet at his habitation; and on their refusal, he waited upon them, and declared that he had particular orders from Mr. Maillart to seize all my effects and papers, in case my life was in danger; and that in consequence of the evident danger in which I then was, he requested them to assist him in carrying his orders into effect. The reply of my officers consisted of a threat of vengeance, if he should ever dare in future to make such a proposal to them. At the moment, however, in which the Sieur Des Assises condemned me to death, a favourable crisis dissipated my disorder, by a spontaneous evacuation of bile, and placed me entirely out of danger. Great indeed was my surprize, when my officers came to express their joy on my convalescence; and when I heard at the same time, from their report, of the conduct which this chief storekeeper had adopted with respect to me, I immediately sent for him, and reproached him for his conduct. Confounded as he was at the disclosure of his proceedings, he avowed, in the presence of my officers, that all which he had hitherto done, had been founded on particular instructions of Mr. Maillart. He at the same time put into my hands these instructions, which might more properly be called a defamatory libel, of which I immediately sent a copy to the Minister, addressing my packet to him by the Chevalier Grenier,

Grenier, Commander of his Majesty's frigate the Belle Poule.

On the 20th, the Sieur Des Assises requested me to sign a verbal proces, declaring, that several considerable thefts had been committed in his Majesty's storehouses; and in particular, that seventeen casks of wine had leaked out since his arrival. I contented myself with replying, that I did not know what it was to affix my signature as authority for misconduct; that I was by no means ignorant of the exorbitant consumption of wine by himself and his people, while my officers could not have a single bottle; and that with regard to the effects which had been stolen, I was well informed of his conduct with the women, and that he was too well acquainted with the thieves to think of forwarding any proceedings against them. This reply confounded him, and obliged him to retire without attempting to make any answer.

This misconduct on the part of the administration, was so much the more infamous, not only because the magazines suffered; but as the articles of trade cost these gentlemen nothing more than the trouble of drawing out a verbal proces, they every day purchased articles at an exorbitant price; insomuch that it became necessary to pay three livres for articles, which before their arrival might have been had for ten sols. I therefore gave orders, that all the provisions which the blacks were desirous of selling, should be exposed in the market; and at the same time forbad the purchase of them at a higher rate than the price settled at the preceeding Cabars.

The Sieur Des Assises, notwithstanding this new prohibition, which was so conformable to found policy, was
the

the first to infringe it, by directing all the provisions which the blacks brought to the Bazar, to be conveyed to him; but the officer of the guard did his duty, and the Sieur Des Assises was punished, by the confiscation of what he had purchased.

We were still but weakly fortified; and the houses which had been constructed according to the manner of the country, began to decay. I thought it necessary therefore to work, both on the fortifications and on the construction of other habitations. I caused to be drawn up, or rather I drew up myself a plan, plate 19, fig. 2. for the construction of a fort; a house for the Governor, built with boards, and one hundred and thirty log houses. I was not a little surprized to hear the Sieur Des Assises, animated by the disposition of Mr. Maillart, openly exclaim against these indispensible labours. He asserted, that he knew no chief but Mr. Maillart; and that his orders were contrary to these augmentations. He not only expressed his desire, that they should not take place, but threatened likewise, that he would inform the blacks that he would not pay any of them who might be employed. This absurd behaviour extorted no other emotion but compassion; and as from that moment I considered this intendant as a designing person, though incapable of executing a project so badly conceived, I caused several chiefs to be assembled, in order to propose this enterprize to them, being determined to apply again to the purse of my friends, to pay their salaries, in case the Sieur Des Assises persevered in his refusal to pay them. Their reply confirmed me in the opinion I had conceived of that gentleman. They all asserted, that they would not work, be-

cause

COUNT DE BENYOWSKY.

becaufe the Sieur Des Affiffes had affured them, that I had only a very fhort time to remain at Madagafcar; but that he would not pay them if they worked for the eftablifhment by my orders. I difmiffed this weak fet of men immediately with indignation.

Such was the execution of the brilliant promifes of the Intendant of the ifle of France, even by a man whom he had nominated his fub-delegate. My troops were exhaufted by continual labour and fatigue, and the officers were threatened to be deprived of the fruit of their labour, by the information which the ftorekeeper gave them, that they fhould foon be difmiffed by a new commander, whom he affured them would be fubftituted in my place in a fhort time.

The iflanders were thus prejudiced againft the eftablifhment, by the public calumnies of thofe whofe duty it was to contribute moft to their union. The individuals compofing the eftablifhment, being extenuated by continual fatigue, and feeing themfelves abandoned and betrayed at every ftep they took; the troops in want of cloathing, badly lodged, and very imperfectly fortified.—Such was our moft critical fituation; and the more efpecially it was to be regretted, as it was the work of perfons charged with orders to give every poffible affiftance to an eftablifhment which was founded on the moft extenfive views.

On the 2d of November, the Sieur Des Affiffes, conftantly animated by the fpirit of Mr. Maillart, affembled at his houfe all the clerks and people employed in the adminiftration, and in their prefence drew out a verbal procefs, importing, that the particular inftructions of the Intendant of the ifle of France, which he had through fear put into my hands, were written by himfelf, and that Mr.

Mr. Maillart had no share in them; but that circumstances having obliged him to draw out this false piece, he avowed its want of foundation. I was immediately informed of this vile proceeding, and went without delay to the rascal, with my Major; and having ordered him to communicate his papers, the original of the private instructions, signed by Mr. Maillart, was found, and admitted by the impostor.

The rest of the month was employed in such works as the volunteers of my corps were capable of, and in which the convalescents were so zealous as to join us. The other absurd circumstances of the conduct of Messrs. Des Assises and his people, which were always founded on the particular and verbal instructions of Mr. Maillart, being only a repetition of those with which he had begun on his first landing, I think it unnecessary to repeat them, but shall only observe, that in order to excite the islanders to work who were disgusted by the pernicious conversation of the principal storekeeper, I employed my own black domestics, and those whom I employed in my house, as I chose rather to deprive myself of their personal services, than omit any occasion of contributing to the good of the establishment.

The first part of the month of December, was employed in the usual works; but on the 11th, I saw with the greatest satisfaction, the arrival of his Majesty's brig Le Coureur, with my spouse, whose presence was so necessary for the abolishment of the cruel custom of destroying of the children born on days which were reckoned unlucky, or which were in some respects imperfect. The same vessel brought the Sieur de la Boullaye, whom I had sent to the isle of France, on the urgent business of the colony, with orders to engage, with the consent of Mr. De Ternay, the proper workmen to forward the buildings, which we could not dispense with. He informed me, that he had brought with him thirteen workmen, six soldiers, and two passengers, in the number of which was the Marquis D'Albergotti De Vezas, Chevalier of St. Louis, and ancient Captain of infantry, who came to offer his services; which, however, I could not accept without having received the consent of the Minister. His long standing in the service, and his misfortunes, which had so much resemblance to my own situation, attached me to this officer, to whom I offered a lodging and my table, which he accepted.

On the 13th, the women of several provinces, being informed of the arrival of my spouse, came to take the oath before her, that they would never sacrifice any child hereafter to their criminal customs; and it was further agreed, that those who should break their oath, should be made slaves, and exported out of the country; and that the children which were born with any defect, which, according to their customs, might have formerly been the cause of putting them to death, should in future be sent to the establishment, to be brought up at our charge, without its being in the power of the parents to reclaim them.

This oath was succeeded by a festival, in testimony of the general satisfaction.

After terminating this business so important to the establishment, and so advantageous to humanity, I directed my views to the perfect knowledge of the Northern coast of the island; in consequence of which, I sent the Sieur Mayeur, with eighty armed blacks to support him in his march,

march, with orders to go in the Periagua, and examine all the harbours, bays, and rivers on that coast, and engage the principal chiefs of the provinces in our interests; at the same time that he should excite them by presents, if necessary, to take part against the Seclaves, whose enemies I knew they had always been; and to finish his mission, by acquiring an accurate knowledge of the island Noffebe; after which he was directed to return by land to Louisbourg, to give an account of his observations.

At the same time I gave orders to part of my troops to proceed upon discovery of the rivers and plains, which were in the vicinity of the chief settlement; and directed the Sieur Garaut de Beaupreau, chief engineer of the island, to embark in his Majesty's brig Le Coureur, to make a plan of the Southern coast, as far as Fort Dauphin. I likewise sent three Periaguas to sound the Bay of Antongil, both on the Eastern and Western shores.

On the 19th, perceiving that the Sieur Des Assises, the principal storekeeper, persisted in not lending any assistance in the works essential to the establishment; and that he persevered in exciting the province of the Saphirobai against me; to the chiefs of which he had insinuated, that by declaring themselves against me, they would do a thing very agreeable to the government of the isle of France, I thought it necessary, at last, to take an effectual resolution. In consequence of which, I assembled the officers of the corps to explain to them our circumstances, and the conduct of the Sieur Des Assises, and requested their advice respecting what they might think proper to be done in the case. Their opinion was agreeable to my own: I therefore gave orders to put him under an arrest, which was done

done the fame hour. But as it was neceffary in the mean time, to keep up a regular account, I nominated Mr. Aumont to fupply his place.

The report of the difgrace of the principal ftore-keeper, deftroyed the hopes of the Saphirobai chiefs; and they came to the number of feven, on the 21ft, with fix hundred workmen, to be employed in the works I had determined to conftruct. Thefe chiefs engaged befides with me, to fupply the fettlement with fix thoufand pieces of wood, and four thoufand madriers, or planks. This profpect of the return of the iflanders to our intereft, tended greatly to diffipate my apprehenfions.

On the 24th, the two detachments which I had fent upon difcovery, returned from their expeditions; and the officers in command gave me an exact account in the form of an itinerary, or journal, from which I was affured, that this immenfe country abounded with the moft beautiful plains, watered with rivers; and that colonifts only were wanting to turn them to the greateft advantage. Sugar, cotton, indigo, coffee, tobacco, and all other productions, were found in abundance.

On the 22d, the brig Le Coureur being ready to fet fail, I gave orders to the Sieur Defmoufleaux, with an interpreter and a detachment, to embark, to make difcoveries on the Southern part of the ifland. The fame day I fent Mr. Perthuis, Lieutenant, with Mr. Rofiere, and a detachment of fix foldiers, and one hundred and eighty armed natives of the country, to make the fame expedition by land.

The latter days of this year offered nothing remarkable; the whole corps was employed in the works, which I had diftributed among them in feveral gangs.

On the 29th, the Surgeon Major informed me, that the Sieur Des Affifes, by his irregular conduct, had contracted a diforder, which his advanced age ought to have fecured him from. Being actuated by compaffion for his fituation, I fent Mr. De Sanglier to him, to exhort him to a more regular conduct; and at the fame time I offered to re-eftablifh him in his charge, on condition that he fhould declare publickly, and in a Cabar of the natives of the country, which I would convene for that purpofe, that all which he had faid and done, was by the direction of a party in the ifle of France, whofe government was jealous of the flourifhing ftate to which Madagafcar would arrive under my conduct; and that he had followed this mode of proceeding, only to gain the favour of Mr. Maillart, who was exceedingly jealous of every good office which could be performed in favour of Madagafcar.

On the return of Mr. De Sanglier, I was furprized to hear that Mr. Des Affifes had accepted my propofition; and that he was truly forry for every thing that he had done, contrary to my intentions; and laftly, that he would accept his charge, and promifed to conduct himfelf in future, with moderation. The voluntary return of fo dangerous a perfon, gave me great fatisfaction; and I immediately fent him an order to continue in the fervice. This domeftic pacification was not, however, fufficient to calm my apprehenfions, as the afflicting view of the ftate of the eftablifhment, perfecuted by the ifle of France,

and

and abandoned by Europe, continually presented itself to my mind.

January the 1st, 1775. Having convened the Saphirobai chiefs, the submission of the principal Intendant was made before them; and I had the satisfaction to see, that many of the chiefs looked on him with contempt. At the breaking up of the Cabar, the chief Raoul asked to speak with me in secret; and informed me, that the Cimanongou chief of the Seclaves, of the province of Antongin, had joined with the King of Bojana to declare war against me; that this chief Cimanongou, had sent envoys to the Saphirobai, to invite them to join him against the establishment; and that several of them were disposed to accede to his proposition, though others were determined to adhere to their resolution of keeping their engagements with me.

This important advice required precaution on my part; for it was certain that the Seclaves were able to bring an army into the field of forty thousand fighting men. But as it would have been dangerous to have shewn my apprehensions, I dissembled, and caused the public works to be carried on with greater spirit.

On the 7th, I received letters from the Sieur Mayeur, dated from Angontzi, in which he gave me an advantageous description of that province. Its rich productions and abundance of cattle, surpassed my expectation; for which reason I determined, notwithstanding my apprehensions of the Seclaves, to send a detachment to establish posts. The details which Mr. Mayeur gave me of the disposition of the chiefs of this province, led me to hope, that I might engage them to assist me in case of need

need. Mr. Maycur informed me in his letter, that he durst not venture to continue his progress without reinforcements. I therefore gave immediate orders to Serjeant Longueteau, to follow him with two hundred and fifty armed natives; and to remain subject to his orders. The following days were employed on the fortifications, and filling up the quay, which I had raised upon the shore within the bay.

On the 12th, I received deputies from the Sambarives and Antimaroa, who offered me five thousand men, to support a war against the Seclaves.

On the 28th, about midnight, I was alarmed at hearing three shot fired on the banks of the river. I gave immediate orders to the picquet guard to repair to the spot, but the detachment returned without having made any discovery. This alarm produced no other consequence, than that of affrighting Mr. Des Assisses, the intendant, who ran intirely naked into the fort. This day I received information, that the navigation of the boats, coming down the river of Tingballe, and from Ranoumena, had become dangerous, on account of the different ambuscades which the ill disposed natives had placed to fire on them. I gave orders, therefore, to open a communication by land, and for this work I engaged the Rohandrian Sance, to send me four thousand men.

From the 19th to the 28th, the settlement was employed on making the above mentioned communication by land.

On the 30th, I received an account from the posts of Foul Point, Massoualla, Mananhar, Tamatava, and Angontzi, that articles of trade were abundant, but that the storehouses

houses were empty. This information induced me to purchase the entire cargo of the brig La Jollie Bourbonoise, amounting to sixty-eight thousand livres, which I disbursed out of my own pocket upon the treasurer's receipt. The same day I received letters from the administrators of the isle of France, which tended to convince me of the intrigues and cabals which they employed, to deprive me of the confidence of the Minister, and to excite the enmity of the natives against me. I received more certain information on this subject from the Marquis D'Albergotti, ancient Captain in the service of France, who was persecuted by the government of the isle of France, and had retired to Madagascar under my protection.

February the 1st. I received information, that Mahertomp, a chief established near our principal settlement, had engaged with the Seclaves to assassinate me. As soon as I was assured of this by sufficient evidence, I went to him unexpectedly with several chiefs, to remonstrate with him on his treachery. He acknowledged his crime, and intreated forgiveness for having failed in his engagements; but his subjects declared, that they would not have any further concern with so perfidious a man. So that he was proscribed, and banished by his own people.

On the 2d, Mr. Corbi, one of my most confidential officers, in concert with the interpreter, informed me, that the old negress, Susanna, whom I had brought from the isle of France, and who in her early youth had been sold to the French, and had lived upwards of fifty years at the isle of France, had reported, that her companion the daughter of Rohandrian Ampansacabé Ramini Larizon, having likewise been made prisoner, was sold to the foreigners;

foreigners; and that she had certain marks that I was her son. This officer represented likewise to me, that in consequence of her report, the Sambarive nation had held several Cabars, to declare me the heir of Ramini, and, consequently, proprietor of the province of Mananhar, and successor to the title of Ampansacabé, or supreme chief of the nation; a title which since the death of Ramini Larizon, had been extinct.

This information appeared to me of the greatest consequence; and I determined to take the advantage of it, to conduct that brave and generous nation to a civilized state, and the establishment of a solid and permanent government. Its situation, its population, the fertility and excellency of its soil and climate, with a variety of other circumstances, conspired to induce me to lay a foundation for the establishment of a power, founded upon national liberty. But as I had no person to whom I could intrust the secret of my mind, I lamented to myself at the reflection how blind the Minister of Versailles was to the true interests of France. I therefore contented myself with giving particular instructions to Mr. Corbi, respecting the answers he should make to such of the natives, as might question him on this subject. On the same day I interrogated Susanna, on the report she had spread concerning my birth. The good old woman threw herself at my knees, and excused herself by confessing, that she had acted intirely upon a conviction of the truth. For she said, that she had known my mother, whose physiognomy resembled mine; and that she had herself been inspired in a dream by the Zahanhar, to publish the secret. Her manner of speaking convinced me, that
she

she really believed what she said; I therefore embraced her, and told her, that I had reasons for keeping the secret respecting my birth; but that, nevertheless, if she had any confidential friends, she might acquaint them with it. At these words she arose, kissed my hands, and declared, that the Sambarive nation was informed of the circumstance, and that the Rohandrian Raffangour waited only for a favourable moment, to acknowledge the blood of Ramini.

The time from the third to the sixth, was employed in digging a canal of communication between the river and the harbour. This was perfected in four days, though it was fifteen hundred toises in length. But as I employed for this purpose near six thousand natives of the country, the whole was performed with the greatest ease.

On the 7th, the chief Ciewi, of the Sambarive nation, came to present two hundred young men of his nation, to serve me in quality of volunteers. I accepted the offer of this brave people, and gave orders immediately for forming them into a regular company. The officers La Tour, La Boullaye, and Evally, were charged with the discipline of this new troop, of which I appointed the son of Rohandrian Raffangour, commander.

On the 8th, Mr. Des Assisses, the intendant, represented to me, that he was desirous of resigning his employment, and retiring to the isle of France. I agreed to his demand with so much the more satisfaction, as he was of no use to me. But as it was necessary that his accounts should be first made up, I allowed him fourteen days for that purpose.

On the 9th, I received an account from an interpreter of the name of D'Ecolle, that an old man in the province of Mananhar, had spread prophecies concerning a general change of government in the island; and that he had asserted, that the descendant of Ramini would rebuild the town of Palmire. He added, that these predictions had occasioned a tumult among the people, who being informed that the Sambarives had declared me to be a descendant of the line of Ramini, required their chiefs to send an embassy to me, to enquire into the fact; and in case it should prove true, to bring me with them, and assure me of the submission of their province. From this resolution, the Rohandrians Anacandrins, and Voadziri, had nominated chiefs, who were immediately to begin their journey by sea.

On the 10th, I made an excursion to the plain, and to fort Augustus, to hasten the works of the fortifications.

On the 11th, Mr. Mayeur, chief interpreter, informed me, that two Saphirobai chiefs had arrived, and demanded an audience. As soon as they were introduced, they declared, that being informed that I had concluded a treaty with the Sambarives, their enemies, they had determined to employ all their powers in preventing the consequences of such an alliance, which, in effect, was an infringement of all the oaths I had entered into with them; and that, in a word, they would rather declare in favour of the Seclaves, than become connected with the Sambarive nation. They ended by representing, that my behaviour to Mahertomp had been violent; and that they had thought it proper to receive him into the Cabar, notwithstanding the sentence against him. Justly irritated at this declaration, I made no other answer, than by an expression of indignation, and commanding them immediately to withdraw.

The same day Raoul Rohandrian of the Saphirobai, who had informed me of the cabals of the Seclaves, came with excuses respecting the proceedings of his nation, at the instigation of old Mahertomp; and assured me, that for his part he was ready to repeat his oath of fidelity and attachment to my person; and he put his son into my hands as a hostage.

After having treated him with the greatest attention, I requested that he would let me know the true reason of the opposition of the Saphirobai chiefs; and he told me, that the ancestors of Mahertomp, and of Rohandrian Onglahe, had been concerned in the massacre of the family of Ramini Larizon, after which they had assumed the Sovereignty of several districts, to the prejudice of the Sambarive nation, who being at that moment assured that they had found a descendant of the blood of Ramini, reclaimed, as his right, the different districts separated from the provinces of Antimaroa.

Upon this information, I asked, whether his interest were not likewise to declare against the Sambarives; and he replied, that it was not; giving at the same time as a reason, that he was descended from the race of Safe Hibrahim, whose family had settled in the place where he dwelt, under the protection of Ramin Ampansacabé, and that he at present was reckoned of the class of the Saphirobai, only because he was desirous of preserving his possessions. I then questioned him, whether he had any knowledge of the heir of Ramini, whom the Sambarives announced;

but

but as he answered, that he knew not a word on that subject, I thought it unneceffary to queftion him further; and affured him of the conftant friendfhip which I fhould always preferve for him and his whole family.

Contented with my declaration, he affured me, that he was defirous of fupporting the eftablifhment with all his force. But he intreated me to confider, that in cafe the eftablifhment fhould be given up, what would be his fituation when expofed alone to the mercy of a body of enraged chiefs, who would not fail to facrifice him and all his family to their refentment. This reafoning appeared juft; and with a view to give him perfect fatisfaction, I declared that my only requeft was, that he would remain neuter.

On the 12th, the engineer who had been employed on the work of the road leading to the plain, and towards Ranoumena, informed me that the whole was finifhed; and I determined to infpect this work myfelf the following day. This day I received an account that the Saphirobai had affembled in troops.

On the 13th, I went on horfeback from Louifbourg to the plain, where I was aftonifhed to find the road finifhed in fo fhort a time. It was four toifes broad, fix French leagues in length, and had a ditch on each fide to carry off the waters. I thought it particularly became me to reward the people who had performed this work; I therefore gave them each a yard of blue cloth, and a bottle of brandy. To fecure the communication of this road, I gave orders immediately to raife a redoubt on the height of Mananbia, on which I built houfes for twenty-four men.

From the 14th to the 16th, I was employed vifiting the pofts dependant on Louifbourg; and I diftributed feveral several pieces of ground to the Europeans at the plain of Health, and at the plain of Fort St. John, on the bank of the great river. All these grounds naturally produced sugar, cotton, indigo, tobacco, and Tacamahaca wood.

On the 17th, having returned to Louisbourg, I gave orders for continuing the building, and increasing the town; after which, on the 18th, I embarked in the country boats for Angontzi. This voyage employed eight days, and I took the opportunity of visiting all the chiefs established on the coast, who expressed the most sincere attachment to me. Upon my arrival at Angontzi, I was charmed with the situation which my engineer had chosen to establish the settlement; my wishes on this occasion for an accession of force to take advantage of the gifts which nature so prodigally held out, were great; but, alas, the hour of their accomplishment was not at hand, and it was in vain that the beauty of the situation, the goodness of the soil, together with the mild and affable character of the inhabitants, led me to form projects I was unable to accomplish.

The Rohandrian of Angontzi assembled a Cabar on the 27th, in which I received in person the oath of attachment and alliance of that nation. The rest of the month passed in entertainments, which were given by the chiefs.

March the 2d, 1775, having received advice by land, that a number of the deputies of the Southern provinces had repaired to Louisbourg, where they waited for me with impatience; and that the Saphirobai had burnt a village belonging to Manonganon, I determined immediately to return; and as the road by land, though difficult, was the shortest, I determined to go that way. The chief of Angontzi,

Angontzi, being informed of my decision, ordered his litter for me, with six hundred armed men for a guard. I seized an instant before my departure, to represent the advantages that would result from a road being made between Angontzi and Louisbourg, he promised six thousand men for this work, provided the people of Antimaroa would same number.

On the 6th, after a rather tedious journey, I arrived at last at Louisbourg, where I was agreeably surprized to find that the marsh at the entrance of the town was intirely filled up. I was indebted for this work to the good will of the same friends who had made the road to the plain. This day I received the reports concerning the different parts of the service of the establishment, with which I was perfectly well satisfied, and convinced that nothing had stood still during my absence. Mr. Sanglier, who had commanded in my absence, likewise informed me, that the deputies of five of the Southern provinces, had demanded a conference in Cabar; and that there were likewise six private chiefs, who had made the same request. In consequence of this, I ordered preparations to be made for holding a Cabar on the following day.

On the 7th, after having rested myself, I conferred with Messrs. Maycur and Corbi, respecting the different interests which had induced the deputies and the chiefs to have recourse to me; and after having received the necessary information, I caused the Cabar to be assembled, at which the deputies were admitted one after the other. The first was from the province of Mananhar; the second from Tamatava; the third from the island of St. Mary; the fourth from Manauzar; and the fifth from Matatava.

After

After the deputies, I received the chiefs; and as their interests were one and the same, I entered into one common oath with them: and when I had made presents to them in return for those they had brought, I dismissed them, because the affairs they were charged with required their speedy return into their respective provinces.

On the 8th, Mr. Gareau de Boispreaux, engineer in chief, proposed to me to erect a light-house on the isle D'Aiguillon, and to erect a flag-staff on the point of land, at the entrance of the river. He likewise requested that the people who had been employed by him before, might continue to serve him. I agreed to his request, and gave him the necessary orders and powers.

On the 9th, having received a visit from the chief Raoul, I proposed to him to employ his subjects in making a road towards Angontzi; and after a long conference, I prevailed on him to promise four thousand men for the service: Manonganon and Mandinque, two other chiefs, promised likewise two thousand men. Being thus assured of sufficient assistance, I gave charge of the work to M. de Boispreaux, the engineer, and his assistant, M. de Rosieres. The plan was made the same day, and M. de Rosieres departed for Angontzi, to begin the operations on that side; while Mr. Gareau de Boispreaux began on the Louisbourg side. This road was not to be of less extent than twenty-eight French leagues.

On the 10th, having learned that the Sieur Des Assises, before his departure, had taken a large quantity of merchandize out of the storehouses, and had distributed them among the Saphirobai, with a view to excite them to rise against me, I sent Mr. Certain to them with a declaration, that the said Des Assisses had stolen the effects out of his Majesty's stores, and that I should consider them as confederates in the theft, and act accordingly.

On the 13th, two Saphirobai chiefs arrived, and brought back great part of the merchandize which I had reclaimed; but they declared, that I ought not to attribute their proceeding to fear, but only to their open and honest character. The value of the effects distributed, with a view to destroy the settlement, amounted to more than twenty-three thousand livres: an exorbitant sum, considering that he had refused the sum of fifteen thousand livres for the necessary works, and constructing houses in the town.

On the 15th, a signal was displayed on the mountain Manghabey, on the isle d'Aiguillon, that two vessels of two masts were in sight. They anchored in the harbour at eleven o'clock. The first was a brig of his Majesty's, commanded by the Sieur Joubert, Lieutenant of a frigate; and the second was the Coureur, which brought back the engineers I had sent to explore the Southern provinces, and survey the coast.

Captain Joubert, having presented his letter, signed by the Governor of the isle of France, and Mr. De Ternay the Intendant, I perceived that he had been sent merely as a spy upon my operations. For the Captain deposed, that his orders were to bring back to the isle of France, the remains of my troops; and that he had been dispatched upon the report that the natives had assassinated me, and cut off the greatest part of my people, the remainder having taken refuge at Manghabey. The Captain, finding that this story had been invented merely to gratify the

chiefs

chiefs of the ifle of France, declared that he was ready to return according to his pofitive orders fo to do, if he found me alive. This proceeding on the part of thofe whofe duty it was to fupport me, put me out of all patience. I gave orders to the Captain to depart inftantly, as his chiefs had fent him only to infult the eftablifhment.

About two in the evening, a fignal was made, that two other veffels were in fight; and at fix his Majefty's frigate the Belle Poule, commanded by the Chevalier De Grenier, Lieutenant, anchored in the harbour. The Commander required provifions and ftores for his veffel, which I caufed to be delivered. This officer teftified the moft lively regret to find, that the chiefs of the ifle of France were fo ftrongly prejudiced againft the fettlement at Madagafcar, and he took charge of my difpatches for the Court of France. I was employed till the 22d, in drawing out my accounts, of which the following is a general ftatement:

Sums advanced for the Eſtabliſhment at Madagaſcar,
1772 *and* 1773.

	Livres	s.	d.
For levying the Regiment of Benyowſky, its tranſport to Madagaſcar, and the ſupplies of articles of trade 1774 and 1775, until the 20th of March	342649	12	5
Bills of Exchange drawn to the amount of	113000	10	3
Total received -	455650	2	8

Expenditures.

For the troops during the years 1772, 1773, 1774, 1775	141432	0	0
For the Marine. To his Majeſty's veſſels the Poſtillion and Coureur -	396864	6	4

FOR THE SETTLEMENT.

Building the Governor's houſe, roads, canals, fortifications, &c. -	315916	11	8
Supplies to the iſle of France in ſlaves	161412	0	0
———————————— in rice -	84000	0	0
Proviſions to ſeveral of his Majeſty's veſſels - - - -	41423	11	7½
	1141048	12	7
Deduct the ſums advanced -	455650	2	8
	585398	9	11
And alſo the ſums advanced by myſelf -	245000	0	0
* Neat profit produced by the Adminiſtration - - -	340398	9	11

* This ſum, which is the difference between the receipts and diſburſements, is not neat profit. The reſult of the above account is, that the ſettlement coſt

This clear account ought to have produced a good effect on the mind of the Minister. For as it was shewn that no more than the sum of liv. 455650 had been advanced, and that the single object of the maintenance of the troops and vessels at sea, amounted to liv. 538296, he might easily perceive the immense advantages that might in a short time be expected from Madagascar.

On the 23d, the Belle Poule set sail, and on the same day I received advice by a courier from Foul Point, that the Fariavas and Betalimenes, had declared war upon Hyavi, and that hostilities had already commenced. The commanding officer at Foul Point pressed me for orders, whether he should assist Hyavi or not. In consequence of this news, I determined to repair to Foul Point myself, in order to pacify the people.

On the 24th, after giving orders relative to the service at the chief establishment, I established a camp of eighty soldiers and two thousand natives, to secure the settlement against any surprize on the part of the Seclaves, and Saphirobai; and then departed for Foul Point, accompanied by two officers and six hundred warriors of the Sambarive nation. As I passed by Mananhar, I was joined by the troop of Sauce, and the people of Antimakol, and found myself at the head of near five thousand armed men,

---

cost the French, liv. 455650 2 8, and liv. 245000, which make together £700650 2 8. This is not equal to the whole charge, or £854212 18 But the settlement paid the difference, £153562 15 4. and also supplied the isle of France, and the King's ships, with £286835 11 7½. This last sum only is the return, and if taken from the whole sum advanced, will leave livres 413814 10, or the loss sustained by the French government, by the effect of this undertaking during the above time. Note of the editor.

On the 27th, my army was reinforced by the troop of Ambarante, and I arrived on the 1st of April at Foul Point.

I found the brig Le Coureur already here at anchor, with my artillery and ammunition. This day I eftablifhed my camp near Tametavi, and in the evening I fent for Hyavi, to enquire of him refpecting the caufe of the war. As he could give me no good reafon, I defered explaining myfelf, until I had heard from the other party; to whofe camp I fent that very night, to engage the chiefs to come and fpeak with me.

On the 2d, I received deputies from the Betalimenes, and Fariavas, who declared to me, that the two nations would abide by my decifion, in the hopes that I would liften only to the dictates of that juftice, which the fpirit of God would infpire me with. They then declared, that Hyavi was the author of the war, by forbidding the Betalimenes and Fariavas to frequent the market at Foul Point; that he had confifcated the cattle, flaves, and provifions of the merchants of their nation, which they had brought for fale to the fettlement; and, laftly, that the foldiers of Hyavi had furprized one of their villages, and taken away feveral young women, whom they had fold to the French merchants.

Being thus informed of the caufe of the war, I difmiffed the deputies with fome prefents, after I had promifed to fettle the whole difpute to their fatisfaction, provided they allowed me the neceffary time for that purpofe. They engaged to do this, and returned to their camp very well fatisfied, at having found me difpofed in their

their favour. For Hyavi had spread a report, that I was coming to assist him.

The next step I took was, to invite Hyavi to my quarters, when I reproached him for his conduct, and the licence he had given his subjects to disturb his neighbours. I spoke so urgently to him, that he confessed himself to blame; but at the same time begged I would act in such a manner, as not to degrade him in the eyes of his enemies. I engaged to regulate my proceedings according to his desire, on condition that he should submit to such terms as I should impose, both on him and the Betalimenes and Fariavas. After I had thus obtained the promise of both parties, I gave orders for holding the Cabar on the 3d, to which Hyavi and his chiefs, and also the Betalimenes and Fariavas were invited.

On the 2d, at day-break, I put my troops under arms, and ranged them in order of battle. About six, the Betalemines and Fariavas arrived, to the number of eight or ten thousand armed men; and a short time after came Hyavi with his people. So that the number of men under arms, who were present that day, amounted to near twenty-two thousand. At eight the Cabar began, and as I was desirous of avoiding all particular debates, I proposed to both parties, to form that day a treaty of alliance and friendship, which I would guarantee, together with the nations of the Sambarives and Saphirobai; and farther I proposed, that they should enter into the following engagements:

1. That trade should in future be free between the three nations, without the reclamation of any particular right, (or impost).

2. That

2. That Hyavi should give up, or cause to be given up, the persons who had lately been surprized and carried off by his soldiers; and that for every one of them who could not be found, he should return two of his own subjects.

3. That the Betalimenes and Fariavas, should not in future, receive amongst them any fugitive subjects of Hyavi; and that they should compel all those, who during the last three months, had taken refuge amongst them, to return two slaves each for his person.

4. That the Betalimenes, Fariavas, and the subjects of Hyavi, should furnish a sufficient number of workmen, to open a road of communication for the general advantage of trade along the coast, from Foul Point to Bohitsmenes.

And in consideration that this last article was one of the most essential for their mutual interests, I declared my intention of appointing several of my officers to superintend the work.

After a continual debate of three hours, which every instant threatened to end in a general engagement, they at last became calm, and agreed to the first article; and with regard to the second and third, they concluded that all past inquiries should be buried in oblivion, without any reclamation being admitted on either side; and that in future, both nations should either give up the fugitives from the other, or at least drive them out of their dominions.

With respect to the fourth article, they agreed to send five thousand men to work on the road proposed to be made. These conditions thus settled, were ratified by an oath, in which the chiefs who came with me joined as witnesses

COUNT DE BENYOWSKY.

witnesses and guarantees. Hyavi then caused fifty oxen to be killed, as did likewise the Betalimenes and Fariavas, and they were cut up and distributed among the troops.

On the 4th, the Betalimenes being desirous of testifying their gratitude, presented my troops with five hundred oxen. The Fariavas did the same, and Hyavi gave five hundred oxen and fifty slaves. The cattle were divided among my followers; but I gave the slaves their liberty, on condition that they should establish themselves near one of my settlements, and pay a tenth of the produce of their lands.

Having thus happily concluded upon a peace to the satisfaction of all parties, I determined to return to Louisbourg; and delayed my departure only till I had received the honours, which the belligerent parties were desirous of shewing me. At the conclusion of the festival, the Fariavas gave my troops forty slaves and two hundred oxen, and Hyavi on his part, gave two thousand piastres.

On the 11th, I arrived happily at Louisbourg, where I found affairs in a good train.

On the 12th, my chief interpreter having informed me of the approaching arrival of envoys from the King of Boyana, at the same time apprized me, that the chiefs of the Saphirobai and Antamboi, had sent deputies to the said envoys, to engage them in their interests against the settlement. I received a farther confirmation of this news from an old woman, a native of the country, who informed me besides, that the Saphirobai had gained the chief of the embassy of the Seclaves by presents; and that the latter had engaged, under the sanction of an oath, to seek means of breaking off the negociation; and to find sufficient reasons to engage his nation in their party. I was perfectly assured of the truth of this information, from other blacks attached to the settlement, who had been present at the making of the oath.

Finding myself thus engaged in the most critical situation, I took the resolution of sending the brig La Flore, to the isle of France, to demand a supply of arms and ammunition; and by the same conveyance I sent back my family, with the greatest part of my houshold, in order to carry on my operations against the Seclaves with the greater activity. The vessel was dispatched without delay to the isle of France, with the Chevalier de Sanglier, Captain in my troop, in order to press the administration of that colony, to forward the necessary supplies with the utmost speed.

On the 21st, the chief Raoul came to me, to request a supply of men, because the Saphirobai chiefs, with the Seclaves, had determined to destroy him, on account of his refusal to enter into the combination against the settlement. The account I received from this chief, of the different preparations the confederates had made to attack the settlement, left me no doubt of the near approach of a war, which there was no means of avoiding. But as I did not expect succours in any short time, and all my force was reduced to the effects which might arise from firmness and courage, I thought it proper still to keep up my hopes.

On the 13th, I went in the night to the Plain of Health, that the enemy might not be informed of my absence; and immediately on my arrival, I put that post into a state of defence. It was guarded by twenty-nine soldiers, and five hundred natives, whom I could depend upon. The command was in the hands of M. de Mallendre, Captain, and M. de la Boullaye, Lieutenant. For a greater security, I caused palisades to be set on that side of the wood, through which the enemy might make an attack, by passing near the foot of the mountain, sheltered from the cannon of the fort. On the river side, I likewise cut down all the trees and underwood, that the artillery might command as far as Cape de Zafaiche. After having thus put this important fort in a state of defence, I embarked in my boats to return to Louisbourg. As I passed by the territory of Mahertompe, I discovered a camp of the enemy, who fired several shot at my boats; but the distance being too great for them to reach us, I arrived safely at Louisbourg, where I found every thing in good order.

On the 28th, I was informed of the arrival of envoys from the Sambarives of the East and West. They demanded a conference, to the exclusion of other nations; and at the same time assured me, that if I listened favourably to them, and granted them my friendship, they would soon deliver me from all my enemies. Such a proposal could not but be very agreeable to me. I therefore gave orders for making the due preparations for holding our meeting.

On the 20th, the Cabar or assembly was held, at which were present on the part of the settlement, the Count de Benyowsky, Commander; Messrs. Perthuis, De la Boullaye, and Rosier, Lieutenants; Unbanowsky, Engineer; Besse, Interpreter; and on the part of the Sambarives, the Prince Raffangour of that nation. The propositions of the Sambarives were delivered in the following speech.

"The nation of the Sambarives, the people of God, established in the provinces Mananhar and Maffoualla, have seen with grief, that the settlement of Louisbourg has entered into treaties of friendship and alliance with other nations, in preference, and to the exclusion of theirs; and that at present, all those nations have united together against their benefactors, and have even invited our people to join with them against the white men. But as the Sambarives have always walked in the paths of justice, our nation has refused their offers, preferring the friendship of the chief of the white men, to every inducement of relationship or alliance, which might exist between ourselves and his enemies. In consequence of this disposition, the Sambarive nation offer to assist the settlement with five thousand men, to be employed against its enemies; and hope, by this action, that they shall be thought worthy of an alliance, the value of which they are well convinced of."

After having heard this harangue, I replied, that I had always been desirous of their alliance, but that the remoteness of their province had not hitherto permitted me to treat with them directly. I assured them, that the offer of supplies inspired me with an high opinion of their sentiments; and that I should accept this mark of friendship with the greatest pleasure, as it would justify the unbounded confidence I was determined to place in the Sambarive nation, respectable for the blood of Ramini.

The envoys then consulted together for a short time, and agreed to enter into the usual oath of allegiance. The rest of the day was employed in rejoicing; and in the evening my interpreter informed me, that the Sambarives

rives had difappeared. This news gave me fome concern; becaufe as the oath of alliance had been taken, they ought to have apprized me of their departure.

June the 1ft, 1775. At four in the morning, my interpreter announced the arrival of the Saphirobai chiefs, who had formed a league with the Seclaves; and likewife informed me, that they had about three thoufand armed men with them, by means of whom he was affured they meditated a furprize. An hour afterwards, the chief Raoul came to demand an afylum for himfelf and family, at the fame time that he acquainted me, that he had been plundered by the confederates, and had only time to fave the lives of himfelf and family; that part of his people had been made prifoners by the enemy, and all his goods were deftroyed by the flames. The unfortunate fate of this chief affected me much, and I begged him to retire with his family into the fort. This chief, in the infancy of the eftablifhment, had been conquered and driven out of his province by my allies, becaufe he oppofed the building of a fortrefs; and in the prefent inftance he fuffered for his attachment to me.

At nine o'clock, the Seclaves and Saphirobai appeared at the diftance of about a cannon fhot. Their troops confifted of more than three thoufand men. They fent deputies to requeft me to come to their camp to hear their complaints. This expreffion rather difconcerted me, as their complaints were backed by an armed force. But at laft, not to give them reafon to imagine that I was awed by their appearance, I put my troops in order to defend the fort, and went to the place of meeting. On my arrival, I ordered my interpreter to attend to their propofals and complaints.

complaints. The confederates then demanded, that I should withdraw my troops from the interior parts of the island, especially from the post at the plain of Health ; and that I should dispense them from the oath by which they had surrendered to me the banks of the river Tingballe, because they said they had been surprized by the promise I had made them of a secure trade, which should afford them the same advantages they had enjoyed with private traders, and of which they had been deprived since the arrival of the military. They concluded their harangue by observing, that their interests did not admit of the troops being allowed a settlement ; and they added that private traders, upon coming amongst them, had always paid a duty, of which they had been deprived since the establishment of the settlement ; and more particularly they declared, that formerly every merchant, and even King's vessel, on its arrival, saluted the chiefs with two guns, a respectful custom which I had maliciously abolished.

After having calmly listened to their speech, and finding myself in a very critical situation, I replied, that they would do well to consider what they were about ; that as they had surrendered to us the lands we were in possession of, they could not reclaim them without violating their oath. Besides which, having entered into an alliance with the settlement, every violent proceeding on their part would authorize me to employ my troops in punishing them ; so that I could not make them any satisfaction without positive orders. That the demolition of the fort, and withdrawing of the troops from the internal parts of the island, were things impossible to be agreed to ; that with regard to the honours, I would give orders to the officers
of

of the shipping to do as they had formerly done; but that with regard to their pretended right to a duty on ships, which entered their ports, it was ridiculous, because it had never been heard that friends and allies received those who came only to trade, from any other motives than to serve themselves.

My speech astonished the people; but some of the chiefs cried out, let us come to business, and took notice that they could not have a better opportunity, as they had one in their hands, and could oblige me to do that by force which I refused to do from good will. In the mean time, I found myself surrounded on all sides, and should certainly have passed a quarter of an hour very disagreeably, if the Commander* at the head of fifty blacks, had not hastened to my assistance. His spirited attack obliged a party of the enemy to oppose him, while another detachment having attacked the fort, and suffered a vigorous repulse, threw their troops into confusion. This gave me an opportunity of making my escape. I saw only two chiefs who opposed my passage. I parried their strokes, upon which they cried out, he is a sorcerer, we are undone. Taking advantage of their stupidity, I rallied the troop of my Commander, among whom I found several of my officers and soldiers, who seeing me surrounded, had sacrificed themselves to assist me. The Commandant of the fort likewise, seeing me clear of the enemy, pointed the cannon, and prepared to fire, which he had forborn to do before, least I should become the victim of his fire. The enemy soon perceived my escape; and for fear of the artillery, hastily retired towards the wood, firing a few shot as they retreated.

* Name not legible.

On my arrival at the fort, I saw my troops again with much satisfaction, as I could not give too much praise to them for their attention to orders. It may here be objected that I did not act prudently, in putting myself in this manner in the hands of the enemy, as it was in my power to have prevented their approach, by making use of my cannon. In answer to which, I must observe in my justification,

1. That in order to be at liberty to act against a nation, which it is intended to civilize, it is necessary to be in possession of facts that prove them the aggressors.

2. A chief cannot dispense with attending to complaints. If I had refused to comply with a request which carried so much the appearance of justice, the party of the complaining nation might have found means of inspiring others with ambiguous sentiments, and my conduct would have afforded them authority for so doing.

3. If unfortunately in a Cabar or assembly, I had made use of cannon, which would have produced a massacre, the other neighbouring nations, being ill informed of the circumstances, would always have suspected that I had premeditated the stroke; and that the assembly had been convened for no other purpose than to exterminate them. An event of this nature, however founded in justice, would have been sufficient to have alienated the minds of every one for a short time; but by avoiding it, my conduct was productive of real advantage. The neighbouring people, informed of the conduct of the Saphirobai and Seelaves, and of the moderation with which I had repelled them, could not delay to join our cause. The war we were about to enter into, would be justified before it could be criticised.

cifed. For this reafon likewife it was, that I determined to make offers of peace to our enemies, which they refufed, and by that means cleared us of all reproach.

On the 3d, the interpreters, whom I had fent to the Saphirobai, with offers of peace, returned with the information, that the confederates had haughtily refufed every propofal of accommodation, and had fent a party of a thoufand men to take the poft at the plain of Health. The next day I received news, that the enemy had been repulfed at fort Auguftus, and at the plain.

On the 5th, the chief Sancé arrived with one thoufand men, to affift the fettlement againft the confederates. This chief was defcended from a pirate named Zan. In the night of the fame day, I was apprized of the arrival of thirty boats of the country, bringing fix hundred armed warriors from the province of Rantabe.

On the 6th, a detachment I had fent to reconnoitre the enemy returned, and informed me, that the Antambour nation, allied to the Saphirobai, had eftablifhed a camp in the plain, and waited only for the junction of the Saphirobai and Seclaves to attack the poft. And that on the other hand the Saphirobai and the Seclaves had formed three camps, between the poft at the plain and the chief fettlement, to cut off the communication. The fame day I was informed of the arrival of fifteen thoufand armed men, of the Sambarive nation, who came to affift the eftablifhment, and requefted to be fent againft the enemy without delay.

On the 10th, the Sambarives being all joined by the Mulatto chiefs, compofed a body of upwards of fix thoufand men, with which I took the field. The campaign
promifed

promised to be laborious, on account of the necessity of climbing rocks and mountains, and passing over marshy lands, which threatened to deprive me of the advantage of my cannon.

Having at last approached the enemy's camp, who were established in the plain of Mahertomp, I sent Messrs. L'Armina and certain officers of my corps, with fifty volunteers, and two thousand blacks, with orders to attack the enemy's post at sun-set. Soon afterwards we heard several repeated discharges, which obliged me to march to support my detachment, who had not been able to dislodge the enemy from the advantageous situation they were encamped in. But the firing ceasing all at once, I supposed the parties had separated. To arrive at a certainty, I sent two volunteers, who reported, that they had observed two camps at a little distance from each other, and that each were busied in forming entrenchments. After this information, I sent Lieutenant la Tour, of my corps, to make a circuit to the other side of the enemy's camp, where he was ordered to remain concealed till midnight; after which time he was to rush impetuously upon them, and at the instant of our attack to fire on them from the other side. My officer performed his orders with great exactness; and I heard several reports of pateraroes at two in the morning, at which instant, as I was ready to march, I proceeded strait to the enemy; but instead of enemies, I met the Sambarives on the road, who, having heard the reports of the large pieces, supposed that I had attacked the enemy. Being thus united by accident to the whole of my forces, I entered the plain of Mahertomp, where we found no enemies, but in their place, my officer, with his detachment. He informed me, that, pursuant to my orders, he had

briskly

briskly attacked the enemy's camp, who, upon hearing the repeated discharge of cannon, imagined the attack to be supported by our whole army, and had made their escape, some by swimming, and the rest into the woods. My detachment collected upwards of two hundred muskets, which the fugitives had left in their haste. Forty prisoners were taken by my people.

Having in this manner become master of the plain of Mahertomp, which is really the most agreeable spot, and the richest part of the whole province of Antimaroa, occupying a space of six leagues along the banks of the river of Tingballe, and more than thirteen in depth, perfectly well cultivated and inhabited throughout, I judged it proper to establish a post to preserve it, and to secure a communication between it, and the chief settlement, and the plain of Health. As I had six thousand blacks under my command, I set them to work without delay on this project; and while I thus employed my people, I determined to send back the prisoners with proposals of peace, to convince them of our good intentions. But these infatuated people still refused to accede to my proposition.

On the 12th, the redoubt was finished at the plain of Mahertomp, in which I left twelve volunteers, commanded by an officer, and defended by four cannon, which I had caused to be brought from Louisbourg. I then proceeded with my whole army to the plain of Health, where on my arrival I learned that the enemy, to the number of seven or eight thousand, was encamped at no more than two leagues distance from us; and that their camp was well entrenched and palisaded. This stopped my progress, until I could receive four field pieces from Louisbourg. But the chiefs of my allies being desirous of proving their valour, without waiting the arrival of the artillery, went and attacked the enemy unknown to me. They made several fruitless assaults, and being at last repelled, they retired as far as to the foot of the mountain, with the enemy close at their backs.

My four pieces of cannon being at last arrived, I marched myself, with thirty volunteers and two hundred disciplined natives, in the pay of the settlement. We departed in the night unknown to our allies, and at day-break, after having erected two batteries, I began a very hot fire on the enemy. In the space of half an hour, one side of their palisade being entirely destroyed, they abandoned their first entrenchment, and filed off behind a kind of redoubt, from which they were likewise dislodged. At last they hastened, in the utmost confusion, to a branch of the river of Ranoumena, which was out of the reach of my cannon. But my allies, being informed that I was engaged with the enemy, ran up, and seeing the camp taken, quickly passed the river, attacked and drove them without resistance. This whole business was performed with only two volunteers wounded, who were my cook and servant. The loss of the Sambarives consisted of eleven men, and of the enemy about sixty-five. The Sambarives pursued them for some days, as far as their frontier; but I remained at the plain of Health.

On the 21st, after having refreshed my people, I raised my camp at the plain, in order to be nearer the second division of the enemy, who had retired into the morass of Ampangou, upon an island of about six leagues in circumference, and surrounded with water.

On

On the 22d, I arrived at the plain of Mahertomp, where I pitched my camp at the foot of the new redoubt. Five days were employed in difcovering the paffage through the morafs, and in reconnoitring the pofition of the enemy.

On the 27th, I raifed my camp at the plain of Mahertomp, and after having paffed the river of Tingballe, I arrived at the entrance of the morafs, from whence we diftinctly faw the enemy's camp, at the diftance of about a league and half, and confifting of four thoufand men.

On the 28th, we received a check at the entrance of the river Ranoufoutchy, which the enemy were obftinately determined to defend. The Seclaves loft fo many men, that they quitted their allies, whofe forces were confiderably weakened by this event.

On the 29th, feveral fkirmifhes took place between our people and the enemy. This night four volunteers, who had been fent to collect wood for the ufe of the camp, paffed the morafs, and thought proper to amufe themfelves by attacking the enemy, to whofe tents they fet fire.

July the 1ft, 1775. Continual rains increafed the waters of Ampangou to fuch an height, that our camp was overflowed, and we were obliged to retreat above a league. Our enemies, attributing our retreat to another caufe, took courage and attempted to harrafs us.

From the 2d to the 8th it rained continually, which gave the enemy time to furround their camp with a ditch and palifade.

On the 9th, I received advice, that a party of about three thoufand of the enemy had rallied fince the defeat of
the

the Antambours, and had joined the oppofite camp; and that another party were very troublefome in the neighbourhood of Louifbourg. On this day I heard of the arrival of a veffel.

On the 10th, the officer commanding the redoubt at the plain of Mahertomp, which I had named Fort St. John, wrote to me, that reports were current to the effect, that the enemy was defirous of forming a treaty of peace with me, to the prejudice of the Sambarives and other nations in alliance, who already began to murmur, more efpecially as I did not attack the enemy, though they did not confider the obftacles occafioned by the overflowing of the waters.

On the 13th, the enemy being in want of provifions in their camp, out of which they dared not fally for fear of my party, began to repent of their warfare. In confequence of this information, I fent feveral boats loaded with rice and bananas, with fome brandy; and let them underftand, that I was fo far from being defirous of exterminating them, that I would leave them a clear paffage to retreat, whenever they thought proper, on condition of their laying down their arms. Accordingly, I withdrew two pofts which guarded the paffage from the ifland to the firm land. This ftep was attended with much fuccefs; for the enemy perceiving themfelves every day more diftreffed by famine, began to retire in troops, and feveral came to me. Thefe I received kindly; and after giving them fome provifions, I fuffered them to go where they pleafed.

On the 14th, I received information from Louifbourg of the arrival of the private fhip the Conquerant, commanded

manded by the Sieur Olivier, from the ifle of France, which brought difpatches from the government of that colony; wherein I was informed, that the Chevalier de Sanglier, Captain of my corps, whom I had fent to demand fupplies, had received an abfolute refufal. This difagreeable news gave me the greateft concern; but as it was a ftep of prudence to encourage my people, I gave out, that this fhip would be followed by two of his Majefty's packets, with a fupply of one hundred men; and I fucceeded in deftroying, in fome meafure, the confternation of my officers.

From the 15th to the 19th, I was informed that the enemy had entered into a treacherous correfpondence with part of our allies. I therefore fet my confidential fpies at work to make difcoveries.

On the 20th in the morning, a detachment, which had been fent out of the camp to obferve the enemy, difcovered two blacks making their efcape; the elder of whom faid to the other, " Run and tell them, that no dependance can be placed on thofe whom they fuppofed to be their friends, and that I am taken." This black, being brought before me, confeffed that he had been fent to feduce part of our allies; but that not having fucceeded, they had been defirous of informing their countrymen, that we intended to attack them. Upon this depofition, I immediately caufed a meeting of feveral chiefs to be held, who condemned him to death. I confented to their decree with greater willingnefs, becaufe the man was found to be the fame, who in the infancy of the fettlement had engaged to fet fort Louis on fire. His fentence was immediately carried into execution.

On the 24th, the commanding officer of fort St. John reported, that a soldier of the name of La Gonivier, lately arrived from the isle of France, had made several mutinous proposals, by assuring the troops that they were abandoned, and that the isle of France was so far from sending any supplies, that on the contrary, its chiefs sought every occasion to destroy us. Being desirous of verifying the fact myself, I gave directions to the officer to take no notice; and with a view to watch the man more narrowly, I ordered him into my own camp. In the night, between eleven and twelve o'clock, hearing a noise, I came out of my tent, and saw the soldier, La Gonivier, make several strokes with a sabre at the officer of the guard, at the same time that I distinctly heard him say, "That the time would soon come, when the soldiers should command the officers at Madagascar." I therefore called the guard, which ran and endeavoured to take the mutineer. The man in despair rushed on them, and wounded two, crying out, "Come on, my friends." This call at first led me to suspect a plot. I observed, however, from all the motions of the volunteers, that they remained composed and steady in their duty, by closing upon the mutineer, who fled towards the wood, but was brought down by a ball. This unexpected event, which tended to disconcert our black allies, induced me to hasten his execution. I therefore called a council of my officers without delay, but the criminal expired of his wound before his trial came on.

On the 28th, the enemy remaining still in a small number on their posts, which they were obstinately determined not to quit, being encouraged by the promise of thirty

thirty thousand men on the part of the Seclaves, I determined to attack them. But as I had no intention of causing a massacre, I advised them of our approach by several discharges of cannon.

On the 26th, 27th, and 28th, our black allies pursued the enemy; who retired to the Northern parts of the island, as far as the frontiers of Antimananhar.

August the 1st. The Sieur Bourdé, to whom the Minister had granted the whale fishery on the coast of Madagascar, not having succeeded in his enterprize, requested my permission to purchase rice, in order to indemnify him for his want of success. I willingly agreed to his request, as the establishment being destitute of merchandize, could not carry on any commerce itself. I granted the same permission to the Sieur Olivier, who brought a vessel from the isle of France.

August the 3d, being delivered from our enemies, and the province of Antimaroa being without cultivation, I proposed to the Sambarives, to replace the Saphirobai, who had been driven out of their province. My proposition was joyfully accepted, and they immediately agreed to pay me an annual acknowledgment for the protection of the establishment.

On the 4th, a general meeting being held for the division of the conquered lands of the enemy, I gave the right branch of the river of Tingballe to the Sambarives, and kept the left branch for the establishment. Several parties of the Saphirobai detesting the offences they had committed against the establishment, now came to request forgiveness. The kind and affable manner in which I received them, soon caused them to forget their losses, and to condemn their chiefs, who had sacrificed their people to their own private interests. From these fugitives I likewise learned, that the Saphirobai were forced to wander in the woods, and subsist upon roots, because the chiefs of the other provinces refused them an asylum. I determined, therefore, to take advantage of this circumstance, to shew the uprightness of my intentions; and for this purpose, on the following day, I sent commissioners to the neighbouring chiefs, to desire them to assist the Saphirobai with the necessaries of life, and to receive them freely, provided they renounced their purpose of continuing the war. This step could not but be productive of manifest advantage.

On the 5th, another embarrassment presented itself. The subsistance of the troops of our allies became chargeable to the establishment, and I determined to dismiss them. But this, according to the custom of the island, could not be done without recompensing them by presents.

The 6th, 7th, and 8th, were employed in the distribution of the presents; and I had the satisfaction to see the different nations with their chiefs, return contented with my manner of proceeding.

On the 9th, I was attacked by a fever.

On the 10th, being no longer employed by the war, I directed my attention entirely to procure the comforts of life for the establishment, on a good footing. Being convinced of the inconveniences to which my people were exposed, in houses constructed with leaves, after the manner of the country, I determined to construct the whole of wood. My troops, with two thousand hired blacks, should have been employed in building new apartments for the Governor, with an hospital, barracks, and store-houses,

and

and two hundred other blacks in building sixty houses, to form the town; and during the building, the troop of Sance, composed of twelve hundred men, should have laboured in filling the morass. But it was unfortunate, that I was then without the means, otherwise Louisbourg would soon have changed its appearance.

On the 16th, my disorder increased, and I felt an universal weakness, which obliged me to place the command in the hands of Captain Mallendre, reserving to myself, however, the communication of all affairs of importance. My illness, however, became continually worse, so that I was not consulted on any business whatever.

On the 20th, I was somewhat better, and received information of the death of the Sieur Garreau.

On the 1st of September, this brave and intelligent officer was carried to the tomb, to the regret of the whole corps. The place of engineer which he possessed, being rendered vacant by his death, I gave orders to the Sieur Rosier, the scholar of the Sieur Garreau, to perform that office.

On the 21st, the officers of my corps waited upon me, and requested, that I would give them orders relative to the intention of the Court, with respect to the establishment at Madagascar; that in case my illness should prevent my being in a situation to attend to the colony, they might act conformably to the good of the service; but finding myself weaker that day than ordinary, I requested them to meet at my house on the 22d.

On the 22d, the fever left me, and I found myself somewhat stronger. This day the meeting was held, for the result of which, see the piece, L. X. at the end of this memoir, by which the council was adjourned to the 25th.

On the 25th, the council met by adjournment, and I received information, that eight wooden houses were finished, in which the troops were lodged.

October the 1st. The Sieur Olivier, master of a private vessel from the isle of France, by whose means the subsistance of the establishment had been provided for, set sail with a cargo of six hundred and fifty thousand pounds of rice; the Sieur Bourdé likewise took in a cargo of eight hundred and fifty thousand pounds of rice. This supply of provisions must have been very acceptable; and if the isle of France had supplied our store-houses with merchandize, a prodigious quantity might have been had, which the islanders wasted for want of sale; and there is reason to apprehend, that this want will diminish their industry next season.

On the 2d, the Sambarive chiefs requested permission to erect flag staffs on their territory, to distinguish the chiefs from each other. I agreed to their request, and at the same time distributed to each chief a white flag, with different stripes of red and blue, to distinguish their degrees. The same day the Saphirobai chiefs, who had always remained attached to the government, requested permission to build a town, under the protection of fort Louis, in order to defend them from the incursions of their adversaries. I agreed to their request with pleasure, as it afforded a means of attaining my purpose, which was to people the province as much as possible, on account of its vicinity to the chief settlement, where the consumption

COUNT DE BENYOWSKY.

tion muſt naturally be more confiderable, than in any other part of the iſland.

On the 3d, I began to perceive a return of my ſtrength, and I found the hofpital entirely empty; a circumſtance which ſhews, that my troops at this time were ſtronger than ever. I do not, however, here ſpeak of that vigour which is natural to Europeans in their own country, but which they lofe in hot climates.

On the 4th, Hiavi, chief of the province of Mahavelou, demanded my affiſtance againſt the Fariavas and Betalimenes, who had declared war againſt him. As this chief had always acted in the intereſts of the Europeans, I determined to affiſt him; and for that purpofe, detached feven volunteers with a fubaltern officer, to Foul Point, to act according to the orders of the commander at that out-fettlement. I was convinced before hand, that the mere report of my having taken part with Hiavi, would put an end to the war.

On the 6th, the hofpital, with all the adjoining buildings, were at laſt finiſhed in a folid manner; but, fortunately, we were at this time in a fituation to keep them vacant.

From the 7th to the 12th, I made an excurfion, to vifit the diſtrict which had been furrendered to the Sambarives, on the banks of the river Tingballe. The lands were excellent, but the territory annexed to the eſtabliſhment by the late conqueſt, were greatly fuperior. What immenfe riches might be derived from a diſtrict of land, twenty-two leagues in length, upon the coaſt of a navigable river? This excurfion entirely reſtored my health.

On the 13th, I gave orders to cover the post of fort St. John, by a broad ditch and double palisade, with a covered way, and to build several houses in wood, for the accommodation of such as might stop there, in their way to the plain of Health.

On the 14th, I received a courier from the Sieur Mayeur, interpreter, and Mr. Corbi, officer of my corps, the latter of whom I had sent in boats round the Northern parts of the island, while the former went by land along the shore, in order to examine all the bays, harbours, and rivers, the inhabitants, their numbers, forces, industry, productions, and mutual interests. I ordered them to continue their journey, until they arrived at the territories of Lambouin, a chief who assumed the title of King of the North. My intention was to engage this chief in our interests, and to purchase of him the island Nossebe, situated to the N. W. of the island of Madagascar, in 13° 15′ S. latitude, and 45° 6′ longitude from Paris. These two officers sent me their journals of the coast. They informed me, that they had joined company in the territories of the chief Lambouin, by whom they were amicably received; that this chief being astonished at the renown of the white men, had determined before their arrival, to send ambassadors to me, to form a treaty with the establishment, and that profiting by his good disposition, they had caused him to enter into an oath of friendship; that they had purchased the island Nossebe of him; and that having in this manner attained the purposes of their mission, they waited only for my orders to return.

Being thus assured of the attachment of Lambouin, whose interest it was to secure himself against the vexations

of

of the Seclaves, I could depend on a refpectable ally, capable of furnifhing fifteen or twenty thoufand men.

From the 15th to the 20th, being in perfect tranquillity, and my troops being recovered from their fatigue, I recommenced the works, and employed them in building a place of refidence for the Governor.

On the 21ft, I received information that feveral bands of the Saphirobai fugitives had approached the eftablifhment, where they had burned feveral houfes of the Sambarives; upon which I immediately detached twelve volunteers, commanded by an officer, and fupported by fix hundred blacks, to clear the woods and their avenues.

On the 22d, my detachment returned in the evening with three prifoners, whom they had taken, after furprizing a party of thefe black robbers.

On the 23d, I received a packet from my officer, who commanded at Foul Point, in which he informed me, that the enemies of Hiavi had made offers of peace, on condition that the commander of that poft fhould be appointed judge, to determine the differences which might arife between them and Hiavi; but that the latter, not having thought proper to confent, my officer engaged to bring Hiavi to reafon, provided he might have permiffion to ufe threats, in cafe he obftinately continued to refufe his compliance. As this manœuvre promifed to gain an entire people to my interefts, and I was well aware of the prudence of my officer, I returned precife orders to him in confequence.

October the 24th. The end of the month now approaching, without the arrival of any news from Europe, and the return of the Chevalier de Sanglier, whom I had sent for supplies to the isle of France, being likewise retarded, produced the most afflicting reflections in my mind; and I had no other resource than my firmness against the unhappy fate which pursued me. I considered the approach of the bad season, during which, if the supplies should continue to be with-held (as it would be out of my power to form establishments in the interior parts of the country), I had every reason to expect that the settlement would be again plunged into the most critical situation. The troops seeing none of the supplies arrive, upon which their hopes had been hitherto supported, must of course consider themselves as abandoned; and that with so much the more certainty, as the reports spread in the isle of France, concerning the reduction of my troops, had been divulged at Madagascar, notwithstanding all my precautions. The courage of my officers, who had adopted the firm resolution of doing their duty, by encouraging their men, was the only circumstance which supported me, and gave me reason to presume that I might still resist the pressure of misfortune. But who could answer for the continuance of my force, which must every day become less effectual? What an unhappy situation it is for a Commander in Chief, who, after having resisted the intemperature of hot climates, suffered dangerous diseases, and undergone infinite fatigue;—who, after having seen his troops diminished one-third, finds himself under the necessity of facing every circumstance, without losing the advantages he has gained, but on the contrary, preserving them against sudden revolutions; and who, instead of the supplies he has requested, is exposed to the jealousy and calumnies of persons in place, who were ordered by the

Government

Government to afford him every affiftance!—A promife was made me, that I fhould receive every year fupplies, and a reinforcement of one hundred and twenty men; and that in the mean time the ifle of France fhould fupport me in every preffing exigency; and in a word, that nothing fhould be wanting for the fuccefs of my miffion. But, alas, two whole years were gone, and I ftill remained without fupplies. If they were ftill delayed, I faw that the fatal inftant would not fail to arrive, in which the fruits of all my labour, care, and fatigue would vanifh, and France be for ever deprived of the power of regaining the confidence of the natives. Such were the reflections that oppreffed me, and on an occafion like this, the pen can never defcribe the fufferings of the mind.

From the 25th, to the end of the month, I employed my time in vifiting the pofts, which I found every where in perfect order. But I found fadnefs and depreffion in every countenance; a fadnefs which certainly did not arife from a fpirit of mutiny. I knew my troops too well to fufpect it. But I could be at no lofs for the caufe. Deftitute of linen, of clothes, or covering, I beheld them difheartened, and had no external refource to relieve them, and reftore their fpirits.

November the 1ft, 1775. Activity and refolution were never more neceffary. I collected a number of the native women, whom I employed in making cloth, and ten volunteers were felected to perform the occupation of taylors, in clothing my poor fellows. I fucceeded in tanning fkins, and being provided with fhoemakers, the profpect of again poffeffing fhoes, began to be more chearing than before. Nothing therefore remained, but to divert my my men. For this purpofe I exercifed them in firing at at a mark, and gave a prize to fuch as diftinguifhed themfelves. This exercife tended to render them more ferviceable, and was at the fame time an object of entertainment. In confequence of this determination, I put a ftop to the ordinary works, and began the exercifes.

On the 4th, I was informed of the arrival of the Saphirobai chief Effonlahé, who was fent by his nation to demand an audience. I referred him to the next day, in order to give time to the Sambarive chiefs to come together, and be prefent at the delivery of the propofitions of this envoy.

On the 5th, the affembly being met, the envoy of the Saphirobai entered. His head was fhaven, as a mark of fubmiffion, and proftrating himfelf on the ground, he pronounced thefe words. "I, the unfortunate chief of the race of the Saphirobai Antimaroa, throw myfelf at the feet of the juftice and mercy of the great Chief, to implore his grace, in the name of my whole nation, which requefts permiffion to fend deputies to expiate its fault. I am come before to offer my life if it be neceffary. Conqueror, in us thou mayeft no longer behold an enemy, but the remains of an unhappy people, who are obedient and fubmiffive to thy laws."

After having liftened to his fpeech, I replied as follows: "I have beheld with forrow the irregularities of the Saphirobai chiefs. I call your own nation to witnefs, with what tendernefs I have conducted myfelf, with a view to maintain an alliance and avoid a war, whofe confequences could not fail to end in your deftruction. And thou, chief Effonlahé, who now fpeakeft with me, fay, waft thou

not

not three times charged to carry offers of peace to thy countrymen? Am I to blame that my offers produced three refusals? Judge then this day, who has acted wrong; and who it is that has deserved the chastisement of heaven. The oaths of fidelity, by which we were united before this unhappy war, have been sported with by you. You have broken your engagements with us. You have dared to infringe a compact made in the presence of the great God. It is he who has punished you, and pursues you with his vengeance.—But I am charged never to refuse the offers of friendship made by the people of Madagascar. It is my duty to protect the unfortunate, and to render justice where it is due, at the price of my blood, and that of my companions. It is by virtue of these orders that I grant forgiveness to the nation of the Saphirobai. They may without fear send any of their chiefs to me during the course of the ensuing month, to regulate the common interests of both nations."

The envoy of the Saphirobai, contented with my answer, repeated his prayers, thanked me, and retired.

The Sambarive chiefs, who were present at the assembly, informed me of their apprehensions, that as I had pardoned the Saphirobai, I should restore them their entire province, and consequently, that they should be forced to abandon their establishment. But when they had received an assurance from me, that that part of the province which had been granted to them, should remain in their possession, by virtue of the treaty concluded with the Saphirobai, they became contented.

From the 6th of November, to the 13th, I was constantly employed in exercising my troops; and their cloathing

cloathing being at laſt ready, was diſtributed among them.

On the 14th, a courier from Foul Point, accompanied with two chiefs, ſubject to Hiavi, arrived. My officers informed me, that Hiavi had at laſt conſented to my requeſt, and that peace was concluded on; but that on the other hand, the chiefs who were ſubject to Hiavi, were meditating a revolt againſt him, as they could no longer bear his oppreſſion. The two chiefs who arrived with my courier, gave me an account of this, and aſſured me, that the people who were ſubject to Hiavi, were perfectly willing to ſubmit to the ſettlement, provided I would declare againſt their Sovereign. I might perhaps have liſtened to this propoſition at another time; but in the ſituation I then ſtood, it would not have been prudent to have engaged myſelf in an affair of ſuch a nature, as might have produced very ſerious conſequences. I therefore contented myſelf with promiſing to theſe two chiefs, that I would bring Hiavi to reaſon, and in the mean time I forbad them to make any attempt againſt him, until I had aſcertained the facts myſelf. My promiſe was accompanied by preſents, with which they were well ſatisfied.

The intereſts of the ſettlement required, that the power of Hiavi ſhould be limited, but a ſudden revolution might probably endanger the government; and it is not till after a courſe of time, that the authority of certain chiefs can be diminiſhed. In the mean time, it is neceſſary to treat them with mildneſs, and to explain to them their true intereſts. For it is certain, that the Madagaſcar nations can never be ſubjugated by force, and the work of civilization cannot be accompliſhed, but by a man who by his
conduct,

conduct, virtue, and juftice, fhall have acquired the confidence of the chiefs and people.

The 15th and 16th, were employed in reparing all the fhallops, boats, and canoes, and putting them in a ftate for fervice.

On the 17th, the Sieur Aumont, ftorekeeper, died. I immediately gave orders to the clerk to feal all his effects and papers, to forward them to Mr. Maillart; and on the other hand, that the fervice might not fuffer, I gave orders to make an inventory of the contents of the ftorehoufes, which I entrufted provifionally to the Sieur Beffe, treafurer, conformably to the intention of the Minifter, who, in his letter took notice, that the treafury and ftores might be entrufted to one perfon. This bufinefs was quickly performed, but I was greatly aftonifhed to hear from the Secretary of the adminiftration, that all the regifters of entry and difburfements were blank. This admirable method of keeping accounts, muft no doubt have been productive of no very agreeable confequences to Mr. Maillart, who chofe thefe people.

On the 18th, I received advice from the blacks, that an Englifh fhip which had failed along the coaft during the courfe of the month, had fuffered fo much by a tempeft, that they were forced to fire feveral guns for affiftance, in the fight of the fettlement of Angontzi; but that the hard weather having driven her off the coaft, they had loft fight of her; and fhe had been fince feen from Andrava, at the diftance of two leagues from the fhore, on fire. No more than feven people were faved in the boat, which came on fhore at Loquez. The following day I fent an order to the Sieur Mayeur, interpreter, (who

was

was not more than two days journey diftance from the place where thefe unfortunate people had landed) to give them affiftance, and afford them the means of coming to the chief fettlement.

On the 19th, feveral blacks from the Weftern coaft informed me, that the chiefs of the Seclaves had held a meeting, in which they had determined to make war upon the French, and to engage all the people of the Eaft in their interefts; in confequence of which, they had fent feveral chiefs into the different provinces, to perfuade them to unite againft the eftablifhment. Thefe reports demanded all my attention. I likewife fent fpies on my part to inquire into the truth, in order that I might have time to make preparations, in cafe the Seclaves fhould fucceed, in forming their league with the people of the Eaft coaft; and they were particularly directed to afcertain, whether they propofed to fall upon us in the bad feafon, which would have greatly embarraffed me.

On the 20th, I fent my fpies with articles of trade to purchafe cattle. Under this pretence, they were to obtain information of the manœuvres of the Seclaves, and the intentions of the different nations.

On the 21ft, the Sambarive chiefs affembled at the fettlement in great confternation, at the news of the war, which the Seclaves had declared againft the eftablifhment. They demanded why the fuccours from France were fo long delayed; and how I fhould act, in cafe I fhould be attacked by the Seclaves in the bad feafon, before their arrival. They obferved, likewife, that with my fmall number of people, I could not make any refiftance againft the enemy; and that they themfelves fhould become their victims,

victims, as being the moſt faithful and zealous friends of the eſtabliſhment. To encourage them, and remove their apprehenſions, I replied, that I was aſhamed of the fear, which ſo brave a nation as themſelves had ſhewn on this occaſion; that the Sambarives ought to have a better opinion of my courage; and that I knew well what would be the propereſt mode of proceeding. My anſwers, however, did not ſatisfy them. They repeated their complaints, and ſaid, " You will abandon us. Your King has not ſent any more people to you. You are ready to quit us, and we alone ſhall be unfortunate, for having been your friends." The voice of the people and of the chiefs was the ſame. They requeſted me to take an oath that I would not abandon them. I gave ſeveral entertainments to the chiefs and people of the Sambarives, and neglected nothing to inſpire them with all the neceſſary confidence. But in my own mind, I had as much need of conſolation; for I found myſelf at the approach of the bad ſeaſon, without ſupplies, without troops, and in a word, entirely abandoned.

On the 14th of December, a periagua arrived from the North, which brought me a Malay woman, who alone had ſurvived the wreck of the Engliſh veſſel. She informed me, that the Engliſh veſſel had left Bombay with ſixteen guns and one hundred men, and that her cargo was compoſed of ſilk and other merchandize of India, with fire-arms and brandy; that after their departure from Bombay, they had put in at the iſland of Johanna; and, laſtly, that on their arrival on the coaſt of Madagaſcar, they had tried to take ſome of the natives to ſpeak with them, but had not ſucceeded, notwithſtanding the repeated trips their boats had made on shore; at the approach of which, the natives of the country were always seen either armed to prevent their landing, or flying into the interior parts of the country; that, lastly, the vessel being overtaken by a tempest, was obliged to stand off the coast, and upon her having caught fire, the whole crew took to the boats to make for the shore; that out of three boats two were sunk by the number of people who crouded into them, and the jolly-boat only reached the shore with seven persons, including the Captain; that the Captain with six others were dead, and she alone remained out of the ship.

On the 15th, my spies having returned, confirmed the report, that great preparations for war were making by the Seclaves against us, and that they waited only for the breaking up of the bad season, to take the field to the number of thirty thousand men; that they had sent several emissaries into the different provinces to engage the chiefs on their side, but that they depended much more on their own forces, flattering themselves that the French durst not face them, and that during the time they should keep them shut up in their forts, they should be at liberty to reduce the provinces of their allies, who would be forced to follow their standards. This information, though very disagreeable, on account of the disposition and situation of the establishment, gave me some consolation; because I was assured, that the Seclaves would leave me in tranquillity during the whole of the bad season, and that the supplies so long expected, would at length arrive.

On the 16th, I sent several messengers both to the North and South of the island, to inform the chiefs of the movements

movements of the Seclaves; at the same time enjoining them, to hold themselves in readiness to join my forces at the first orders I should give. I signified to them besides, that all those who should receive the Seclaves among them, under any pretext whatever, would be considered as enemies of the establishment.

On the 18th, I received information of the arrival of the chiefs of the Saphirobai and Antambour, who requested a meeting, and demanded peace.

On the 21st, the Saphirobai and Antambour chiefs were admitted into the Cabar. They represented to me, that the misfortunes and power of war, having dispossessed them of their province, and being reduced to the vile and abject condition of vagabonds, who have no country, they had unanimously determined to surrender themselves to my discretion; that they requested only a part of their province for cultivation, without pretending to the propriety, the right of which belonged to the Sambarives. They concluded by observing, that if they were to be unhappy, they intreated at least, that they might be permitted to die in their own country. Being informed from my interpreters, of the sincerity of their repentance, and the interests of the establishment requiring, that the province should be as fully peopled as possible, I pardoned them, and the chiefs entered into an oath of submission and fidelity.

On the 24th, a signal was made on the mountain, that a two-masted vessel was in sight.

On the 26th, the vessel anchored near the isle Aiguillon, about noon, and the Chevalier de Sanglier, Captain, whom I had sent to the isle of France, being come on shore, presented to me four recruits he had raised, which composed the succour the isle of France sent me. I employed the whole day in reading my packets, in hopes of finding some order or letter from the Minister; but I found nothing but the railleries which the letters of Messrs. de Ternay and Maillart were filled with. Mr. de Sanglier informed me, that several suits at law were carrying on against me in the isle of France; and, lastly, that every outrage, calumny, and imposture, was used to overwhelm me. I here pass them over in silence, as they form no part of my operations.

On the 27th, the four persons whom Mr. de Ternay forwarded to me to be employed as volunteers of honour, were presented to me. This commander pretended to serve the state, by sending men to me whose past conduct had consisted of highly reprehensible irregularities, and unnatural crimes. I do not here mention their names on account of their families; but I do not think they escaped at Madagascar. This island is a true touchstone for the conduct of men. I received information of the death of his Majesty, Louis XV. of happy memory, and the joyful accession of his Majesty Louis XVI. to the throne. I likewise understood that the Ministry was changed; and I was apprehensive that for this reason my supplies would be retarded, and the plan of my operations might probably be changed. In a word, all these circumstances opposed my progress. I had no other dependance than patience and firmness, and the hope that the veil which covered the future, would at last fall.

January

January the 1st, 1776. I was busied in adjusting the accounts of my troops, and those of the general storehouse, which I discharged out of my own purse.

On the 10th, his Majesty's packet le Dauphin, commanded by Ensign Tromelin, left the isle of France to go to the Secheyles islands, and put in at the settlement for provisions, which I caused to be delivered to them.

On the 11th, his Majesty's brig le Coureur, which I had sent to Mozambique arrived. The Captain of this vessel informed me, that he had been forced to anchor at the isle of France, and that he could purchase but very few slaves. This information astonished me, as the articles of trade with which we had been supplied from the general storehouse, had been very considerable. I therefore sent an officer on board to examine the officers and crew, respecting the trade at Mozambique; and I went on board myself to assist in the examination. In this way I learned, that the Captain had sold forty-two blacks at the isle of France, which were the produce of his cargo, and the rice. I therefore caused him to be put under confinement on board the vessel. Three men from the isle of France were sent on shore, one of whom called himself a taylor, the other a cabinet-maker, and the third a writer. They were all three sick, and had been taken out of the hospital, doubtless with a view to augment the number of the dead at Madagascar.

On the 12th, I received advice that the Rohandrian Cunifaloues was on his way to put himself under the protection of the establishment, in order to resist the Seclaves, who threatened him, and several parties of whom had already set whole villages in flames upon our frontiers.

On the 13th, two Sambarive chiefs, who were ſtrongly attached to my perſon, informed me, that the King of the Seclaves had ſent a ſecret meſſenger to Hiavi, King and Chief of Foul Point, to engage him to act againſt the intereſts of the eſtabliſhment; and that Hiavi had held a meeting on this buſineſs, in which the envoys of the Seclaves had propoſed to Hiavi, to ſupport him in the ſovereignty over the whole Eaſt coaſt, on condition that he ſhould make war on the eſtabliſhment. But that Hiavi would not conſent to make war upon the white men; becauſe he ſaid, it was impoſſible for the King to reſiſt the French, whoſe Fangafoudi, or ſorcerers, were ſtronger than thoſe of the blacks; and that moreover the Baron, having a knowledge of the ſtars, knew every thing which was contrived againſt him; and that he (Hiavi) having engaged by oath to be faithful to the eſtabliſhment, durſt not make any attempt againſt it, as he was ſure to die immediately, in caſe he ſhould break his oath.

On the 14th, were in the midſt of the bad ſeaſon. If it ſhould weaken us, ſaid I to myſelf, and the ſupplies be ſtill detained, I may ſay with Virgil, *Sic vos non vobis nidificatis aves.*

I received information that Hiavi, notwithſtanding his anſwer to the Seclaves, was inclined to their ſide, and that he had furniſhed them with arms and ammunition. This conduct induced me to depreſs his authority, which was eaſy to be done, by aſſuring the Mulatta chiefs, who were deſcended from Europeans, that the alliance of Hiavi with the Seclaves, would reduce them to ſervitude; and that when they were reduced to the obedience of Hiavi, they would ſoon be confounded with his ſlaves. Their proud ſpi-

rit

it would have eagerly seized the inftant to withdraw themfelves from the fubjection to Hiavi, by attaching themfelves entirely to the eftablifhment; but I preferred gentle methods to preferve peace and tranquillity along the Eaft coaft.

From the 15th to the 20th, I held different Cabars, and fent feveral emiffaries to obferve the motions of the enemy.

On the 21ft, the new dwelling for the Governor was finifhed, and I went to refide there with the more fatisfaction, as I had long been very inconveniently lodged, and had felt the confequences in the effect it had on my health.

On the 22d, the Sambarive chiefs informed me, that the Seclaves had invited them to join them againft the whites; but that their nation had anfwered, by fending them powder, ball, and gun flints (the fignal of war), declaring at the fame time, that the Sambarives had allied themfelves to me with fincerity; that they confidered my enemies as their enemies, and that they would not give the Seclaves the trouble of coming to them, becaufe they intended to meet them. I gave an entertainment to this brave nation.

On the 23d, I was informed by my interpreter, that the Sambarives had fent feveral of their chiefs into different provinces, to engage the people to join them to make war on the Seclaves. This brave nation gave public notice, that all thofe who did not join them fhould be confidered as their enemies, and that their troops fhould carry flames and fire into their provinces. This mark of fo eminent a degree of attachment affected me greatly, and I ardently

wifhed

wished for an opportunity of convincing this good people of my affection.

On the 14th, I learned positively, that the Fariavas and the Betalimenes had recommenced the war against Hiavi, and that his own people mutinied against him, for having entered into an oath with the Seelaves. This news was soon followed by a demand on the part of Hiavi for assistance, which was what I expected.

On the 25th, the chiefs of the Antambours sent me word that several chiefs of the Seelaves, established upon their frontiers, had refused to take arms against the establishment; and that to avoid the rage of their King, a party of them had taken refuge amongst the Antambour, and others with Cunifaloues the chief, who had sent me this information, and was himself coming.

On the 29th, Diafaick, chief of the Machineranon, and confidant of Hiavi, came to demand assistance against his enemies, at the same time that he complained that reports were current that I had abandoned Hiavi, for which reason it was absolutely necessary that I should declare in his favour, in order to appease the troubles and revolts which had been excited among his own subjects. I replied, that Hiavi had brought himself into the difficulties he now experienced; that he had himself given reasons for his enemies to declare against him a second time, in consequence of the league he had made with the Seelaves against the government; that his own proceeding had served as a warning to the Betalimenes and Fariavas, with regard to their behaviour, from whom it was that I had received information of all the intrigues of Hiavi. The chief Fauna, confounded at my answer, threw himself at my feet, begging pardon for Hiavi, and protefting that he would recall his mafter to his duty. In my definitive anfwer, I infifted that Hiavi fhould fend his brother to me with five hundred armed men, with orders to march againft the Seclaves, and fhould publickly renounce the alliance of that nation. I promifed, that in the mean time I would prevent his enemies from making any attempts againft him, but that on the flighteft appearance of refufal on his part, I would openly join his opponents.

It cannot eafily be imagined, with what precaution I found it neceffary to act with regard to the inhabitants of this ifland. Revolutions are fo fudden, that to prevent them, I was forced to become an orator, to conform to the character of this nation. It was a very unhappy circumftance that I was without forces; the fmalleft augmentation would have been fufficient to have enabled me to have effected whatever revolutions I thought proper; but having no more than one hundred men, and thofe exhaufted by fatigue, who could not be able to guard one hundred and eighty leagues of coaft, which was the fpace contained by our different fettlements. It was impoflible therefore to remove fo many obftacles as prefented themfelves, without employing ftratagem or cabal; a fituation very afflicting for a military man, when his operations can only be carried on in the cabinet in a tedious and difgraceful way.

February the 1ft, a fignal was hung out at the mountain, that a fhip was in fight.

On the 2d, the fignal ftill appeared; but I difcovered nothing but a fmall veffel, which feemed to be a banion, or the veffel of fome perfon, whofe wretched fortune required

quired the affiftance of piracy, or the employment of a fpy.

On the 3d, the Antambour and Saphirobai chiefs came to declare to me, that being determined to give invariable proofs of their attachment to the eftablifhment, they requefted me to accept fifteen hundred armed men of their nation, to be employed againft the Seclaves. Good news, exclaimed I, the example of my brave Sambarives will invite the other nations to imitate them.

A private veffel named the Lizard, anchored in the harbour, and the Captain, Mr. St. Etheard, made me an offer of his cargo on the King's account. It confifted of cloth, brandy, and fugar.

On the 8th, I received pofitive information of the march of the Seclaves, who directed their courfe towards our frontiers.

Between the 9th and 15th, I vifited my pofts, and faw that the artillery was in a proper fituation for fervice.

My officers, being informed by the natives of the approach of the Seclaves, and perceiving their troops to be greatly weakened, were in no fmall confternation, and could not avoid repeating fome of the circumftances to me; becaufe as they faw me apparently at my eafe, in fuch a critical fituation, they imagined that I was unacquainted with the proceedings of our enemies.

From the 17th to the 23d, I cleared the environs of fort Louis, in order to difcover the approach of the enemy more readily; and I was particularly bufied in making fire balls, rockets, fuzees, and fire lances, in order to prevent the enemy from harraffing us.

On the 23d, the chiefs of the province, Antivarai and Angontzi, came to offer me five hundred warriors. This news afforded me some small comfort, and I began to collect myself against the unhappy events that threatened the establishment. The greatest part of the bad season was now over, and our sick were not so numerous as I expected.

The envoys of Lambouin, King of the North, arrived, and demanded an assembly. They declared on the part of their Prince, that he was already in the field to attack the Seclaves on his side, and waited only for my orders for that purpose. The desire of this chief to establish a constant trade with the settlement, in order to secure its protection, which was necessary to him against the Seclaves, and to preserve his authority, could not fail of being productive of the greatest advantage to the establishment.

On the 2d, I was informed of the arrival of envoys from the chief Cunifaloucs, who informed me of the approach of their chief, together with Rozai, cousin of the King of the Seclaves, who was driven by his relation out of his native country, and probably came to take advantage of the present circumstances, and adapt them to his desire of revenge. After having shewn every sign of friendship to the envoys of the chief Cunifaloucs, I sent several spies to meet him, in order to observe his conduct, and prevent a surprize.

The chief Cunifaloucs, possessor of the province of Santianak, had been tributary for the space of eighteen years to the Seclaves, who often had ravaged his province, under the specious pretence of collecting the tribute. I therefore had reason to think, that the motive of his journey was founded on the hope of throwing off the subjection to the Seclaves, by the assistance of the establishment. The coincidence of this chief in my views, promised greatly to diminish the forces of the Seclaves, because his example would lead others. Rozai, the chief of the Seclaves, who came with him, is of the reigning family of that nation, of which the father of the present King usurped the crown, after having rendered himself master of the country, by a sudden revolt of all the inhabitants, and having, without compassion, reduced the ancient royal family to servitude. I was assured that Rozai had many partizans in the nation, who, if they saw him at the head of some forces, would join his party. All these circumstances gave me reason to hope, that I might derive great advantages this year from a campaign, and I might have undoubtedly struck a fine stroke, if the supplies had arrived. As the war I am about to describe, relates to the country of the Seclaves, it may be proper to give a slight notion of that kingdom and nation.

An Account of the Kingdom of the Seclaves, called Boyana.

March, 1776. The kingdom of the Seclaves extends from the Bay of Massaheli, on the West coast of Madagascar, lying between 44° 20'. and 42° longitude from Paris, and 14° and 16° South latitude, upon the same Western coast of the island. Here it must be observed, that this kingdom is not to be confounded with the ancient country of the Seclaves, which extends much further to the Southward,

and

and no longer depends upon the same chief. The authority of the first chief of the Seclaves, who from time immemorial has possessed the title of King, is despotic. His whole people are slaves, and the chiefs who govern the different provinces, are nominated by him. Their property and lives are in his hands. He always keeps an army of three thousand warriors on foot. His authority which he often abuses, renders him formidable to his unhappy people, who mortally hate him.

The Arabians of the islands Johanna, Comoro, and Mayotto, have established a factory at Maronvai, the capital of the Seclaves, which is at all times supplied with effects and merchandizes, consisting of Surat cloth, combs, silver bracelets, gold buckles, razors, knives, glass beads, &c. in exchange for which they receive skins, incense, benjamin, amber, wax, and wood in planks. The facility which the King of the Seclaves finds in the commerce of the Arabians, and that which he has hitherto found in obtaining arms, gunpowder, and brandy, from private ships, which touch at Madagascar, and which he receives in payment of tribute from different provinces on the Eastern coast, renders him averse to the establishment of a direct trade with the French. It may likewise be true, that the Arabians, jealous of our rival commerce, may have inspired him with sentiments contrary to the interests of the establishment. But, as since my arrival, all the provinces of the East coast have shaken off their yoke, and no longer supply them with arms and warlike stores, the Seclaves cannot but be quickly reduced.

The country of the Seclaves enjoys a very wholesome air. It is flat, has few woods, and is watered with an infinity of fine rivers, and abounds with immense plains, inhabited by thousands of wild oxen, which belong to any one who can take them. The King of the Seclaves might raise an army of thirty thousand men, if he possessed the affections of his people; but upon the least appearance of war, it is usual for them to fly into the mountains, towards the Eastern coast. From these emigrations several different nations have been formed. Since my arrival in this island, I have always maintained detachments, either in the country of the Seclaves, or on its frontiers; and they have experienced none of those disorders which prevail near the sea coast to the Eastward. For this reason I am convinced, that the Western coast would be more favourable to the Europeans. Such an advantage, added to that of possessing several excellent harbours, by which a communication might be formed with the coast of Africa, renders it highly deserving of the utmost exertions of a Governor established at this place, to secure this country; for which purpose nothing more is necessary than to engage the whole of the Eastern coast in his interest against the Seclaves. The happiest occasion now presented itself; for the King of the Seclaves, having declared war against the establishment, and its allies, it became unnecessary to confine ourselves to defensive operations. But the weakness and extreme wants of my troops, tended but too much to check my ardour.

A courier from Foul Point brought me the good news, that Hiavi had expressed the most sincere repentance at having

having entered into an oath with the Seclaves; and that in order to repair his fault, he had sent twelve hundred warriors to my affiftance.

The chief Cunifaloues at length arrived on the 6th, I ordered the meeting to be held on the 8th, to which I invited the chiefs of the Sambarives, Saphirobai, Antambours, Antavacas, and Antavolifbei. When the affembly met Cunifaloues, addreffed me as follows: I write down the proper words of the difcourfe of the blacks, in order that thofe who fucceed me might be familiarized with their expreffion. " I Cunifaloues, the unfortunate chief of the noble race of Santianak, being fubjected by the laws of war to the Seclaves, come to render what I owe to the great warrior and great chief of the white men, whofe name be bleffed, and arm fupported by the force of God. Being affured that the reports which were fpread of the war, which the Seclaves propofed to make againft thee were true, I have haftened to offer thee my arm with thofe of my people. Difpofe of our goods at thy pleafure. Thy will fhall ever be mine, and that of my children. Deign to receive our oath, to affure thee that Cunifaloues acknowledges no other mafter but thyfelf."

This harangue was fucceeded by a fhout of joy, which the followers of this chief, confifting of about three hundred warriors, repeated feveral times. After which I made the following anfwer: " Thy reputation, my friend, and thy misfortunes, have long fince affured thee of my protection. I am unacquainted with none of thy pretenfions, and the juft vengeance which thou entertaineft againft the ufurper of the Seclaves; and thou mayeft be affured that my arm fhall fupport thine. But with regard to the fubmission thou hast made to me, I say that thou art in an error. Know then that it is not conformable to my principles, to reduce the brave nations of Madagascar to servitude. I demand only thy friendship towards myself; but I require thy attachment to the union which exists at this day, between the nations whose deputies are here assembled. My only intention is to inform thee of our interests; to explain the advantages of commerce, and of a well-established government, and to communicate light which may lead to happiness. If thou art resolved to unite in our common interests, thou wilt make an oath of fidelity to the union, and receive orders from my mouth, or the mouth of those who may succeed me."

The chief had scarcely heard my answer, before he demanded to enter into the oath of fidelity, obliging himself to pay to the establishment the same tribute which he had paid to the Seclaves, and offering one thousand warriors of his nation to be directed by my orders, according to circumstances. Upon his declaration, I proceeded to the ceremony of the oath, which was performed with all the decency imaginable. It was scarcely ended before Rozai, the chief of the Seclaves, who arrived with Cunifaloues, directed a second speech to me as follows: "I, Rozai, the unfortunate prince of Boyana, seeking amongst strangers a support against the injustice of the usurper of my kingdom, who, not content with having deprived me of my country, retains my wives and children in slavery, throw myself at thy knees for protection. The people say of thee, that thou callest thyself the father of the unhappy: Reject not then the prayer of a prince who reclaims thy assistance. As a proof of my submission, thou shalt receive

ceive my oath, and mayeft depend on me from henceforth among the number of thy faithful friends."

The following was my anfwer: " I grant to the prince Rozai, who reclaims the protection of the eftablifhment, and that of the united nations, the conftant and permanent fupport of our arms, with fo much the greater fatisfaction, as his misfortunes plead in his favour; a plea which at all times has found a fupport againft injuftice and oppreffion. In the mean time, the prince Rozai may affure himfelf of our protection by oath."

After having thus fatisfied the unfortunate chief, I addreffed myfelf to him and the chief Cunifaloues, advifing them to reflect well on what they had done, by connecting themfelves under oath to the interefts of the eftablifhment, whofe protection they had thereby fecured as long as they fhould continue faithful to their engagements: But that, if they fhould have the misfortune to break their oaths, it would be no longer in my power to prevent the unhappy confequences which might refult to them, their families, and fubjects.

On the 9th, 10th, and 11th, the chiefs of the Eaftern coaft, gave an entertainment to Cunifaloues and Rozai. My brave Sambarives particularly diftinguifhed themfelves. The chiefs, Cunifaloues and Rozai, afterwards required to be difmiffed in order to take the field againft the Seclaves. They informed me likewife, that they fhould lofe no time in fending emiffaries into all the different provinces which were fubject to the Seclaves, to engage them to join the part of Rozai, and demanded favour and protection for thofe who fhould enter into their league.

On

On the 12th, the chief Lambarault arrived with twelve armed boats and two hundred warriors. He informed me, that he came to the affiftance of the eftablifhment; that being the fon of a white man, he was defirous of being one of the firft in the combat; and that feveral of his fubjects, who had returned from the country of the Seclaves, had reported to him, that the enemy was no more than five days march from our frontiers; for which reafon, if I would accept his affiftance, he would go forth to reconnoitre them. I received this chief in a friendly manner, but for feveral reafons I kept him near me.

On the 13th, my interpreter informed me, that his people had reported, that the chiefs of the different provinces propofed to fend deputies to me to inquire, whether my intention was to remain fhut up till the arrival of the Seclaves, or whether I was afraid to go forth to meet them? They informed me likewife, that all the chiefs had the moft unbounded confidence in me; but that they were apprehenfive that by remaining fimply on the defenfive, I fhould facrifice their provinces to the outrages of the Seclaves. This report determined me to avail myfelf of the ftate of affairs, to engage all the coaft in my intereft, whofe chiefs would join me with fo much the greater readinefs in the field, as by fighting the Seclaves, their poffeffions would be defended from their ravages.

Being thus at length engaged again, in an important affair, which required a decifion, whether without fupport or affiftance from the Europeans, with a handful of men, I fhould undertake an operation of the greateft confequence. Fortunately, however, the unhealthy feafon

was

was over, and my troops were in sufficient health to make up by their courage, for the unfortunate position they were in.

On the 14th, the Sambarive chiefs waited upon me, and presented to me several deputies of the different provinces, which their nation had sent to inform me, that they were all ready to take the field, and waited only for my naming the day on which they were to join me. Upon which I replied, that having forces more than sufficient about me to prevent the Seclaves from continuing their hostilities upon my frontiers, I had at first resolved not to engage my allies to follow me, least the cultivation of their lands might be interrupted. But that being unable any longer to resist their pressing instances and voluntary offers, I should accept their assistance to partake with them the glory of having punished the Seclaves; and that in consequence I should dispatch my couriers, to inform the whole coast of my resolutions to take the field at the end of the following month; to march directly to the enemy, and force them to come to battle.

I had hardly concluded my answer, when they all with one voice cried out, " The Seclaves shall be vanquished, and become our slaves." The rest of the day was consumed in dancing and war songs. For my own part, I was rather uneasy. I found myself on the point of becoming engaged in a serious affair, without the assistance or orders of the Court, which might at that moment be ready to decide upon giving up the establishment, and recalling my troops, in consequence of the false reports which the chiefs of the isle of France had made. Three years had already

already paſt without my having received the ſmalleſt order relative to my ſervice.

On the 15th, after many deliberations, I at laſt determined to declare war againſt the Seclaves; and to order all the chiefs to repair to the ſtandard at the end of April, with their principal warriors.

Not having a ſufficient number of troops to ſerve the field pieces, I began to inſtruct the Mozambique ſlaves in working them.

On the 20th, I commanded all my officers to aſſemble at fort Louis, to hold a council on the firſt of April, in order that I might have no reaſon to reproach myſelf in an enterprize of ſuch delicacy, the engaging in which might be imputed to me as a fault by my adverſaries. The Mozambiques made great progreſs in this exerciſe, and began to be uſed to the noiſe, as well as the manœuvres of the guns. In order that the pieces might be the better ſerved, I appointed a cannonier to each, from among my volunteers, with one workman and four Mozambiques. I had nine pieces ready for ſervice, two of which carried a pound ball. I had great reaſon to be ſatisfied with the progreſs of the Mozambiques, for on the 25th, they worked the guns very well, without any aſſiſtance or command from the Europeans.

On the 27th, my ſpies having returned from the Seclaves, reported, that the enemy had halted in the province of Antanquins, to wait for the junction of a ſtrong party; that their deſign was to fall directly on the eſtabliſhment, and in the mean time to ravage the frontiers, whoſe inhabitants had taken refuge in the woods, and waited only for our arrival to join us.

On the 1ſt of April, a general aſſembly of the corps was held, in which the annexed reſult was determined on (LXX); in which it was concluded, that the troops ſhould be formed into two diviſions, one under the order of the Chevalier de Sanglier, Captain of the corps, and Commander in my abſence, which ſhould be appointed to guard our poſts at Louiſbourg, fort St. John, and fort Auguſtus; while the other ſhould immediately take the field under my orders, and carry the war to the frontiers of the Seclaves, in order to check them, until ſupplies or the orders which I expected, might arrive. Immediately after this deciſion of council, I diſplayed the red flag as the ſignal of war well known in this iſland.

On the 2d, I was buſied in exerciſing my troops. The artillery was well ſerved, and there were very few of my volunteers on whom I could not depend for bringing down his man at the diſtance of two hundred paces, which aſſured me that I ſhould give a good account of my enemies; but, in order that the campaign might not be carried on in a confuſed manner, I appointed the following order, in which is included the whole force under my command, conſiſting of four thouſand one hundred and thirteen men, in three diviſions, which I called the forces of the eſtabliſhment.

The Left.		The Centre.		The Right.	
Commander.		Commander.		Commander.	
Mr. le Cerf, Captain	1	Baron de Benyowfky	1	De Melandre, Captain	1
—— Corbi, Lieutenant	1	Chev. de la Tour, Lieut.	1	De la Bouillage, Lieut.	1
Le Maitre, Interpreter	1	Evali, Enfign	1	Diard, Interpreter	1
D'Ecole, Interpreter	1	Mayeur, Interpreter	1	Volunteers	72
Volunteers	112	Volunteers	64	Artillery, three pieces, Served by	
Artillery, three Pieces, Served by		Artillery, three pieces, Served by		M. de la Min.	1
Cannoniers	3	Cannoniers	4	Cannoniers	2
Mozambique Commanders	2	Mozambique Commanders	2	Mozambique Commanders	2
Mozambique Slaves	6	Mozambique Slaves	6	Mozambique Slaves	6
Malgagos Commanders	2	Malgagos Commanders	2	Malgagos Commanders	2
Malgagos Warriors	1000	Malgagos Warriors	1800	Malgagos Warriors	1000
	1129		1822		1088

In the Hospital Service.

Popengui, Surgeon-Major — 1
His Aide Major — 1
Mozambique Slaves — 12

Such were the forces with which I proceeded to take the field; but it must be observed, that my three divisions were to be reinforced with the troops our allies were obliged to furnish; that is to say, for the right division, three thousand six hundred natives; for the centre, five thousand; for the left, three thousand six hundred; which, on the whole, amounted to not less than sixteen thousand three hundred and thirteen men.

On the 3d, I was busied in drawing out orders for Mr. de Sanglier, Commander in my absence, in order that he might conform to my intentions in every thing which related to the security of the posts entrusted to his care. I left with him seventy-six white men, with four officers; one hundred and twenty Mozambiques, and six hundred and eighty Malgagos, which was a sufficient number to defend the posts under his command.

On the 4th, I established a camp in the plain, at the distance of one league from Louisbourg, with a view to habituate my troops to obedience of orders. From this place it was, that I this day sent my orders to the chiefs of our allies, to repair at the end of the month to Hirbay, near Mananhar, at the distance of fifteen leagues from the plain, where I then was. I made choice of this place of rendezvous on account of the facility of procuring subsistence for sixteen thousand men, whose supplies would have exhausted the magazines of the establishment.

On the 10th, my envoys returned, and assured me that all the chiefs were ready to march, and would be at Hirbay before me. On the same day the Sambarives gave a great festival of war, according to the custom of the country,

country. The Saphirobai did the same, and nothing was seen but fires through the whole extent of the coast.

On the 11th, I made up my packets for the Minister, to whom I gave an account of my operations.

From the 12th to the 15th, I was employed in making my final visits to the posts.

On the 16th, being desirous of accelerating my march as much as possible, I caused all the boats to be repaired for the transport of the artillery and ammunition. My allies had engaged to send sixty other boats for the transport of my troops; so that I had reason to hope that I might set sail on the 30th, and arrive at Hirbay on the 2d of May, from which place I had determined to depart on the 4th, with a view to reach the other side of the mountains on the 8th or 9th, and offer battle to the enemy on the 10th or 11th. The rest of the campaign would depend on their decision, or rather on the orders of the Court, which I waited for, and the uncertain tenor of which obliged me not to proceed too far in the present juncture.

On the 18th, being the eve of my departure, and my determination being made, nothing remained but to follow it. Adieu then to reflections; for when a military adventure is once began, it must be followed with spirit.

This day Mulem, the brother of Hiavi, arrived, with twelve hundred and fifty warriors, to remain subject to my orders; these were intended to form my guard, and Hiavi had distinguished himself by selecting young men, among whom there was not one under five feet eight inches in height.

On the 20th, two couriers from the North informed me, that the chiefs of the provinces of Antimananhar, Angontzi, and Antiamak, were already on their march with three thousand warriors, one half of whom were coming by land, and the other half in boats. They assured me likewise, that these chiefs had made an oath not to quit my colours, until Cimanour, King of the Seclaves, was made prisoner of war. D'Ecole, my interpreter, was at the head of this army.

The preparations for the campaign, and the movements I was obliged to make, will not permit me to continue my memoir regularly from day to day, I shall therefore resume it after my return.

History of the War against the Seclaves.

I set sail with my little squadron, composed of one hundred and ninety-three boats of the country, on the 30th of April, and stopped at the isle d'Aiguillon, where I inspected the loading, and rectified the considerable inequalities I found in the several boats.

May the 1st, 1776. We set sail for Manambia, distant seven leagues from Louisbourg, where I found a very agreeable plain to pitch my camp. In the evening of the same day, I received a visit from the chiefs of the place. The principal chief, named Tacalounin, presented me with three hundred warriors to follow me, and also with six boats loaded with provisions, and thirty oxen.

May the 2d. I raised my camp, and sailed for Tanson, where, on my arrival in the evening, I found the troop of Tacalounins already encamped, and supplied with provisions and cattle. At the close of the night the chiefs of this country came to salute me; they brought us ten boats, loaded with provisions, and drink made of honey and melasses, with three hundred young men for the military service.

On the 3d, just as I was embarking to continue my journey, I received envoys from Cunifaloues, who informed me, that there were several parties of the Seelaves about, who only waited for a favourable instant to surprize me. They assured me likewise, that their chiefs were already in the field, but that they were greatly apprehensive that the Seelaves, whose forces were much superior to theirs, would attack them with advantage before my arrival. After I had heard the report of these envoys, I ordered them to follow me; and to prevent my troop of blacks, who conveyed our provision, from being surprized in some of the defiles, I ordered Mr. de Malendre, Captain and Commander of the right division, to protect them with his troop.

After this precaution I embarked, and continued my route towards Hirbay; but the wind blowing strong a-head, forced me to anchor at Fontzimarou. One of my boats, loaded with artillery, struck on a rock and sunk; another was bulged, and several others run aground, which obliged me to leave the left division behind, to recover the cannon and their carriages, and bring them to Hirbay. The chiefs of the place supplied me with divers, and boats to conduct my division to the rendezvous, where we arrived in safety on the 4th. But I had scarcely time to pitch my camp, before several blacks informed me, that
the

the divifion commanded by Mr. Malendre, had been attacked by the Seclaves. In confequence of this news, I detached twelve boats, with a part of my troop and Malgagos, to their affiftance. They foon returned with the information, that they had difcovered the divifion on its march, at a fmall diftance from us, and that the troops appeared undifturbed. Thefe laft arrived likewife about midnight, fafe and found; and their Commander informed me, that he had indeed been attacked by the Seclaves in a defile; but that the enemy had always kept at a very great diftance firing at his party, though their fhot could not reach him; and that he, perceiving that to be the cafe, had preferred marching ftrait to me, inftead of ftopping to caufe any embarraffment.

On the 5th, my left divifion at laft arrived, and all my people were then together. The number of warriors which the chiefs had promifed me, increafed every day, and the continual confumption of provifions becoming an object of great confequence, obliged me to quicken my operations.

On the 7th, I fent back the envoys of Cunifaloues, to inform him of my march; and on the fame day I received information, from a party whom I had fent upon the fcout, that the Seclaves had difappeared, and had withdrawn towards the frontier of the province of Antonguin.

Upon this report, I fent my right divifion to clear the paffage of the mountains, and foon afterwards followed them with my whole army. With much fatigue and difficulty, we paffed the mountains Vohibey. Our pieces of artillery, mounted on carriages, were very ill calculated for fervice in fuch mountainous and irregular countries as this.

I should have been much better satisfied, if they had been mounted on swivels, after the manner of pateraroes.

After I had passed the mountains, I encamped near a river called Mananhar, where I was joined by the chiefs Antimogols, Antivoiefon, Antivohibey, and the Sambarives. Their number amounted to near four thousand men, well armed.

In this place I rested my troops two days; and after having established a store of provisions in the place, and appointed a party of my left division for a guard, I raised my camp, and marched in three columns, through a wood of six leagues extent from East to West. When I came out of the wood, I discovered the camp of my first division, and three other camps of the Seclaves posted opposite them. But as all my people were fatigued, I determined to remain concealed in the skirts of the wood, that I might not be discovered by the enemy, whom I proposed to attack as soon as my army had taken some repose. To this effect, I acquainted the Commander of the first division with my intention, in order that he might not be alarmed at a brisk attack on my part.

At three in the morning, I established a rear guard for the security of our equipage, and marched directly to the first camp of the enemy. At sun rise, I was within cannon shot of them. At my approach, they arranged themselves in several divisions at the head of their camp, where they appeared disposed to receive us, and immediately began to fire. The black troops of our allies, notwithstanding my prohibition, answered their fire, which obliged me to bring forward my cannon. Twenty shot from these put the enemy to flight, and caufed them to abandon their firft camp, which I paffed without ftopping, and proceeded to the fecond, which I found in the hands of my firft divifion.

The enemy perceiving their two camps deftroyed, quitted the third of themfelves, which was foon confumed by the flames.. This affair coft the Seclaves eighty men killed, and fifty wounded, who were made prifoners, while none of my party were hurt, excepting a few natives, who were wounded. The allied chiefs, encouraged by this fuccefs, demanded permiffion to chace the enemy; and I agreed to their requeft with great willingnefs, as their Cabars or affemblies had become very chargeable.

After the departure of the blacks, I advanced my camp into an agreeable plain, filled with orange trees, banana trees, and cardamon plants.

On the 14th, the chief Cunifaloues joined me with fifteen hundred warriors. He told me that the Seclaves, who had fled, had fpread a report every where, that it was not the white men who had vanquifhed them, but devils which were mixed among them, and had vomited dreadful flames upon their army.

On the 17th, feveral parties of the Seclaves arrived, and intreated forgivenefs; at the fame time that they begged that I would come into their province to defend them from the ravages of my black allies.

On the 18th, I difpatched Mr. de Malendre to Antonguin, in order to reftrain the allied chiefs within the limits of difcipline; and the fame evening I raifed my camp to proceed in perfon to the province of Antonguin.

On the 19th, I came in sight of a village of the Antongueze, composed of about five hundred houses well pallisaded, and defended by a ditch. Beyond the village, I discovered six camps, which the chiefs of our allies had established. For my part, I rather chose to form my camp on the side where I was, in order to enjoy a state of tranquillity, which must be entirely renounced on mixing with the natives.

On the 20th, all the chiefs of my party waited upon me to congratulate me, and to give me a pompous account of their warlike exploits. They assured me, that the Seclaves, not thinking proper to rally upon their frontiers, had fled as far as the Western coast of the island.

On the 22d, the chief of Antonguin, named Tihenbato, came to my camp in person, having his head and beard shaved in token of submission. He intreated forgiveness for having followed the Seclaves, and immediately entered into the oath of fidelity, acknowledging his province to be conquered: at the same time that he requested it should be entrusted to him on condition of his paying an annual tribute. It was from this chief that I obtained more particular information concerning the Seclaves, which convinced me that the King of that nation was cured of the desire of making war upon the Europeans. He also informed me, that the King of the Seclaves had sent envoys to Hiavi, to request his intercession with me to procure peace at any rate.

Some days afterwards I received envoys from the King of the Seclaves, who proposed a treaty of peace; but as I did not think proper to consent, I dismissed them with the simple

simple anfwer, that the chiefs of the Seclaves ought not to afk for peace, but pardon; that I propofed to ftay in the province to allow them time to make their determination, and that their King ought not to hefitate in fubmitting himfelf to the laws eftablifhed among the chiefs of the Eaftern coaft.

After the departure of thefe envoys, I remained encamped on the fpot, until the end of the month; during which time I fent feveral officers to make difcoveries in the country. Their reports convinced me more and more of the expediency of forming an eftablifhment in this charming, rich and agreeable country; but being without forces and fupplies, I had no power to act.

June the 1ft, 1776. I received advice from M. le Cerf, Commander of the left divifion, that certain blacks who came from Louifbourg, had affured him, that they faw two fhips enter the harbour. This news gave me great encouragement.

On the 5th, the long expected courier at laft arrived with packets from the Court, in which I learned with inexpreffible fatisfaction, that the Minifter had fent from France his Majefty's veffel la Sirenne, with ammunition, provifions and money for trade; and that this fupply would foon be followed by others of greater importance. But alas, my joy was of fhort duration; for on the other hand, I learned by the difpatches from the ifle of France, that the corvette was loft to the Southward of fort Dauphin, and confequently, that I could expect no fupplies. And to crown the whole, the Minifter, in a private letter, informed me, that his Majefty had referved the communication of his intentions with regard to Madagafcar, until the end of
the

the year; for which reason I must confine my operations to the preservation of the posts, &c.

All these events tended only to encrease my solicitude, and more especially, as my presence was become necessary at Louisbourg, I found myself forced to suspend my military operations. I therefore assembled my officers, in order to come to a final decision respecting the steps proper to be taken in our present situation.

On the 6th, I held a council, and conformably to its decision, I determined to return to Louisbourg, leaving my troops under the orders of Mr. de Malendre, with all our black allies, whom I had persuaded to remain satisfied with the advantages and the victory gained over our enemies. The chiefs Cunifaloues and Rozai, alone were discontented, because they feared the resentment of the Seclaves; but I encouraged them, by a promise under oath, to come to their assistance as soon as ever I should hear that the Seclaves marched against them. Cunifaloues was at last satisfied with my promise; but the unfortunate prince Rozai was inconsolable, and declared that he would quit me no more, because as he had once had recourse to me, all his hopes depended on the alliance of the Europeans. As I saw this chief was so greatly oppressed with his misfortunes, I promised to send to the Seclaves to reclaim his wives, his children, and all his family; and assured him, that he might depend on receiving speedy satisfaction in this respect. This assurance set his mind at ease.

On the 7th, I distributed presents to the chiefs, and likewise divided the captures we had made; and after having secured the submission of the province of Antonguin, I departed on my way to Louisbourg.

On the 8th, at the close of day, I began my march, and on the 12th, I arrived at Louisbourg, where my time was intirely taken up in preparing my dispatches for the Minister, excepting only that I was occasionally interrupted by the festivals which the chiefs gave to their people, in celebration of our victory over the enemy.

On the 21st, his Majesty's corvette the Iphigenia, set sail on her return to the isle of France.

On the 26th, a squadron of boats appeared in sight, directing their course towards the harbour.

On the 22d, the squadron anchored in the harbour, and put my whole troop on shore with shouts of joy. The same evening the black troops landed, and established their camp round Louisbourg. Mr. de Malendre informed me, that after my departure he had received envoys from the Seclaves, who, in the name of their King, had proposed preliminaries to a treaty of peace; but that as he had no authority from me to act in a business of that nature, he informed them that their King might be convinced by my sudden departure, that I was not disposed to carry on the war against them with efficacy; and that consequently, he would do well to send envoys directly to me, to take advantage of my good disposition towards them, and bring this affair to a termination, in which he would certainly succeed, if, as a mark of good faith, he should send the family of the prince Rozai to me. My officer likewise informed me, that the envoys were very well satisfied with his answer, and immediately returned; and that the whole of the allied chiefs had exactly obeyed his commands. The rest of the month was consumed in entertainments, which

which greatly diminished the stock of liquor I had purchased, and imported from the isle of France.

On the 1st of July, all the chiefs refused to depart for their provinces with their troops, and declared that they had reasons for not leaving me at that moment.

From the 2d to the 9th, I was employed in visiting the posts, while my troops who had returned from the campaign, availed themselves of the time I had granted to rest themselves after their fatigue.

On the 10th, I divided my troops to encrease the garrisons of my posts, and caused the different materials for building to be collected.

On the 11th, Mr. Mayeur, my principal interpreter, having been charged by me to discover the reason why the chiefs had determined not to quit me, informed me, that Hiavi had received a letter from the isle of France, by which he understood that I was to be relieved, and sent to France to take my trial; and that the brother of Hiavi, having communicated this news to several of the chiefs, they had determined to oppose by force all those who might attempt to carry such a design into execution. This information, which convinced me of the sincere attachment of the whole nation, afforded me some consolation in my disgrace; but was not sufficient to dispel my disagreeable reflections.

On the 12th, several bodies of the natives from the Seclaves, requested permission to establish themselves on the territory of the establishment, subject to its regulations. I granted them the lands on the left branch of the river of Tingballe. The power of this province daily increasing, I
could

could eafily perceive that it will hereafter poffefs one third of the population of the ifland.

From the 18th to the 19th I made an excurfion on the bufinefs of difcovery, into the interior parts of the ifland to the northward, where I found feveral confiderable rivers, between the chain of the mountains of Ramangafi and Volifbey, at the feet of which I found various minerals, and very fine rock chryftals, fome of which were coloured.

Auguft 1, 1776. As the tranquillity of the country afforded me that repofe which I had not experienced hitherto, I vifited the habitations and fettlements, which I found in good order and cultivation. I therefore determined to allot lands to the individuals for the formation of villages. Several foldiers and others requefted grants, which I accordingly made out, to the number of fixty-four.

On the 3d, I affembled the chiefs, and reprefented to them, that their refidence on the fpot tended to exhauft the country; and obferved, that if they were abfolutely determined to refide near me, I would advife them to fend back their people into their provinces, as they would always have time to collect them together. In confequence of this infinuation, they demanded when I expected veffels to arrive from Europe; and as I could not anfwer pofitively, they requefted me not to make any propofal to them for their departure, as, in this affair, they only followed the impulfe of their friendfhip for me, and were determined to perifh, rather than quit me.

On the 9th, I received news that a private fhip was loft to the northward; I therefore fent his Majefty's veffel, the Coureur,

Coureur, to collect the people, and bring them to Louisbourg.

On the 14th, I was informed of the arrival of envoys from the Seclaves, who presented to me the family of the Prince Rozai, as a proof of the good disposition of that nation. These envoys likewise presented three hundred oxen, and sixty slaves, in the name of their nation, and demanded that I would make oath not to enter into a war against them in future. I accepted the presents, and received the family of Rozai with pleasure; but the promise not to make war, being an engagement which related to the interests of the settlement, I replied, that I was ready to enter into such an oath, provided the King of the Seclaves would likewise make the same, and give assurances that he would accede to the union of the chiefs and people of the east coasts, and would acknowledge himself a member of that union, and subject to its decisions. I moreover insisted, that he should permit the free entrance of all merchandize sent from the establishments into his country, for the purpose of carrying on an uninterrupted commerce with his people; and as the preservation and safe keeping of merchandize required particular care, that he should permit me to build in proper places, store-houses, which might serve as places of entertainment to my troops, and to travellers. The envoys replied, that they could make no stipulations in these respects, but that they would depart without delay, to inform their master of my intentions, in order that he might determine how to act. When these envoys were about to depart, I loaded them with presents; and they promised me, upon their oath, to use every exertion to induce their master

master to accept my propositions, and attach himself entirely to me.

On the 16th, the Sieur Mayeur informed me that the chiefs Raoul, Manding, Raffangour, and Ramaraombe, demanded an audience, as deputies from their nations. This extraordinary communication, which had been hitherto unusual, gave me some surprize: in consequence of which I immediately granted the audience, and rose up to meet them, as I supposed they were already on their way. But the Sieur Mayeur informed me, that the said chiefs were still in their camp, busied in preparations to present themselves in ceremony; and that he would go and acquaint them, with my permission. Immediately after his departure, I invited several officers of the troops, and of the administration, to be present at my audience, which seemed likely to be productive of consequences; for the manner in which the deputies were announced to me, convinced me that they had some affair of importance to propose, and in this I was not deceived. About ten, the guard of the fort discovered two bodies of armed troops, marching in columns, with drums beating and colours flying, and called out to arms; but the officer of the guard being in the secret, as I afterwards learned, did not oppose their march, but only challenged them, and sent a report to me. I soon discovered the troop myself, which consisted of 1,200 men, with the chiefs and deputies at their head, preceded by the standards of their provinces. On their arrival at the parade before the Governor's house, after they were drawn out, and had grounded their arms, the deputies advanced towards the hall, where they were received and conducted to me by my officers. After the first salutation, I caused seats, which consisted of low chairs, used in this country on occasions of ceremony, to be presented to the chiefs; three seated themselves, but the chief Raffangour remained standing, and spoke the following words, which I here give accurately:

"Blessed be the day which brought thee into the world.
"Blessed be thy parents, who have taken care of thy in-
"fancy; and blessed be the hour in which thou didst set
"thy foot upon our island.

"The Malgagos chiefs and captains, whose hearts thou
"hast gained, who love thee, and are faithfully attached
"to thee, have received information that the French King
"intends to appoint another in thy place; and that he is
"angry with thee because thou hast refused to deliver us
"to his slavery: they have therefore met, and have held
"cabars, to decide upon the manner in which they should
"act, if this should prove true. Their love and their at-
"tachment for thee, have obliged me, in this circum-
"stance, to reveal to thee the secret of thy birth, and thy
"rights over this immense country, all whose people adore
"thee. Yes, I myself, Raffangour, reputed the sole sur-
"vivor of the family of Ramini, I have renounced this
"sacred right, to declare thee the only true inheritor of
"Ramini. The spirit of God, which reigns over our ca-
"bars, caused all the chiefs and captains to make oath,
"that they would acknowledge thee their Ampansacabe;
"that they would no more quit thee, but preserve thy
"person, at the price of their lives, against all the violence
"of the French."

After

After this declaration he sat down, and caused the chief Raoul to rise, and deliver his message, which was as follows. " I, Raoul, chief of the Saphirobai, sent to thee
" by the chiefs and captains of several united nations, de-
" mand, that thou wilt grant to-morrow, a public cabar, to
" render thee homage of our fidelity and obedience. I am
" likewise charged to request, that thou wilt not display
" the white standard, but the blue, in sign that thou
" heartily acceptest our submission.

" The chiefs and captains, assembled in cabar, have like-
" wise commissioned me to request, that thou wilt keep
" the officers and soldiers at a distance from the place in
" which this cabar shall be held; and that, in the mean
" time, thou wilt keep, as a guard, the twelve hundred war-
" riors, which the nation will constantly maintain around
" thee."

After this exposition, he likewise seated himself, in expectation of my answer. This unforeseen proceeding was not a little embarrassing; but as I was desirous of time to reflect, and form proper combinations, I immediately replied, that I should with pleasure see the chiefs and nations united in cabar, and that I would then declare my sentiments in public. In the mean time, I requested them to remain convinced of my friendship for them, my zeal for their interests, and my readiness to make any sacrifice for the good of the nation.

My answer was satisfactory to them, and they all prostrated themselves before they quitted me; a mark of submission which no chief had hitherto shewn. After their departure, I examined Mr. Mayeur respecting the causes which had produced this revolution among the chiefs; but
he

he excused himself, and said that several of my officers knew more of the business than himself. During my conversation with the Sieur Mayeur, I perceived three officers, who came at the head of fifty men, and declared, that having learned what steps had been taken at the isle of France, they had all determined to give up their lives, rather than see me quit the island; that with regard to themselves, as they were connected with the natives, they had determined to fix their abode on the island, and therefore requested that I would no longer consider them as soldiers, but as men devoted to my interests. This direct proceeding on the part of officers of distinction, embarrassed me still more. It was in vain that I desired them to reflect on what they were about; and observed, that I could not but blame them for persisting in a resolution of such delicacy: for they replied, that as they had made the step, they could not now go back; that, being connected with the interests of the chiefs, and particularly attached to me, they would carry their design into execution, whether I approved it or not. On this occasion they repeated the conduct of the minister against me; insisted upon the intrigues and cabals which the Government of the isle of France had employed, to induce the natives to cut us off; and they concluded, that what had passed was sufficient to justify their conduct. The manner in which all this was said, left me no hope of dissuading them. I therefore directed my discourse principally to induce them to remain steady in their duty, and promised to get their discharges, in order that they might attach themselves to the country, without having any cause to reproach themselves. One of the

officers

officers informed me, that I should not find ten soldiers who would quit Madagascar; and that even among the officers, there were not above two or three who were not of their mind. This information convinced me that the connivance of the troops with the chiefs, arose from the habitude they had contracted of living with the natives of the country, during the preceding campaign, against the Seclaves.

After the departure of the troops, I employed myself in forming a plan to appease these people, and to take the best advantage of the favourable disposition which the natives of the country had shewn towards me. This plan naturally led me to that of civilizing the Madagascar nations. Towards the evening I gave orders for covering the floor of the hall of cabar, and to make every preparation for celebrating a festival at the breaking up of the meeting.

On the 17th, in the morning, twenty-one guns were fired from the fort, without displaying the standard; but on the great flag-staff before my house a blue flag was displayed, agreeably to my orders. I gave directions that all the troops should remain in the fort. At seven, a detachment of six hundred blacks arrived, and formed a square about the hall. At nine, the chiefs quitted the camp, with all their people, to come to the cabar. On their arrival upon the parade, they sent twelve chiefs to me, with the same number of standards, to conduct me. As I was ready, I followed them; but before I entered the cabar, I went to the chiefs, to thank them for their politeness and attention. Sixty-two chiefs were seated in cabar, and their attendants remained under arms, in order. The first chief who spoke, was Manonganon, to the following effect:

" We

"We, the princes and captains, who are assembled, and represent the whole nation, being determined by the rights of thy birth, by thy wisdom, and by thy affection for us, do declare at this instant, that we acknowledge thee for our Ampansacabe, and intreat thee to accept this title and rank, with the assurance of finding fidelity, affection, and constancy in our hearts.

"Answer us."

I then arose, and replied, that the same zeal which the whole nation had acknowledged me to possess for their welfare, induced me to accept their offer, in the hope that the princes, chiefs, and captains of the nation, would always assist me in the great enterprize of civilization. I then explained to them the advantages which they, and more especially their children, would derive from the establishment of a solid government. I addressed myself to their passions, by displaying that immortality with which their names would be transmitted to posterity, in consequence of their having established wise and humane laws; and enlarged on that glory which the Madagascar nation would possess in future times. But that which affected them most strongly, was the display of advantages which a well-directed commerce, supported by an effectual cultivation of their lands, could not but procure in a very short time. In fact, this part of my speech, relating to a subject which was best known by the people of Madagascar, was naturally the best calculated to produce the most effect upon their minds.

As soon as I had finished my harangue, the chiefs deputed a captain to announce my nomination to the people; immediately after which the discharges of musquetry began, and continued near a quarter of an hour. As soon as tranquillity was restored, a second chief, named Sancé, spoke, and informed me that his nation required me to quit the service of the King of France, and to cause all those to quit the same service who were desirous of fixing their residence at Madagascar. And lastly, that I would declare what province I chose for the place of my residence, in order that they might build a town. When I perceived that he spoke no more, I replied, that it was my intention to quit the service of France, and to cause all those who were desirous of remaining at Madagascar likewise to quit it; but that I could not carry this design into execution before the arrival of his Majesty's commissaries; for which reason, I requested the cabar to defer the performance of the oath, because, as I was hitherto engaged in the service of the King, I was not yet master of my actions. With regard to the town in question, I expressed my opinion, that it would be most convenient to fix it in the centre of the island, that I might be as near as possible to each province: and in order to render them better acquainted with my intentions, I declared to them, that having accepted the charge of Ampansacabe, my first duty would be to establish good laws, to maintain peace and tranquillity throughout the land, and to defend the country from foreign incursions; after which, my attention would be directed to the establishment of commerce in the most flourishing state, by increasing cultivation; but that all these things could not be done simply by my will alone, but that I depended upon the assistance of the chiefs of the nation, some of whom would be nominated to the council, others to governments, others to the departments of war, the marine, &c.

This difcourfe led the chiefs to propofe a variety of queftions, and it required much converfation to make them comprehend the true fenfe of what I faid. I fucceeded at laft in this, and feveral of them proftrated themfelves, and thanked me for having infpired them with the difpofition to form a refolution of nominating me their Ampanfacabe.

The third chief who fpoke, was Diamandrifs. He obferved, that the French would be angry with me for having quitted them, and that confequently a war might be expected on their part; on which bufinefs he requefted my opinion.

My reply was, that the King of France had a power over me during the whole time I fhould continue in his fervice; but the moment I fhould quit his fervice, I fhould be my own mafter. I admitted the truth, that the French might probably become jealous, when they faw the ifland of Madagafcar formed into a folid government; but that I fhould be forry for them if they fhould adopt the plan of acting by force againft a whole nation. I obferved likewife, that in a cafe of this nature, I had a plan to propofe in due time, which would fecure a folid friendfhip between the French and the Madagafcar nations. Here the chief Raffangour interrupted me, by obferving, that the French could never be good friends with the Madagafcar nation, as they muft conftantly recollect feveral maffacres of their nation on this ifland.

Raffangour ended the cabar, by propofing, that an oath fhould be mutually entered into only between me and the chiefs,

chiefs, with the declaration that it should be publickly repeated as soon as I should quit the service of France. This oath was immediately made; and, in order to render it more sacred, it was confirmed by the oath of blood. This oath is performed by opening the skin of the left breast with a razor, and each of the assistants sucks a drop of the blood of him who is received as chief; at which ceremony maledictions and imprecations are pronounced against him who shall fail in his engagement.

After the oath, the chiefs commissioned the chief Sancé to command their troops, and to be watchful that, on the arrival of the King's commissaries, no attempts should be made against my person. Before the cabar broke up, the chief Sancé went out, doubtless for the purpose of informing the troops and people how to behave. He sent word by one of his captains, that all was ready; whereupon we went forth. At my coming forth, the troops lowered their colours, and the Madagascar soldiers, having their musquets pointing downwards, laid their left hands on their breasts, in sign of engagement, or oath. As I understood that there were near eleven thousand men assembled in cabar, I ordered twenty oxen to be killed, and gave them twelve casks of brandy. With respect to the chiefs, I entertained them alone. The troops having at last received permission to come out of the fort, followed their officers, to compliment me upon the performance of what they called an agreement of union and harmony between the establishment and the chiefs of the country.

The Sieur D'Ecole, my second interpreter, observed to me, that all those of the troops who had blue ribbons on their white cockades had determined to fix their refidence at Madagafcar. The reft of the day was employed in rejoicing. Towards the evening, near twelve hundred women and girls prefented themfelves upon the parade, in compliment to me, where they afterwards amufed themfelves by dancing. I prefented them all with handkerchiefs, ribbons, and brandy with fugar.

On the 18th, I convened the chiefs, and propofed to them to return into their refpective provinces, to their families, except fix, whom I was defirous of having near me, to affift in quality of counfellors. The chief Sancé, who was to remain, encamped with three thoufand men, fubject to my orders. This precaution appeared to me to be more particularly neceffary, as a merchant, who came from Foul Point, and arrived at this port, had affured me, that it was publifhed in the ifle of France, that orders had been given for arrefting me, and fending me home to be judged criminally.

Between the 19th and 22d, my time was continually employed in take leave of the chiefs, who agreed that they would affemble the moment they fhould perceive fires lighted at Mangabey. Every chief engaged to forward the execution of this fignal, by lighting feveral fires on the coaft, or upon the mountain.

On the 23d, I at length arrived at that tranquillity I had fo much defired fince my fettling on the ifland. I faw the whole eaft coaft perfectly united to the eftablifhment, and the weftern coaft ready to join in the fame common intereft. The cultivation of the country being every where doubled, afforded a promife of real advantage ; and

nothing

nothing was wanting but a more ample supply from home, in order to take advantage of the happy situation of affairs. But, unfortunately, the most proper time for establishing the colonists was suffered to elapse; and I saw myself, with grief, reduced to the simple movements of an Automaton. I had, besides, every reason to be apprehensive of the consequences of the prejudices excited against me; for I could attribute the retardation of the supplies only to the false reports which the administration of the isle of France had forwarded to the Court, respecting the establishment at Madagascar; and I had reason to fear that the ministry, being prejudiced by the reports, might defer the supplies, for no other purpose than that of ruining me. I likewise saw the principles upon which I had founded the settlement at Madagascar reduced naturally, by the want of force, to a crisis, which led the natives to a knowledge of their own strength, and to form a government amongst themselves, which, when once established, would no longer permit them to suffer a foreign force to reside amongst them. The first step towards this resolution being made, if the minister has executed the plan which was announced to me, France cannot fail of seeing herself deprived of all the advantages which were acquired by treaties of commerce and friendship with the natives of the country.

On the 27th, a private vessel, the St. Vincent, commanded by the Sieur Blanchard, arrived from the isle of France, laden with articles of trade from India, which were well calculated for the trade of barter for rice. I therefore directed the store-keeper to purchase his cargo, for the use of the establishment. I could not dispense with this

this proceeding, because I durst not give up trading with the natives; because the consequences would undoubtedly have been a neglect of the cultivation of the country, if the regular trade had been interrupted.

On the 10th, the ship Desire entered the harbour, with the news that Messrs. Bellecombe and Chevreau had already arrived at the isle of France, on board his Majesty's frigate the Consolante, and that these gentlemen had orders to repair, without delay, to Madagascar. This unexpected circumstance convinced me, that the minister had determined to send these gentlemen in quality of commissaries, to secure my person, in order to pursue violent measures for the reduction of the islanders by force. My suspicions were at last justified; for I received a letter from a friend, containing information that these inspectors had orders to bring me to Europe, in case they could be assured that such a proceeding, on the part of Government, towards me, would not excite the natives of the island to drive all the French out of their country. The dependance I placed on the attachment of the natives, set me entirely at ease in this respect; but I was strongly affected with indignation at the decision of the minister, and determined to resign my charge, in order that I might have it in my power to serve my friends more effectually.

On the 20th, the chiefs of the country having received information of the arrival of new orders from the Court, and observing some consternation among my people, waited upon me to enquire whether I had received orders for my departure, and how such orders could be reconciled with the promise I had made; that I would never abandon them.

These

These reproaches were followed by lamentations, which affected me very sensibly, because I was convinced they arose from real attachment. I used every exertion to render them easy, by observing, that the movements they had doubtless taken notice of among the white men, were only made as preparations for the honourable reception of a General officer, who came from his Majesty to enquire into the state of the settlement, and to assure them of his powerful protection. This answer removed their apprehensions in some measure, but did not entirely destroy them.

On the 21st, a signal was made on the mountain, that a three-masted vessel was in sight. Soon after, I saw her myself, and knew her to be the Consolante. In the evening she anchored off the isle Aiguillon; and two hours after I received a letter from Messrs. Bellecombe and Chevreau, jointly, informing me of their quality as commissaries on the part of the King, and inspectors in their several departments. This letter was accompanied with an order, in the King's name, for me to come on board. As I had been forewarned of the instructions which these commissaries had received, I did not think proper to go on board, but answered, that I was ready, conformably to the orders of his Majesty, to put the command of the settlement into their hands, that they might proceed to act according to their instructions; but that, until I had made an act of resignation, I neither could, nor ought to leave the shore. Together with my answer I sent a particular letter to Mr. Bellecombe, whom I intreated to come on shore without fear, and without landing his troops; and at the same time I solemnly promised to conform to every request

I could

I could honourably comply with. Upon receiving this anfwer, he replied, that he would come on fhore, to infpire me with every confidence, by furrendering himfelf up to my politenefs and delicacy. At the end of his letter, he infinuated, that if he had thought proper to give credit to all that he had heard, he fhould not have taken this ftep; but that, as a military man, he would depend on my word of honour.

On the 22d, Meffrs. De Bellecombe, marefhal des camps, and Chevreau, commiffary general of ftores, came on fhore. I received them conformably to his Majefty's orders, fpecified in the letter of the minifter, and immediately afterwards I prefented my troop to Mr. De Bellecombe, acknowledging him, at the head of the troops, as infpector. In the evening of the fame day, the commiffaries put into my hands a paper, containing twenty-five articles of queftions and demands relative to their miffion, to which they demanded my anfwers to each feverally. The reft of the day was employed in converfation refpecting the different parts of the eftablifhment.

On the 23d, I prefented my anfwers, likewife reduced into twenty-five articles, to the gentlemen commiffioners. This piece, marked *L. X. A.* is annexed to the prefent Memoir. The reft of the day was employed in vifiting the fort, the publick buildings, and the hofpital; and, in the mean time, Mr. Chevreau was bufied in examining the accounts, together with thofe who had charge of the adminiftration.

On the 24th, I gave an ample account of every thing relating to the military fervice.

On

COUNT DE BENYOWSKY.

On the 25th, the chiefs of the country, to whom I had sent an invitation to assemble at the settlement, conformably to the intention of the commissaries, demanded some days to collect those who resided at a distance. The commissaries, in order to save time, made an excursion with me to visit the two posts, Fort St. John, and Fort Augustus at the plain. The fear of contracting the disorders of the country occasioned them to hasten their return.

On the 26th, after our return to Louisbourg, they held a cabar, or assembly, with the chiefs, at which I declined being present, in order that the natives of the country might be at liberty to speak their minds. The result of this meeting is likewise annexed to the present Memoir.

On the 27th, the commissaries, after having given me a discharge respecting my past conduct, and accounts, and a certificate for the sum of four hundred and fifteen thousand livres which I had advanced to the treasury, prepared to go on board. I believe their departure was hastened by the fear of disorders, which they had been informed, at the isle of France, as being very common at Madagascar. This circumstance probably disgusted them with our residence on shore, and might cause their reports, though very well written, to be less favourable than otherwise they might have been.

On the 28th, I delivered to Mr. Bellecombe my act of resignation, and surrendered the command of the troops to Mr. De Sanglier.

On the 29th, Mr. Bellecombe retired on board, and sent me an order in the King's name to confine my operations to the preservation of the chief settlement, until I should receive further

further inftructions from Court; to put a ftop to all the works whatever; to continue the prohibition of trading with the blacks, and laftly, permitting me to abfent myfelf from Madagafcar. But as I did not think proper to receive charge of any orders, becaufe I had refigned my office, I forwarded this order to Mr. De Sanglier, and declared to the infpectors, that being determined from thenceforth to take charge of nothing relative to the eftablifhment, I could no otherwife forward the new intentions of Government than by the good offices I might render them with the natives of the country. Upon this declaration the infpectors addreffed to me a requifition, that I would promote the advantage of the eftablifhment; but they at the fame time declared, that as they could not accept my difmiffion, I was bound to perform the duties of my office until the arrival of precife orders from his Majefty, which would not fail to arrive upon their report. After thefe proceedings I faw no more of the commiffaries, who departed for Foul Point, where I am unacquainted with their proceedings. For my part, I retired immediately into one of my habitations, where I was vifited by feveral Rohandrians and Woadziri chiefs, who, having been informed that I had quitted the fervice of the King of France, required me to enter into the oath of Ampanfacabe; for which reafon they gave orders for a general meeting of the nation, on the 12th of the next month.

On the third day after my retreat, feveral of the officers came to beg I would affift them with my advice; and the troops fent deputies to me to declare, that if I did not refume the command over them, they were determined to

leave

leave the fort, and declare themselves independent. Mr. De Sanglier, the commander, likewise urged the same requeft very ftrongly, and aſſured me, that the troops would infallibly revolt, in cafe of my refuſal; and the natives would, of courſe, ruin the pofts already eſtabliſhed. Theſe repreſentations, and the imminent danger of the fettlement, determined me at laſt to refume the command, at the ſame time that I made a declaration, that I was actuated to this proceeding by a wiſh to preſerve the Europeans, and to keep up the connection of friendſhip and commerce; but that this refumption ſhould not be confidered as a renewal of any obligation on my part, as I confidered myſelf as entirely out of the ſervice of France.

Such was the confequence of the precipitation with which the miniſter acted. My conduct has fince proved, that all my actions aroſe from the moſt perfect delicacy, and that I did not, in any reſpect, depart from the attachment due to France; and if I refuſed to aſſiſt in fuch ſteps as Government was defirous of taking, to the violation of thoſe treaties of alliance and commerce which I had ftipulated with the Madagaſcar nation, I only did my duty. And certain it is, that I was defirous of ferving the French by this conduct, for I was well convinced from the knowledge I had acquired refpecting the characters and manners of the people, that every attempt by force againſt the liberty of that nation, would be pernicious to the eftabliſhment and general intereſts of the nation. Future times will prove, that Madagaſcar can never be fubdued by force, and that mildneſs and equity alone can lead this nation to a civilized ſtate, which, when once eftabliſhed, cannot fail of procuring immenſe fortune and proſperity to its allies.

allies. But, alas! after what has paſſed, I have no reaſon to hope that the miniſter will change his ſyſtem, though I am determined to uſe every effort to perſuade him to do ſo.

October the 1ſt, 1776. Being deſirous of placing the eſtabliſhment in a ſituation to maintain itſelf, until the arrival of new orders from Court, I returned to Louiſbourg, where having aſſembled the troops, I declared, that I reſumed the command merely with a view to provide for the ſubſiſtence of the eſtabliſhment, to which buſineſs I ſhould afterwards attend jointly with Mr. Coquereau, the principal ſtore-keeper. And in order that my regulations might be duly performed, I aſſembled a committee, compoſed of the principal ſtore-keeper, two captains, and a ſub-commiſſary of the marines, in which we regulated the proviſions for the ſubſiſtence and continuation of trade, as well as the conduct we ſhould in future adopt with reſpect to the natives. With regard to the military ſervice, few alterations were neceſſary, becauſe I had always attended cloſely to that department.

The 2d and 3d were employed in writing out inſtructions for the reſpective individuals.

On the 4th, an aſſembly of the chiefs of the Sambarives, Saphirobai, Antavocny, Antivohibey, Antimaroa, Antambour, Antimokol, Antimananhar, Safeibrahim, and Saferahimina, was held, in which I declared, that having quitted the ſervice of the King of France, I thought it proper to inform his Majeſty, by his miniſters, reſpecting the poſition of the eſtabliſhment, in order that I might have no cauſe to reproach myſelf for the conſequences, in caſe

COUNT DE BENYOWSKY.

cafe the French minifter fhould perfift in his intention of fubjugating the inhabitants of Madagafcar by force; for which reafon I requefted them all to confefs, fincerely, whether they were defirous of the continuation of the eftablifhment, or its recall; and I promifed, upon oath, to tranfmit their decifion, word for word, to the King of France. Upon this propofal, the chiefs held a confultation of near an hour, and afterwards, having refumed their places, anfwered as follows:

" Wife and prudent as thou art, can'ft thou doubt our
" attachment towards thee? Haft thou not feen with
" what ardour we have fought againft our brothers, when
" they had rebelled, in order to bring them to their duty.
" Whence, therefore, is it that thou fheweft fo much dif-
" truft towards a people which is attached to thee? If
" thy heart tells thee that thou wifheft well to the French,
" fay, and write to their King, that we offer him our hearts
" and our friendfhip. But we wifh to live under thy
" command. Thou art our father and our lord. Let the
" French love thee, as we do, and our arms fhall be united
" to theirs; our colours fhall be united with thofe of the
" white men, and we will fight valiantly againft the com-
" mon enemy: but if thou muft fuffer the hatred of the
" French, we will never acknowledge them as our bre-
" thren, but their enemies fhall be our friends. Thefe
" are our thoughts, and the words of our hearts. Promife,
" therefore, before that God, whom we all adore, to write
" them to the King of the French, and engage that thou
" wilt be more attached to us than to the French nation,
" and wilt never defert us."

Being

Being assured of this unanimous reply, I made preparations for the cabar and oath, and engaged to inform the King of France of the thoughts of the Madagascar people, and to live with them in future. The chiefs, on their side, engaged to obey my orders exactly, and to live in good harmony with the establishment.

After the ceremony was ended, I gave an entertainment to the natives, at which all the Europeans were present. This series of events preceding a revolution, which fixes the epoch of the civilization of Madagascar, led me to make many reflections. I knew, by experience, how little I could depend on the propriety of the decisions of the Cabinet of Versailles. My firmness alone was left me to bear up against the apprehensions of the political artifices which France would employ against me, to calumniate and destroy my reputation. But being assured of my loyalty, I determined, after having fixed my system of conduct amongst the chiefs and people of Madagascar, to return into France, in order to present in person an account of the interests of the settlement, and to combat the prejudices of the minister. I was well aware of the risk I ran; but at length the care of my reputation, and my affection for the people who had adopted me, led me to this resolution. I determined, therefore, that as France could not charge me with rebellion, and could only blame her ministers for their ignorance of her real interests, I would employ my fortune, my credit, and even the interest of Madagascar, to procure friends to that island, and bring the great work of civilization to an happy conclusion. This is my resolution, and I will adhere to it as long as I live.

On the 5th, I received from the different chiefs considerable presents, in slaves, cattle, and rice, which I distributed to the troops. This day, having convoked all the people of the establishment, I declared to them, that having secured their tranquillity with the natives of the country, and provided for their subsistence until they could receive orders from Court, I should now quit them, and would no longer retain any command. Their tears were an unequivocal answer, and I heard but one exclamation, " No, we will not lose our father!"

On the 6th, the interpreter announced that six deputed chiefs had arrived with a considerable number of armed men. Upon receiving them, they informed me that the great day of the oath approached, and that the chiefs and people in assembly, desired that I would meet them, for which purpose they had detached the troops for my safeguard and service. To conform, therefore, to their desires, I quitted my French dress, and assumed that of an Indian; after which I set out. It was necessary for me to pass through a long row of natives of the country, who shouted, and invoked Zahanhar. My friends, the officers of my troop, and the whole people of the establishment, followed me. As soon as I had arrived at the camp, I was received by all the chiefs, and conducted to the tent which was designed for me, with six others for my domestics. I caused six four-pounders to be brought into my camp, which were placed before my tent, and a daily appointment of two hundred men was ordered for my guard.

On the 7th, 8th, and 9th, I was employed in drawing out my proposals to the assembly, for the establishment of a permanent Government. The 10th at laſt arrived, and I was awakened by a triple diſcharge of cannon. At ſix in the morning the chief Raffangour, with ſix others, all cloathed in white, preſented themſelves at my feet, and requeſted to ſpeak with me. I received them without my tent, being likewiſe cloathed in white. The diſcourſe of Raffangour expreſſed the teſtimonies of confidence with which the Madagaſcar nation had intruſted me with the ſupreme power, and the advantages they hoped to attain from my knowledge and ſervices. After his ſpeech, he begged me to follow him; and we went out of the camp into the plain, where we entered into a circle formed by an aſſembly of thirty thouſand armed men. The chiefs being each at the head of the people of their own nation, and the women without the circle, the chiefs immediately formed the firſt circle round us, and Raffangour harangued them to the following effect:

"Bleſſed be Zahanhar, who has returned to his people. "Bleſſed be the blood of Zafferamini, to whom our attach- "ment is due. Bleſſed be the law of our fathers, which "commands us to obey a chief deſcended from the blood "of Ramini. Our fathers and ourſelves, have expe- "rienced, that diſunion is the puniſhment of God. Since "the long time we have been deprived of a chief of the "ſacred race of Ramini, we have lived like wild beaſts; "ſometimes killing our brethren, and at other times pe- "riſhing by their violence. Enfeebled by our diſunion, "we have always been the prey of the ſtrongeſt. We "have been wicked, without being deſirous to liſten to "the voice of juſtice and equity. Yes, we have in our
"own

" own times beheld the wretched defcendants of thofe
" who fpilled the blood of Ramini, call in the French to
" affift them in oppreffing and deftroying their brethren.
" We know how Zahanhar has punifhed them, by per-
" mitting one of their flaves, fupported by the French, to
" fpill their blood, in expiation of their crimes. You all
" underftand me; but I have thought proper to bring thefe
" facts to your recollection, in order that you might take
" the union of hearts for your law. To preferve this, you
" muft follow the law of your fathers, which commands
" you to fubmit to the defcendant of Ramini—I here
" prefent him to you; I give him this fagaie, that he may
" be the only Ombiafiobe, as was our father Ramini. At-
" tend to my voice, ye Rohandrians, Anacandrians, Vo-
" adziri, Lohavohites, Philoubey, Ondzatfi, Ombiaffes,
" Ampouria. It is the law of the blood of our fathers.
" Acknowledge the Ampanfacabe; fubmit to him, lif-
" ten to his voice, follow the laws which he fhall give,
" and you fhall be happy. Alas! my old age does not
" permit me to fhare your happinefs, my friends, and my
" fpirit fhall not perceive the teftimonies of that gratitude,
" which you may fhew to my tomb." He then turned
to me, and proceeded—" And thou, worthy fon of the
" blood of Ramini, implore the affiftance of God, who
" enlightens thee with his fpirit. Be juft; love thy peo-
" ple as thy children; let their happinefs be thine, and
" be not a ftranger to their wants and misfortunes. Go-
" vern and affift with thy councils the Rohandrians and
" Anacandrians; protect the Voadziri; watch with pa-
" ternal care over the Lohavohites and Philoubey; em-
" ploy,

" ploy, for the general good, the Ondzatſi and Ombiaſſes;
" and do not deſpiſe the Ampouria; cauſe them to conſi-
" der their maſters as their fathers, as it was in the time
" of our father Ramini."

Having finiſhed this diſcourſe, he put the ſagaie into my hands, and proſtrated himſelf before me, as did like-wiſe his companions, and all the chiefs that were aſſembled together; and at laſt I ſaw upwards of fifty thouſand men proſtrated before me. Raffangour requeſted me to make a public anſwer, which he repeated in theſe words----" Ve-
" loun Raminiha, Veloun Ouloun malacaſſa, Veloun Ro-
" handriani, Anacandriani, Voadziri, Lohavohites, Phi-
" loubey, Ondzatſi, Ombiaſſes, Ampouria, Veloun, Ve-
" loun Zaffé Aminiha, Mitomba Zahanhar:"----which implies, Long live the blood of Ramini, Long live the Ma-dagaſcar nation, Long live the Rohandrians, &c. Long live the blood of our fathers, and may the God who created the heavens and the earth long preſerve us all. The people gave repeated ſhouts whenever I named any claſs; and at laſt aroſe; and when every one was ſtanding, I continued my ſpeech, by ſaying, that I acknowledged the favour of Heaven, which had brought me again to the land of my fathers; that I ſhould employ my whole life in attending to what the ſpirit of God ſhould inſpire me to do, that every individual of the Madagaſcar nation might conſider me as a father. I then intreated the Rohandrians, and the other chiefs, to the Voadziri incluſive, to aſſiſt me with their counſels. I engaged the Lohavohites faithfully to execute the orders they ſhould receive; and I aſſured the Ampouria, that the laws would abate the inconveniences

of

of their unhappy state of slavery. I promised the Ondzatii and Ombiasses to employ them in the welfare of the nation; and I concluded my discourse by declaring, that I considered it as my duty to devote all my time to the establishment of a form of Government, in order that union and harmony might be preserved. I was continuing my harangue, when Raffangour begged me to stop. The orders then separated from each other, the Rohandrians assembling together, and Anacandrians likewise apart, as did all the others. I was first led to the Rohandrians, where I found an ox, whose throat I cut, at the same time pronouncing the oath of sacrifice, and every Rohandrian took a drop of the blood, which he swallowed, repeating, with a loud voice, imprecations against himself and his children, in case he should fail in the obedience he had sworn to me. I was then conducted to the circle of the Anacandrians, where I killed two oxen, and the same oath was repeated. In this manner I passed through all the classes of the people, where I killed three oxen for the Voadziri, four with the Lohavohites, six with the Ondzatsi, two with the Ombiasses, and twelve with the Ampouria. These last dipped the ends of their sagaies in the blood, and licked them, at the same time pronouncing the oath. This whole ceremony passed without the least confusion; and I was again conducted to the circle of the Rohandrians, who made a second oath with me, which was performed in this manner:----each person made an incision, with a razor, under the left breast, as I did likewise myself, and each mutually sucked the blood of each other, at the same time pronouncing the most horrible maledictions against whoever should violate his oath, and benedictions in favour of those who should continue faithful to their engagement. All this ceremony was ended in the course of two hours. After noon the chiefs announced to their people a moment of recollection, to invoke the spirit of God, and to thank Zahanhar for his goodness and protection.

At a quarter past two the Rohandrians conducted me to my tent, where I detained them to dinner. I invited the Anacandrians and Voadziri to drink after dinner, and sent four casks of brandy to the Lohavohites, to be distributed among the Ondzatsi, Ombiasses, and Ampouria.

About six in the evening, near three hundred women, natives of the country, appeared, and requested to make an oath with my spouse. The ceremony was performed by moon-light, and their oath was made by dancing. The purport of it was, that they would obey the orders of my spouse, and would appeal to her in all the disputes and quarrels, in which it was not proper for men to meddle. This oath being finished, their rejoicings began, and the night passed in dances and songs.

On the 11th, I requested all the chiefs to assemble, to hold their first cabar. At eight, the assembly being full, I required the execution of an act of engagement, under oath, to be made with the insertion of all the names of the chiefs and people present. This act was written in the language of the country, with Roman letters, and was as follows:

"This act of oath of the Kings Rohandrian, of the
"Princes Voadziri, of the chiefs Lohavohites, and the
"people of Madagascar, made the 10th of October, 1776,
appointing

" appointing and confirming the election of Maurice Au-
" gustus Count of Benyowsky, to the rank of Ampansa-
" cabe, or supreme chief of the nation, the Kings, Princes,
" chiefs, and people undersigned, being assembled in ca-
" bar:

" In presence of our people, having consumed the sacri-
" fice, and made the oath of blood, we proclaim, declare,
" and acknowledge Mauritius Augustus for our supreme
" chief Ampansacabe, titles extinct since the decease of our
" holy family of Ramini, which we revive in him and his
" family. It is for this reason that, having consumed the
" sacrifice, we submit inviolably to his authority; in con-
" sequence of which we determine to erect, in our province
" of Mahavelou, a monument to perpetuate the memory
" of our union, and to immortalize our holy oath: In
" order that our infants, and their children, unto the most
" remote posterity, may be obedient to the sacred family
" Ombiasse of the Ampansacabe, whom we all sanctify
" by our submissions. Cursed be our children who shall
" not obey our present will; cursed be their inheritances,
" and the fruits of the earth on which they shall subsist:—
" may the most horrid slavery confound them."

This oath, having been three times read aloud, was signed, in the name of the nation, by

  Hiavi, King of the East.
  Lambouin, King of the North.
  Raffangour, Rohandrian of the Sambarives.

A List of the great Men, or Chiefs, and the People present at this Cabar.

Raffangour Rohandrian---Cievi Voadziri,
Of the province of Zaferamini, with their people.

Sianique Rohandrian---Mandingue Anacandrian,
Of the province of Zaphirobay, with their people.

Raoul Anacandrian---Diamanong Voadziri,
Of the province of Antambour, with their people.

Manongamon Rohandrian---Mamon Anacandrian,
Of the province of Antivoiefou, with their people.

Manacandrin Anacandrian----Diamandrifs Lohavohits,
Of the province of Antifapherobay, with their people.

Raffenou Anacandrian---Leloatou Anacandrian,
Of the province of Antivohibey, with their people.

Sancé Rohandrian Malata---Damo Anacandrian,
Of the the province of Sambarives, with their people.

Lambaranthe Rohandrian---Francé Anacandrian,
Of the province of Antfirac, with their people.

Hiavi Rohandrianabé,
King, with his troop of Ondzatfi.

Lamboiun

Lamboiun Rohandrianabé,
King of the North, with his troop.

Ramaraombe Rohandrian---Diamboulmafie Anacandrian,
Of the province of Maſſouala, with their troops.

Raffidzimon Anacandrian---Diafaitfche Lohavohits,
Of the province of Antavacayr, with their people.

Dianbandze Anacandrian---Siomba Lohavohits,
Of the province of Rantabay, with their people.

Romain Lohavohites---Mamay Lohavohits,
Of the province ſubjected to Hiavi, with the Ondzatſi.

Diane Sara Rohandrian---Ravoye Lohavohits,
Of the province of Manoarou, with their people.

Mumere Rohandrian---Ravoye Lohavohits,
Of the province of Mananzari, with their people.

Ravouſow Anacandrian---Belaze Lohavohits,
Of the province of Mahafali, with their people.

Diane Souloat Rohandrian---Fanhamenon Anacandrian,
Of the province of Matanany, with their people.

I employed the reſt of the day in conferring with the chiefs, in order to perſuade them to adopt a conſtitution, which I had determined to propoſe the following day, the hour of meeting being fixed at ten.

This

This day likewife was employed in feftivals and rejoicing; and nothing paffed of any importance, except the delivery of a petition, figned by thirty-eight foldiers, five fubaltern officers, three officers, and fix perfons employed in civil affairs. They entreated that I would grant them my protection, which I could not refufe. They had previoufly fecured an affurance of protection from the greater part of the Rohandrians. Towards the evening I received advice of the arrival of two private veffels upon the coaft, and I immediately fent an interpreter to purchafe the faid veffels and their cargoes.

On the 12th, the chiefs of the province of Rantabay prefented the Europeans who formerly belonged to the fettlement, and requefted me to receive them under my protection, and permit them to fettle amongft us. I confented to this, and their oath was received in cabar. At ten, the meeting being full, I opened the bufinefs, by a motion for the eftablifhment of a form of government and conftitution. My propofal was to the following effect:

"In confequence of my election to the office of Am-
" panfacabe, I find myfelf charged with a prodigious
" weight. When I confidered the duties annexed to my
" office, by accepting this charge, I forefaw that the ge-
" neral good of the nation muft be my firft aim. To at-
" tain this, I am convinced that the power ought to be
" lodged in the hands of a fupreme Council, compofed of
" members of known wifdom, prudence, and activity.
" Let this Council exercife all the acts of fovereignty, and
" poffefs the fole right, with the confent of the Ampan-
" facabe, of convening the general affembly of the nation.

In

"In order that they may adopt and agree to the constitu-
" tion, when it shall be drawn out, or whenever it shall be
" required, to administer the oath of fidelity to the
" Ampanſacabe. From among the members of the ſu-
" preme Council, who ſhall always be taken out of the
" rank of Rohandrians and Anacandrians, whether Indians
" or Europeans, nomination ſhall be made to the places
" of governors of provinces, as well as to the offices of
" miniſters of State, whether in the departments of war,
" marine, finance or trade, juſtice or agriculture. And
" as it is likewiſe neceſſary to watch with the greateſt
" exactneſs to the execution of all the orders and reſolu-
" tions appointed by the ſupreme Council, the Ampanſa-
" cabe, with the advice of the Council, ſhall eſtabliſh a
" permanent Council, compoſed of one or two Rohandrians,
" and all the reſt of the Voadziri and Lohavohites. Let
" there be provincial Councils likewiſe, whoſe members
" ſhall conſiſt of a Rohandrian governor, five Anacandrians,
" two Voadziri, four Lohavohites, and the reſt of the
" Ondzatſi and Ombiaſſes. The buſineſs of the ſupreme
" Council will be conſtantly to prevent all diſſentions,
" which might ariſe from miſunderſtandings between the
" Rohandrians, or between the ſeveral provinces; it will
" be incumbent on them to uſe only the ways of juſtice.
" They muſt watch, left foreign armies ſhould make at-
" tempts againſt the liberty of the Madagaſcar nation, by
" forming eſtabliſhments on ſhore. Their conſtant endea-
" vour muſt be, to render induſtry and trade flouriſhing;
" and, in a word, their utmoſt exertions muſt be directed
" to ſecure the moſt perfect proſperity to the community."

I con-

I concluded my discourse, by assuring the cabar, that with the aid and assistance of God, I hoped to see, in a short time, happiness, riches, and prosperity, return to the nation; and, by means of due order and form of government, established on good principles, I hoped that the island would be for ever freed from discord, the scourge of war, and the unhappy state of slavery.

As soon as I had ceased to speak, all those who were present cried out, " Velou Ampansacabe, velou Ramini;" which implies, Long live our lord, long live the descendant of Ramini. The chief Raffangour begged that I would permit him to announce my discourse to the people; and he went out for this purpose, and returned in the space of an hour, with all the people. On his return into the cabar, he assured all the chiefs, that the nation entrusted all their rights to the assembly, the individuals of which gave me full authority to form a supreme Council, and to do every thing I thought proper for their common welfare. I therefore proceeded to nominate to the charges of the supreme Council, the number of which was fixed at thirty-two persons.

Four Europeans were immediately nominated, and eight natives of the country, whose names were as follow:

    Raffangour Rohandrian,
    Sianique Rohandrian,
    Raoul Anacandrian,
    Manongamanon Rohandrian,
    Raffenou Anacandrian,
    Sancé Rohandrian, a Mulatto,
    Hiavi Rohandrian,
    Lambouin Rohandrian.

The two laſt mentioned Rohandrians ſolemnly renounced all pretentions to ſupremacy.

The nomination of the twenty other members was deferred, in order to afford employ for ſuch Europeans as might hereafter arrive, and thoſe natives of the country who might be found to poſſeſs abilities.

After this nomination, which was univerſally approved by ſhouts of joy, I proceeded to that of the permanent Council, which was confined to eighteen individuals.

Two Europeans were immediately nominated, and ſix natives of the country, whoſe names were as follow:

 Ramazaombe Rohandrian,
 Rafidzimon Anacandrian,
 Diamanong Voadziri,
 Zievi Voadziri,
 Diamandriſſe Lohavohits,
 Diafaiche Lohavohits.

This nomination was likewiſe applauded; and the nomination of the ten other members was deferred, for the ſame reaſon as was mentioned reſpecting the ſupreme Council.

Being ſatisfied with the buſineſs of the day, having eſtabliſhed theſe two pillars which were to ſupport the burthen of the conſtitution, I adjourned the cabar till the following day, at eight o'clock. This day I received a demand from the ſettlement, to furniſh a cargo of rice for the iſle of France; but the commander at Louiſbourg informed me that the ſtorehouſes were empty, and unprovided with any articles of trade, and that it would be impoſſible for him to extricate himſelf without my aſſiſtance. In conſequence of this reprefentation, and to fhew how much I had the good of the fettlement at heart, I requefted the Saphirobai chiefs to open a trade for bills, of which I formed a model, and fent a fufficient number to the commander of the fettlement.

In the night of this day I received advice, that the King of the Seclaves had fent prefents and envoys towards me, to conclude the peace. I difpatched a Rohandrian to meet them.

On the 13th, the Council being affembled, I propofed to determine upon a place for the erection of a town: the place appointed was at the head of the river Manangouzon. It was likewife propofed to erect fix governments, from the harbour of Moroava to the point of Itapere. But as I was in want of people capable of fulfilling thefe charges, I deferred the execution of the act of Council. This circumftance afforded me an occafion to reprefent to the members of the Council, that it would be of the greateft advantage for the interefts of the nation, to form treaties of commerce and friendfhip with the King of France, or fome other European power, in order to fecure the exportation of our productions, and the importation of articles neceffary for the inftruction of youth in the different fciences, arts, and trades, by engaging Europeans of fkill in thofe refpective employments, to come and eftablifh themfelves among us. I accompanied this propofition with an affurance, that I would go on this bufinefs myfelf; and there was only the old Raffangour Rohandrian who teftified his difpleafure, and faid openly, that I was going to feek my death. He intreated his countrymen to oppofe my departure; but, unfortunately, I was too ftrongly attached to my principles;

and

and I declared that it was my intention to repair to Europe, in order to conclude treaties of commerce and friendship with any European nation whatever, and that I had only deferred the execution of this project until the form of Government I had established should be in a regular train.

The 14th, 15th, and 16th, I was constantly employed in establishing the rules and orders of Government. This day the envoys of Cimanounpou, King of the Seclaves, were presented to me. They announced a present of eighty slaves, and five hundred oxen; but as they declared they were sent by their King to the French commandant, after having assured them that this title no longer belonged to me, I caused them to be conducted, with their attendants, to Louisbourg; but their astonishment was extreme, when they heard that I was chosen Ampansacabe, and descendant of the line of Ramini; for it was not till after the death, or rather the massacre, of Ramini Larizon, that the Rohandrian of Boyana, assumed the title of King of the Seclaves.

On the 17th, I purchased the cargo of a private vessel, of the value of forty-five thousand livres, for which I gave one hundred and twenty-eight slaves. This cargo was afterwards consigned to the disposition of Ramaraombe Rohandrian, member of the permanent Council.

On the 18th, judging it necessary to establish an order for the military service, I nominated Sancé Rohandrian, a Mulatto, Miaditompe Generalissimo, and established twelve companies, each of one hundred and fifty Ondzatsi, with orders to look to the preservation of the peace, conformably to the instructions which should be prescribed by the supreme Council. At the instant of this formation, each
Rohandrian

Rohandrian demanded permission to establish, in his respective district, a company of war. I not only granted this request, but ordered them so to do; and, with a view to give a sanction to this military establishment, I determined to make the resolution in full cabar, which I had appointed for the 19th. This day I caused twenty-two standards to be made, in order to be distributed to the different Rohandrians and Anacandrians. These colours had a blue ground, with a white moon in the middle. Those of each legion had a blue square on a white ground, with a moon and six stars in the middle.

On the 19th, the people being assembled in cabar, I gave my sanction to the establishment of bodies of troops; and the colours were distributed with a degree of solemnity which was truly striking.

On the 20th, having a corvette ready to sail, and having regulated the direction of my houses, and provided for the affairs of the nation, I determined to renew the proposals respecting my departure, and demanded titles and powers relative to my mission. The following was concluded on in the Council.

The chiefs Rohandrian, Anacandrian, Voadziri, Lohavohiti, and the people Ondzatsi and Ombiasses, assembled in general cabar of the nation, having agreed to the proposition made by their Ampansacabe, and consented that the said Ampansacabe shall absent himself to make a voyage to Europe, in order to conclude a treaty with the King of France, or any other nation; and to empower him to engage men, skilful in different arts and occupations, to come and dwell at Madagascar; it is in consequence that they have determined to give him entire authority, and absolute power.

power. They promise to him to follow exactly the order which he has prescribed for the form of Government, during the whole time of his absence; and they swear to be faithful to him; that they will not admit any foreigner into their island; and still less will they suffer any of their people to make particular treaties with any person whomsoever. They declare likewise, that after the expiration of the term of one year and a half, if they do not see their Ampansacabe return, they will not suffer any French settlement upon the coast of their island.

But they require that their Ampansacabe oblige himself to return, whether he shall succeed or not in his enterprize; and that, in case of any retardation, he shall send them news of his safety.

These engagements and resolutions were confirmed by the oath of blood, and the cabar broke up with lamentations, which strongly shook my resolution; but, alas! my destiny was too strong, and I followed its impulse in what appeared to me to be just and reasonable.

After the cabar had risen, Raffangour came to me, to represent once more the danger to which I exposed myself. He assured me, that he knew the French to be ambitious of rendering themselves masters of the island, sooner or later, and that they would make attempts against my life and liberty. He urged examples of their ferocity, by repeating what had been their behaviour upon the island. In a word, he spoke to me in the language of a friend, who was aware of the calamities that awaited me. His reasoning was well founded, and rested upon the highest probability; and I can only blame my zeal to promote the interest of France, at the risk of losing my fortune, my

estate

estate, and my life. This day was employed in drawing out the full powers, which were read in the committee, and duly expedited. Here follows a copy of the full powers.

October 23, 1776. In the plain of Mahavelou, the Kings, Princes, chiefs, and people of Madagascar, upon the north and eastern coasts of the island, being united in cabar, or general assembly, having heard the propositions of their Ampansacabe, placing an entire confidence in his affection towards them, and his sworn fidelity to perform his engagements, give unto him absolute and irrevocable powers to treat in Europe with the King of France, or any other King or nation, and to form commercial or friendly alliances, relations, or engagements. In consequence whereof we declare, in the present cabar, our approval, agreement, and ratification of whatever he shall sign and conclude, in his quality of an Ampansacabe. And, to consolidate our submissions, we have unanimously resolved, and do appoint, that in case the King of France shall not accept our offers, the Ampansacabe shall enjoy full authority and power to address himself to any other Sovereign or nation, and to conclude treaties of commerce and friendship with them, and to make other engagements relative thereto. And, in the mean time, during the absence of our Ampansacabe, we solemnly bind ourselves, not to receive any foreigner into our island, nor to form any treaty or connection with any other nation; in testimony of which we have executed the present instrument, after having caused it to be read and interpreted in full cabar, and have put the same into the hands of our said Lord Ampansacabe. Signed the year, the month, and the day above written, in the name of the whole nation.

> RAFFANGOUR, Rohandrian,
> HIAVI, King of the East,
> LAMBOUIN, King of the North.

On the 21st, I informed the chiefs, that being desirous of making preparations for my departure, I should take my leave of them; and I proposed to them to acknowledge, for the whole time of my absence, Raffangour chief of the supreme Council, or, in his absence or failure, the chief Sancé. The rest of this day was taken up in a festival, at which more than forty thousand people were present.

From the 22d of this month to the 10th of December, I was employed in arranging a variety of affairs, of a public as well as private nature.

On the 11th, I went to Louisbourg to assist the commanding officer of that settlement with my advice; and on the 14th, being at last informed, that every thing was embarked on board the brig, the Belle Arthur, which I had freighted to carry me to the Cape of Good Hope, I took my leave to go on board. When I came to the sea side, I found myself surrounded by most of the chiefs of the country, and all the people of the settlement, wishing me a good voyage; and the natives invoking Zahanhar to assist me in my undertakings. At the conclusion they all wept; and, at this single moment of my life, I experienced what the heart is capable of suffering, when torn from a beloved and affectionate society to which it is devoted. At length I went on board, not without paying a tribute to nature, which I had never experienced during the moſt dreadful ſufferings of my tyrannical exile. The north wind at length began to blow afreſh; and towards evening I ſet ſail for the Cape of Good Hope, at which place I propoſed to freight another veſſel, to carry me to France. This voyage may probably give birth to happy circumſtances, ſuch as my wiſhes have formed, in favour of the ſettlement at Madagaſcar, and may perhaps repair the faults committed by the miniſter.

THE END.

PIECES referred to in the MEMOIRS.

1775. The Piece L. X.

AT a meeting of the corps of the officers of the Volunteers, under the Count de Benyowsky.

On the twenty-second day of September, in the year one thousand seven hundred and seventy-five; the Baron de Benyowsky, Colonel of the said corps of Volunteers, named after him, and Commander in Chief of the establishments of his Majesty the King of France, upon the island of Madagascar, being informed, by the Surgeon Major, of his critical situation during his illness, which, by the daily and very evident diminution of his strength, threatened to come to a fatal determination: and being desirous, in consequence, to prevent the alarms of the gentlemen officers of his corps; who, beholding their chief sinking under the violence of a dangerous disorder, and being likewise aware of the weak situation of the troops, exposed to an infinity of unhappy consequences, as well on account of the want of pay as cloathing, have desired that a meeting might be held, for the purpose of rendering them acquainted with the will of their chief, and those orders which they should follow, in case of his decease: From these causes and reasons the said Baron de Benyowsky, Colonel of the corps of Volunteers, and Commander in Chief for his Majesty upon this island, has appointed the twenty-fifth of the present month, in order to consult upon the steps which may be most proper to be taken in such critical circumstances; and in consequence thereof, he has given his orders, that the reasons which have determined him to call the meeting, as well as the results then and there determined upon, should be written down, and entered in the register of the corps.

The Baron de Benyowsky, notwithstanding the violence of his illness, finding himself in possession of perfect understanding and tranquillity of mind, required the consent of his Surgeon Major, that he might preside at the assembly, which at length, after several consultations with the other surgeons, was granted. He therefore ordered the officers of his corps to meet, at the general quarters, on the twenty-fifth of the present month, that is to say, Mr. De Mallendre, Captain; Mr. Le Cerf, Captain; Mr. Perthuis, Lieutenant; Mr. Certain, Lieutenant; Mr. De la Boullaye, second Lieutenant; Mr. De La Tour, second Lieutenant; Mr. Lermina, Quartermaster; Mr. Evali, Ensign; Mr. Rosieres, Lieutenant, Aid de Camp, and performing the function of Secretary; and Mr. Besse, Treasurer, invited to be present at the assembly, in quality of principal officer of the administration, in lieu of principal Storekeeper, or Commissary.

In the year one thousand seven hundred and seventy-five, on the twenty-fifth of September: Present the following officers of the corps of Volunteers of Benyowsky; Mr. De Mallendre, Captain; Mr. Le Cerf; Captain, Mr. Perthuis,

Perthuis, Lieutenant; Mr. Certain, Lieutenant; Mr. De la Boullaye, second Lieutenant; Mr. De La Tour, second Lieutenant; Mr. Lermina, Quartermaster; Mr. Evali, Ensign; Mr. Rosieres, Lieutenant, Aid de Camp, and performing the function of Secretary; and Mr. Besse, Treasurer, invited to be present at the assembly, in quality of principal officer of Administration, in lieu of principal Storekeeper, or Commissary—Mr. De Sanglier being detached to the isle of France; Mr. De La Boullaye senior, Lieutenant, and Corbi, second Lieutenant, being absent with a party upon this island. The Baron De Benyowsky addressed the assembly as follows:

"The apprehensions, gentlemen, which you have entertained concerning my illness, are new proofs of your attachment; but as I find them guided by the zeal which you all possess for the service of the King, our master, it becomes me to pass over the emotions of gratitude with which my mind is impressed, and to speak, in the first place, of the interests with which the Court has entrusted me, in order that you may be enabled to proceed with certainty, in case it should please Divine Providence to require my life.

"At the end of the year one thousand seven hundred and seventy-two, the King gave orders for raising our corps, and appointed me to the command. At the beginning of the following year, I received his Majesty's orders, by the ministers, to repair with the said corps to this island; but as I was at the same time enjoined to keep the subject of our mission a secret, I durst not acquaint you with the place of our destination, of which you were not informed but in a very confused manner, at the isle

" of France. You will obferve, that it was no want of
" confidence on my part, which left you ignorant of the
" fubject of our enterprize. The conduct which I have
" held towards you during our paffage, and my diligence
" in inftructing you in the art of tacticks, convinced you
" of my zeal for your common good, which you have re-
" paid by marks of attachment and efteem, which will ne-
" ver be effaced from my mind. Since our arrival at our
" place of deftination, we have fuffered together a variety
" of diftreffes and fatigue, and have combated againft the
" intemperance of a fultry climate, and the violence of a
" people jealous of their liberty. We have armed ourfelves
" with courage to execute the orders we received, and
" fuccefs has attended our endeavours, in fpite of the en-
" vious fate which purfued us. Excufe me, my dear
" companions, if I forbear to name the authors of our fuf-
" ferings; you know them; and the fhame which they
" ought to feel, at feeing themfelves difcovered and de-
" feated, is revenge fufficient. The conduct to which I
" have adhered in this ifland, is fo well known to you,
" that I need not fpeak of our paft fufferings. You are
" convinced that I have done my duty, in diminifhing
" them, by applying my own fortune to fupply the wants
" of the eftablifhment which we have formed. You,
" yourfelves, by advancing the fums you had received,
" have fupplied me with means of adminiftring to the pref-
" fing neceffities which were fo unjuftly refufed to be fup-
" plied, and without which we muft have been entirely
" reduced. As a recompence for my zeal and fufferings, I
" now find myfelf repaid by the blackeft calumnies, on
" the part of the ifle of France. There is no difgraceful

" action

" action which they have not accufed me of. Exclamations
" are made againft the exorbitant expences which are pre-
" tended to have been made in this ifland, and againft the
" cruelties committed by me, or my order, againft private
" traders, by whom it has been publickly afferted, that they
" were compelled to fign certain writings, while a piftol
" was held at their breafts. But the moft mortifying cir-
" cumftance is, that every means has been ufed to perfuade
" the public at the ifle of France, that fufficient fupplies
" have been forwarded out of their treafury, for the exi-
" gencies of the fervice of the troops here ; but that I have
" appropriated thefe fums, and have left the foldiers with-
" out refource, overwhelmed with labour, and threatened
" with every horror that tyranny can inflict. Thefe ma-
" licious reports, in which every effort is made to deftroy
" my reputation, would give me no concern in any other
" circumftances. I fhould look upon them with con-
" tempt, if the hope of recovering from the illnefs which
" I now fuffer, could permit me to indulge the expecta-
" tion of rendering an account of my conduct, at fome
" future period, to the King and his minifters: but as I
" am well aware of the dangerous confequences which
" may attend my prefent illnefs, and which every day
" threatens to take me hence, I conjure you, gentlemen,
" by your honour, to render that teftimony to the truth,
" which may fruftrate the views of thofe who are defirous
" of blackening my fame. As a foldier, and as a chief, you
" know me from experience:—render to my name, when
" I am no more, that juftice which I have deferved by my
" conduct, and which you cannot refufe.

" After

"After this short recital of past circumstances, I must proceed to our present situation. With a view to secure the establishment till the arrival of new orders from Court, and to prevent its suffering from external attacks, which I foresaw, I dispatched the Postillion packet for France a twelvemonth ago, in order to render an account of our position at Court, and to request supplies. In the mean time, I have reclaimed the assistance of the isle of France, pursuant to his Majesty's orders, which you may see in the letter which his minister wrote to the chiefs of that settlement, and which I here produce to convince you of the fact. You would doubtless have concluded, as I did, that the supplies would speedily have been forwarded; but, alas! in reply, I received only a refusal, which I have hitherto concealed, with a view to avoid giving you embarrassment and disquiet. This refusal, in the present juncture, is more particularly distressing, because I have already employed my whole property in the King's service, and am therefore incapable of administring to our present wants. The stores are filled with useless effects, which have been sent us from the isle of France, but are unprovided with the most necessary articles; the treasury is without money, and the troops without either pay or cloathing. Such is our present situation, which is deplorable indeed for men, who for two years incessantly, without a pause of twenty-four hours, have been kept in continual motion; and who, in the last war against the islanders, have so valiantly distinguished themselves under your conduct. The success of this war, the event of which has secured our good fortune and the tranquility of the country, has filled us with joy. We ought, "therefore,

" therefore, to take advantage of the present good dispofi-
" tion of affairs, for the further encouragement, and raising
" the spirits of our soldiers: they are attached to us, gentle-
" men; nothing is impossible for them to attempt, under
" our direction. I conjure you, therefore, to animate
" them, by directing their minds to glory, which is the
" great mover of the French nation. An animated soldier,
" to whom his officer sets the example, suffers with wil-
" lingness: I will even say more, he runs with avidity to
" the greatest hardships. In this manner, therefore, you
" will succeed in keeping up the ordinary service, which
" is urged by the different parties we are obliged to main-
" tain. With regard to the nine months pay due to your-
" selves and the troops, I will endeavour partly to dif-
" charge it, by difpofing of my small stock of necessaries
" to a private vessel, which is now upon the coast. We
" may perhaps, likewise, by the same channel, supply our-
" selves with articles of trade, for the daily exigencies of
" the hospital. In this manner, ballancing our resources
" against our misfortunes, we may hope for new orders
" from Court, which, according to all appearance, can-
" not be longer delayed than till the return of the Postil-
" lion. Besides this, the spot we now inhabit being ren-
" dered more healthy by the works we have executed, will
" secure the health of those who at present are tolerably
" well, and are not entirely exhausted. Our experience
" this year confirms this probability. Last year we lost
" one hundred and thirteen men; this year, the number
" of deaths is no more than eleven; which is a difference
" we have great reason to value ourselves upon. We have
" expofed ourselves, by labouring for the advantage of
" others,

"others, who will enjoy, with safety and without fear, the fruits of our exertions. No one will dispute the glory we possess, of having laboured for the common good, at the peril of our lives.

"I shall now leave you, gentlemen, for a short time, to recover my exhausted strength. In the mean time, you will consult together upon the properest means to be adopted in our present situation. It is unnecessary to observe, that it is by the orders of his Majesty that we have exerted ourselves upon this spot; and that it is not enough to have succeeded, but that it is likewise equally necessary to preserve the advantages we have acquired. There is no difficulty which a determined courage cannot overcome. Adieu, my friends; I leave you for an instant."   (Signed)

THE BARON DE BENYOWSKY,

With his paraph or flourish.

The commander being then exhausted by his illness, retired, after exhorting the gentlemen present to consult together, and lay their opinion before him. Whereupon the meeting deliberated, and determined to draw out their opinions in separate articles, and submit them to their commander in chief.

THE OPINIONS OF THE OFFICERS, WHICH THEY SUBMIT TO THEIR COMMANDER.

PRIMO. The officers of the corps of Volunteers, having attended to the speech of their Commander, are unanimously

mously penetrated with grief to hear, that the zeal which he has shewn, and the numerous exertions he has made, at the expence of his fortune and health, in favour of all those who have had the honour of serving under his orders, have been recompensed by attempts to tarnish his reputation, by acts of imposture and the blackest calumny. As witnesses of his conduct, they think it an act of duty and justice to protest solemnly, by the present resolutions, against all the imputations and pretended malversations. And they mutually engage and bind themselves, in case of the decease of their Commander, to represent this affair to his Majesty and his ministers.

2dly. They have the honour to represent to their Commander in Chief, that, after all the magnanimous efforts with which he has been pleased to maintain the royal establishment, and corps of Volunteers, by furnishing means for the support of every individual hitherto, they shall consider it an honour to follow the example of their Chief; and they intreat his permission, that they may themselves contribute a sum, to be advanced to the treasury, in order that they may by this means be considered as worthy his esteem, and may contribute, to the utmost of their power, to the good of his Majesty's service.

3dly. With respect to the troops and the service, they will omit nothing which may justify the opinion of their Commander; and they request that, in consideration of the small number of men, he will withdraw the troops from the two intermediate posts of Massoula and Mananhar, in order that the main body, being reinforced, may be better enabled to act in the vicinity of the chief settlement, and defend themselves from the robberies which have been committed by vagabonds since the last war.

4thly.

4thly. They respectfully entreat that the Commander in Chief will be pleased to consider, that the arrival of a vessel from Europe may be frustrated by several unforeseen events, and that consequently it would be very necessary to send a summons to the isle of France, in the name of his Majesty, to obtain a supply, as well of men as of money and effects for their subsistence.

5thly. The present meeting of officers, perceiving that the health of their Commander is greatly altered; and being likewise informed, by the surgeon-major, that it cannot but be still more impaired by the fatigue and exertions which he continues to make, notwithstanding their opposition; they take the liberty unanimously to entreat, that he will, for a certain time, desist from this continued labour. They are more pressing in this respect, as they are actuated by the impression of that friendship, which he has ever been pleased to shew to the corps of Volunteers, as well as for the interests of the establishment, in which he is bound to consult the advantage of his Majesty's service, by forbearing to make exertions which tend to deprive the settlement of his future services.

6thly. The officers, in the last place, take the liberty to represent, that, exhausted as they are by past and present distresses, there is not one among them who does not feel his strength greatly impaired, and that a change of garrison is very necessary for the whole corps: they therefore deposit their general interests in the hands of their Commander in Chief, and entreat that he will be pleased to intercede with his Majesty and the ministry in favour of the corps, to procure them a just recompence, and a certain time to recover themfelves from the exceffive fatigues they have been oppreffed with.

Signed with the following names.

> DE MALLENDRE, with paraph;
> LE CERF, with paraph;
> PERTHUIS, Lieutenant;
> LE CERTAIN, Lieutenant;
> DE VEZIERS, Lieutenant;
> DE LA BOULLAYE;
> DES GRAVES, fecond Lieutenant;
> The Chevalier DE LA TOUR, fecond Lieutenant;
> LARMINA, Quartermafter, with paraph;
> ROZIERES, Lieutenant, performing the office of Secretary;
> BESSE, Treafurer, with paraph.

DECISION OF THE ASSEMBLY OF THE CORPS OF VOLUNTEERS OF BENYOWSKY.

PRIMO. The Commander in Chief being fatisfied with the promife of the gentlemen officers of his corps, with regard to what concerns his reputation; and reclaiming only their viva voce teftimonies, in cafe of his premature deceafe, referves himfelf in perfon to clear himfelf of all calumnious imputations, and to carry his complaints to the foot of his Majefty's throne.

2dly. The Commander in Chief will take the firft opportunity of forwarding a fummons to the chief of the ifle of France, to obtain the supplies necessary for the subsistance of the establishment.

3dly. The Commander in Chief will distribute among the officers the several departments of daily employment, that he may be enabled to repose himself. He likewise declares, that, having disposed of every particular of business relating to the settlement, as well as to his own private affairs, they will find, in case of his decease, his last Will, sealed up in the box marked A, which is in his cabinet, which is placed in the office: the same box contains several papers addressed to the minister, and an order in the King's name, which enjoins that gentleman, who, by his rank among the officers, shall be entitled to succeed him, to conform, until new orders from Court, to the instructions he will find annexed to the order. By this provision, the officers in command will avoid that embarrassment which otherwise might become of great consequence to the establishment. He therefore exhorts them to arm themselves with courage, to support the interests of their master; and as they have all faced death to acquire glory, so at present it becomes them nobly to submit to suffering and distress, in order to maintain it.

4thly. The gentlemen officers of the corps of Volunteers, are requested to form a sum of twelve thousand livres, to be remitted to the treasury, for the payment of the troops; and the Commander in Chief engages to furnish a like sum, for the purchase of different effects and merchandize, for the subsistence of the hospitals, and daily exigencies.

5thly. The posts of Massoula and Mananhar shall be withdrawn, to reinforce the chief settlement, and to defend

fend the cultivated lands of the allied natives from the devastation and fire of the vagabonds.

6thly. The Commander in Chief will forward his pressing representations to the minister, concerning the distresses and fatigues which his corps have endured; and will demand, for the refreshment of the said corps, a garrison better calculated for their recovery, in the internal part of the island.

7thly. An act, in form, shall be drawn out, of the proceedings of this present assembly of the officers of the corps of Volunteers, which shall consist of three parts, one of which shall be forwarded to the minister, the second to the isle of France, with the summons, and the third shall be deposited in the archieves of the corps.

Done in our general camp on the island of Madagascar, the twenty-fifth of September, 1775.

Signed,
 The BARON DE BENYOWSKY, Colonel and Commander in Chief of the French settlements on the island of Madagascar;
 DE MALLENDRE, with paraph;
 LE CERF, Captain, with paraph;
 PERTHUIS, Lieutenant;
 LE CERTAIN, Lieutenant;
 DE LA BOULLAYE;
 DES GRAVES, second Lieutenant;
 The Chevalier DE LA TOUR, second Lieutenant;
 DE LARMINA, Quartermaster;
 ROZIERES, Lieutenant, performing the office of Secretary;—and
 BESSE, Treasurer.

The Piece L. X. X.

AT A COUNCIL OF THE OFFICERS OF THE CORPS OF VOLUNTEERS OF BENYOWSKY, CONVENED BY ORDER OF THE BARON DE BENYOWSKY.

April the 1st, 1776. Present in council convened by order of the Baron de Benyowsky, Colonel of the regiment named after him, and Commander in Chief of the French establishment on the island of Madagascar; namely, the Chevalier de Sanglier, Captain; De Mallendre, Captain; Perthuis, first Lieutenant; Corbi, second Lieutenant; De La Boullaye, second Lieutenant; the Chevalier de La Tour, second Lieutenant; Larmina, Quartermaster; Evali, Ensign; Rozieres, performing the office of Engineer; Mayeur, Lieutenant, and first interpreter of the establishment; Bessiere, performing the office of Secretary; and Besse, invited to be present in the assembly, in quality of principal officer of the Administration, in lieu of principal Storekeeper or Commissary. The Baron de Benyowsky being president at this Council; and Messrs. Le Certain and De La Boullaye, senior, Lieutenant, being absent; the former detached to the isle of France, and the latter being commander at Foul Point.

The Baron de Benyowsky opened the meeting with the following speech:

"I have called you together, gentlemen, to consult
" upon the critical circumstances of our situation, the se-
" curity of our posts, and the preservation of the several
" provinces

"provinces allied to the settlement, as well as the part
"which it becomes us to take in the present situation with
"regard to the war with the Seclaves; whose chief, having
"declared war against the French standard, has already
"commenced hostilities, by ravaging the people who are
"allied by oath to the establishment, and who, if unassisted
"by us, may be compelled by force to yield to our ene-
"mies, and become subject to them. All these circum-
"stances require the utmost attention of the settlement;
"and that more especially, as their increase will threaten
"us with the loss of the fruits of all the laborious exertions
"we have made for the space of three years; and as
"they happen at a time when the forces of the establish-
"ment are exhausted. These positions, therefore, require
"a minute discussion, in order that we may form a well-
"digested plan; and that, without having the rash-
"ness to face every event, we may exert that courage
"which will be sufficient to answer our purposes; and by
"collecting our forces, we may maintain our labours with
"glory, and crown them by the titles of brave soldiers,
"and faithful servants of the King who has employed us.

"It is unnecessary to enumerate, at present, the vari-
"ous checks and vexations to which we have so unjustly
"been subjected, and which have placed the settlement in
"the most unhappy and critical situation, and reduced
"our people to a state of extreme weakness. All these
"circumstances are well known to you, as we discussed
"them in the last meeting, held on the 25th of Septem-
"ber, 1775, and provided a temporary remedy, in the
"hope of speedy assistance either from the isle of France
"or from Europe. But, since that period, six months have
"elapsed,

"elapsed, and the small assistance we have derived from
" the isle of France being scarcely sufficient to main-
" tain us until this time, our distresses cannot but increase,
" and must at last overwhelm us. At present it is necessary
" to oppose them with determined courage. For this pur-
" pose, let us suppose that the supplies, though daily ex-
" pected, are still far from their arrival; let us make our
" account from the actual situation of things; let us cal-
" culate the forces we really possess, and upon this estimate
" let us decide what conduct is the most proper to be held.
" Our own assurance of having employed all the resources
" of our courage, in the service of his Majesty, will be an
" ample recompense for our labours.

" If we consider the number which usually composes a
" troop, and look to ourselves, we shall see only a feeble
" remnant, worn out by the severe pressure of long and
" assiduous fatigue; scarcely equal to the ordinary service;
" no longer daring to quit their forts and retrenchments.—
" But it is a consequence of that valorous spirit, which
" ought to be natural to a soldier, that we should raise our
" courage beyond that of common minds: the more the
" vicissitudes of events oppress and overwhelm us, the
" more it becomes us to collect our force and firmness.
" Bound as we are by the ties of honour, and of duty,
" to justify the confidence of the Court, which has ap-
" pointed us to form a solid establishment in this island,
" we can do nootherwise than resolve to vanquish and subdue
" all obstacles. Three years have now elapsed since we bad
" adieu to the pleasures of a life of tranquillity; we have
" familiarized ourselves to hardships, labours, and war,
" and we have withstood the rigours of this unwholesome
" climate.

" climate. Thousands of enemies, whom we have con-
" quered and dispersed, have acquired us that reputation
" through the whole extent of this vast island, which has
" procured the alliances of more than one third of its whole
" people.---What risque then shall we now run, by dividing
" our troops, and appointing one half to guard our posts,
" which are fortified and provided with artillery; while the
" other half takes the field, and carries terror to the ene-
" my, keeps the neutral powers in respect, and preserves
" the allies of the settlement? Such an engagement, well
" made, may open to us resources we have hitherto been
" unacquainted with. The supplies, so long expected,
" will at last arrive, and then every difficulty and obstacle
" will be surmounted. The troops, when reinforced, will
" resume their primitive vigour; and having kept the ene-
" my in check, they will then entirely destroy them. The
" storehouses being furnished, will increase the confidence
" of the natives of the country; who having, since our ar-
" rival here, been amused with mere promises, and seeing
" no supplies arrive, may join the Seclaves, the only na-
" tion which remains for us to fight and subdue; because
" its natural obstinacy will never suffer them to be surprised
" by negotiation, and because they neglect no opportunity
" of engaging all the other nations of the island in their in-
" terest, either by promise or threats. We have therefore
" only the strength of our arms, and our superiority in the
" art of war, to oppose against them. To purchase peace
" is contrary to the character of the French; and would,
" besides, diminish our reputation, and debase us in the
" eyes of all the nations of this island, who would revolt,
" when they saw us undecided and embarrassed in our pro-
" ceedings

" ceedings with one national one; whereas several nations
" have been reduced at the mere sight of us, and have not
" dared to collect their forces in opposition to our enter-
" prizes, but have all attached themselves, by treaty, to
" the settlement. Their attachment must be preserved by
" civilization, and justice duly administered to them.
" The mild treatment they have received from us, and the
" assistance we have given them against their enemies, have
" secured their esteem; and, forgetting the name of foreigner,
" they now behold in us the friend and the ally. But the
" instant we refuse to assist them against the Seclaves, and
" they lose that respect for us which fear produces, they
" will indubitably arrange themselves on the stronger side,
" and encrease that force.

" All these circumstances, gentlemen, require a speedy
" decision, on our part, in order that we may act in the
" most becoming and certain manner. As far as I can see
" into our situation, and the position in which we stand
" with regard to the natives, we cannot dispense with en-
" tering into the war against the Seclaves. It is therefore an
" object of discussion, whether we ought to confine our-
" selves merely to the defence of the frontiers of our allies, in
" conjunction with them, or whether we ought to begin
" an offensive war, by entering into their country: for it
" is impossible for us to remain in our forts, and behind our
" entrenchments, in a state of expectation, until our ene-
" mies come upon us. We should by that means ex-
" pose our allies, who dwell on their frontiers, to conti-
" nual ravages and slavery, and the establishment will
" not be able to clear itself of the blame, as it is engaged to
" support its allies against all the attempts of their enemies.
                                                " These

"These are just reasons, which ought to determine us to take the field, and to carry the war to the frontier of the Seclaves. By this manœuvre, we shall cover our own possessions, with those of our allies, and we shall be in a situation, on the arrival of the first supply of men, in consequence of the knowledge we shall have acquired of the country, and of the means necessary to be employed against the enemy, to attack them in our turn, subdue them, and compel them to accept of such terms as we shall prescribe.

"After having thus given a detail to you, gentlemen, of our present circumstances, and communicated my views, I request that you will discuss the part which it is necessary to take in an enterprize of such delicacy, and let me know your sentiments without delay."

Done at Louisbourg, April 1, 1778.

Signed,

The Baron de Benyowsky.

The corps of officers of the Volunteers, after having maturely considered and discussed the steps practicable to be taken, to prevent the inconveniences probably to arise from the violence of the enemies which threaten the establishment, perceive no better than to take the field immediately, and to carry the war to the frontiers of the Seclaves; and in this manner to keep the enemy in continual movement, until the arrival of the final orders of his Majesty, and the supplies, which cannot fail to arrive soon. They are confident in affirming, that though the number of the troops,

troops, to be divided for the service of war, and the defence of the chief settlement and out-posts, be small, yet the valour and courage of each company will justify the opinion of the Commander in Chief; and that the corps desires nothing more ardently, than to receive orders which may give them an opportunity of performing their duty in a manner worthy of themselves.

With regard to the alternative of an offensive or defensive war, the corps of officers, not being desirous of anticipating the will of their Commander, will always follow with spirit the decision he shall make, and upon which the success of the campaign will probably depend.

Done this 1st of April, 1776, at the general camp of Louisbourg.

Signed,

The Chevalier SANGLIER;
DE MALLENDRE;
LE CERF;
DE LA BOULLAYE;
DES GREVES;
CORBI;
The Chevalier DE LA TOUR;
ROZIERES;
MAYEUR;
LARMINA;
EVALI;—and
BESSE.

ESTABLISH-

ESTABLISHMENT AT MADAGASCAR.

ADMINISTRATION GENERAL AND PARTICULAR.

* Demands, Obfervations, and Queftions, propofed to the Baron de Benyowfky, Colonel and Commander of the Eftablifhments of his Majefty, the King of France, upon the ifland of Madagafcar, by Meffrs. De Bellecombe and Chevreau, by virtue of the powers vefted in them, as Infpectors and Commiffaries for his Majefty upon the faid ifland of Madagafcar.

ARTICLE I.

WE demand of the Baron de Benyowfky, that he do communicate to us the original of the orders of the King, with the difpatches and inftructions of the minifter, by virtue of which he came to take poffeffion, in his Majefty's name, to form an eftablifhment and command at Madagafcar, at the place called the Bay of Antongil; and alfo the ordonnance for creating a corps of Volunteers, in his name,

---

* This appears to be the piece *L. X. A.* referred to at page 256 of the prefent volume, though the mark is omitted in the manufcript. In the original, the Queftions and Replies are arranged in columns oppofite each other; but I have, for the convenience of printing, fubjoined each Anfwer to the Queftion, which precedes it. NOTE OF THE EDITOR.

which

which bears date the 30th October, 1772; and a communication of the dispatches and correspondences of the marine and colonies, and of Messrs. the chiefs of the Administration of the isle of France.

Answer to ARTICLE I.

I have the honour to present to Messrs. the commissaries, hereunto annexed, under cover *L. A.* the orders of Court, which they demand, and also the ordonnance of my corps, and my correspondence with the ministers and the chiefs of the Administration of the isle of France. As I received no orders to take any possession in the island of Madagascar, I have confined myself to the establishment of posts, for the facilitation of trade, and the cultivation of the ground; and have formed connections and treaties of friendship and mutual interest with the natives of the country, who have voluntarily granted the lands upon which the different forts and the chief settlement are situated.

ARTICLE II.

We demand of the Baron de Benyowsky, an accurate and full statement, or list, by name, of the officers, subalterns, and volunteers, people employed, sea-faring men, and other subjects of his Majesty whomsoever, that have been subject to his orders at Madagascar, or who are at this present time under his command; together with their places of residence, and respective functions.

Answer to ARTICLE II.

I have the honour to present to Messrs. the commissaries, the register of the corps of Volunteers, in order that they may

may receive information of the names of all the foldiers who came hither with me, or have been enrolled either in the military or fea fervice fince that time, and thofe who are at prefent actually under my orders. The marginal notes indicate their places of refidence, and their functions. As to the perfons who are employed in the Adminiftration, their regifters will exhibit their number, and other particulars. *L. B.*

ARTICLE III.

We likewife demand another accurate and full ftatement, or lift by name, of all the officers, fubalterns, and Volunteers, people employed, fea-faring men, or other fubjects of his Majefty, who have either died, or have departed, together with the day of their death, or defertion, from the commencement of the eftablifhment until the prefent day: and as it is very interefting to their families to poffefs the titles and accounts of fuch as have died or deferted, we demand details for each individual man, inventories, verbal proceffes of fales, and accounts of the fucceffion of each; in order to tranfmit the fame to the minifter, who has exprefsly inftructed us on this head, as well as on that of remitting the refpective amounts, in bills of exchange, to France.

Anfwer to ARTICLE III.

Lifts of all the perfons who have died upon this ifland, fince the formation of the fettlement, are hereunto annexed, *L. C.* With regard to the inventories and produce of the fucceffion of thofe who have died, and were of the military, I have remitted to the minifter the amount, in bills of exchange, with inventories of fales, agreeably to his orders. I here

I here speak only of the military, as I have no concern with those who have been employed in the Administration.

ARTICLE IV.

What is the present state of his Majesty's treasury and stores, at Madagascar? We demand of the Baron de Benyowsky, to present to us, or to cause the persons accountable (the treasurer and storekeeper) to present to us, lists or inventories, signed by him and them, of the nett residue in hand, at the time of our arrival.

Answer to ARTICLE IV.

The cash and stores, at Madagascar, having been entrusted, since the departure of Mr. Des Assises, the principal storekeeper, to Mr. Aumont, the principal storekeeper, and to Mr. Besse; the lists and inventories will ascertain its situation. The treasury and stores have been supplied, for three years past, only by advances I have made.

ARTICLE V.

What are the public works, such as roads or canals, begun or finished: what are the fortifications and civil buildings, erected upon his Majesty's account, in the island of Madagascar, since the arrival of the Baron de Benyowsky? We demand a full statement, with values annexed; and likewise an account of the artillery and warlike stores attached to the settlement.

Does not the island of Madagascar afford all the necessary materials, such as lime-stones, bricks, and wood, for every kind of building?

Answer

Anfwer to ARTICLE V.

The public works, roads, fortifications, and civil erections, made by my orders, on account of his Majesty, will appear by the engineer's ftatement, who is charged with this department. I have the honour to prefent this ftatement, under cover *L. D.*; and alfo a full account of the artillery and ammunition of war.

The ifland of Madagafcar affords bricks, lime-ftones, wood in planks, as well for exportation, as for every kind of building.

ARTICLE VI.

We likewife demand of the Baron de Benyowfky, a communication of all the regifters of receipts and difburfements whatever, made on the ifland of Madagafcar, and on the occafion of the feveral pofts which he has eftablifhed fince his arrival; together with a table of comparifon of all the fums he received in Europe, at the ifle of France, and at Madagafcar, under what title and denomination foever they may have been received; whether fince he was appointed colonel and chief of this great undertaking; whether in effects of trade, filver, piaftres, calebafhes, paper money, or letters of exchange; with all the expenditures and confumptions, of what nature foever they may be.

Anfwer to ARTICLE VI.

I have the honour to prefent to the commiffaries, a general ftatement of the balance of debits and credits, drawn out in the month of May, in the prefent year. The difburfements fince made, will be eafily known by the regifters of the treasury. The statement shews, that the receipt, until the arrival of the commissaries, amounted only to six hundred and forty thousand livres: and the piece *B.* contains expences; the amount of which forms the sum of two million nine hundred eighty-three thousand one hundred eighty-six livres, seven sols, and eleven deniers, of which sum the royal treasury is indebted to me four hundred and fifteen thousand livres. By comparing these two statements, the commissaries will be convinced, that the sum of one million seven hundred twenty-eight thousand one hundred and eighty-six livres has been procured by commerce, and the voluntary presents of the natives of the country.

ARTICLE VII.

To what sum per month do the whole expences, made up on the account of his Majesty, in the bay of Antongil, and the other settlements dependant thereon, amount to, reckoning from the first of October, in the actual state of affairs? We request the Baron de Benyowsky to supply us with accounts at large, distinguishing the different nature of the expences under these heads:

Effective troops;

Administration—the persons employed, and other servants, whether black or white men, who receive wages;

Hospitals;

Marine;

The maintenance of public buildings;

Subsistence;

What is the manner of paying these expences; in money, in paper-money, in letters of exchange, or in articles of trade?

Answer

Answer to ARTICLE VII.

In the actual state of the corps of Volunteers, their subsistence and pay will amount to the sum of eleven thousand eight hundred and sixty livres.

Administration.---With regard to the subsistence and pay of those employed in this department, and other Europeans who receive wages, I can speak nothing, as their quantum is regulated by the chief of the Administration.

Hospitals.---Cost per month, one thousand eight hundred livres.

Marine.---About two thousand livres.

Maintenance of public buildings.---Value in merchandize, one thousand six hundred livres.

Blacks in his Majesty's pay.---Value in merchandize, nine hundred livres.

The most ready manner of acquitting these expences, is to pay in money, which being laid out in the purchase of necessaries at the storehouses, will of course return into the treasury: by this means, the provision of subsistence will diminish; their consumption will be more proportioned to the state of each individual, and the specie will either be kept in circulation, or return into the treasury, by the sale of effects from the storehouses.

ARTICLE VIII.

The trade for rice and cattle being, by the account we have received at the isle of France, one of the motives which have determined Government to form an establishment at the isle of Madagascar, we demand of the Baron de Benyowsky, what are the causes of the want of success hitherto;
and

and why the ifle of France has not been fupplied with thefe two objects, rice and cattle, for three years paft; efpecially after the confiderable remittances which have been made in articles of trade for this purpofe?

We demand accounts of the confignments he has made to the ifle of France, in flaves, cattle, and rice; and alfo an account of the fale of thefe three articles, which he may have made to individuals on the King's account.

Anfwer to ARTICLE VIII.

The caufe of the want of fuccefs in fupplying the ifle of France in rice and cattle, can only be attributed to the ill will which the chief of the Adminiftration of the ifle of France has fhewn towards the fettlement at Madagafcar. The firft confignment which he made in piece goods and mufquets, the only articles neceffary for the rice trade, was fcarcely fufficient to pay the firft expences of the neceffary things required for the foundation of this eftablifhment. Moreover, he has never fatisfied the demands, which I have repeatedly made, to furnifh articles of trade. The invoices of his confignments, which I have the honour to prefent to the commiffaries, under the mark *L. E.* will juftify my affertions. Befides which, although I have often repeated to the chiefs of the ifle of France, that rice and cattle were in great plenty, they have for a long time left me ignorant of their difpofition in this refpect; until at length they declared, that they renounced all thefe fupplies. Their correfpondence, which I have the honour to prefent to Meffrs. the commiffaries, will evidently convince them of this affertion. Befides which, with regard to the article of trade, I cannot enter too minutely into it, becaufe this part was under the care of Mr. Des Assises, the commissary and sub-delegate, who naturally must have possessed instructions *ad hoc*. The correspondence of this administrator with the chiefs of the isle of France, must itself justify my assertions, that the trade of rice, slaves, and cattle, and the necessary supplies, have been neglected by the fault of the isle of France. I again request the commissaries to examine the invoices of the consignments from the isle of France to the establishment at Madagascar; and I hope they will then acknowledge, that the supplies have certainly not been considerable.

· The papers of the Administration must contain details of the consignments made to the isle of France, in slaves, cattle, and rice; and likewise of the sales of these three articles made to private traders, on the King's account. This department being absolutely foreign to my charge, and Mr. Maillart having required me to leave the entire disposition of the same to his sub-delegate, I am not acquainted with the detail, excepting so far as it was necessary for me to render myself acquainted with it, to develope the motives which determined Mr. Maillart so earnestly to counteract my operations.

ARTICLE IX.

What number of men does the Baron apprehend to be necessary as a garrison, to maintain themselves in the chief place, which he has chosen, and its dependencies?

Answer to ARTICLE IX.

I am at a loss to reply to the commissioners questions, contained in their ninth article, being entirely ignorant under what point of view the settlement at Madagascar is considered. I shall assume three:—

1st. The establishment at Madagascar, may be considered as intended to acquire the dominion of this vast island, to form a solid colony of Europeans, which, when once master of the whole island, will form a part of the power of the parent state; and by its natural fertility, will supply the indispensible wants of the other French colonies, by including in itself a military force, may be advantageously employed against the enemies of the parent country in India. The conduct of the minister, and the mission of the commissaries, induce me to make this digression.

2dly. The establishment at Madagascar, may be considered as a pacific military post, intended to gain the confidence of the natives of the country; to form treaties of friendship and commerce with them; to secure the trade which the merchants might carry on in this island; and to watch over and regulate them, in order that the trade of private vessels may not, in future, occasion those irregularities and disorders, of which formerly there existed so many examples.

3dly. The establishment may likewise be considered under the point of view of being tolerated by the natives, and under this head I cannot explain myself.

Upon which of these three principles the minister may consider it as most expedient to found the establishment, must rest with your own opinions, gentlemen. My operations and labours have hitherto been directed to form the establishment upon a fundamental basis, which is the second of the three points of view which I have proposed: I have pursued it, and can venture to assert, that the means
which

which I have employed, have been neceffary for its fuccefs; the particular inftructions of the Court have led me to it: I have the honour to prefent thefe to the commiffaries, and beg that they will pleafe to examine their purport.

ARTICLE X.

What are the chief places or pofts upon the coaft, or in the interior parts of the ifland, which depend upon the principal fettlement? In what fituation are they with refpect to public buildings, or erections; more efpecially that called the Plain of Health; what advantage is derived from them, or what ufeful purpofe do they anfwer?

Is it eafy to crofs the ifland from eaft to weft, from the Bay of Antongil to Bambetok?

What pofts has the Baron eftablifhed to fecure the communication?

Anfwer to ARTICLE X.

The chief places and pofts, dependant on the principal fettlement eftablifhed at the Bay of Antongil, are fort St. John, fort Auguftus, Antfirac, Mananhar, Maffoula, fort St. Maurice at Angontzi, Fenerif, fort Francis at Foul Point, and the fettlement, or factory, at Tamatava. As the commiffaries have infpected the works at Louifbourg, fort St. John, and fort Auguftus or the Plain of Health, it is unneceffary to defcribe them. The others confift of pallifades, furrounding houfes, built after the country fafhion, for the neceffary lodging. Each poft has its advantage with regard to trade; but my principal object in eftablifhing them, was to fecure fuch pofts as, by their fituation, might render us mafters of the trade of the country, by fecuring

curing the navigation of the principal rivers. The situation in which the commissaries now find me, by taking the second principle as the basis of my settlement, will shew the propriety of my operations. The passage from east to west, is easy; and its difficulties may be removed by a very moderate exertion of force. This operation having been one of the principal parts of my plan, I have begun it; but the want of force has checked my exertions. There are five posts to secure this communication; but as I thought proper to give up to the chiefs in alliance with the establishment, the posts of Ranoumena, Antangnin, and Angonum, I have kept only two, namely, that of fort St. John, and that of the Plain.

ARTICLE XI.

What is the name of the chief of the territory upon which our settlement is formed; what is the extent of his dominions; do we possess property in land, or concessions acquired, or in farm, at the bay of Antongil, and the dependant posts? In this case we request the Baron de Benyowsky to communicate to us the titles.

Answer to ARTICLE XI.

The name of the prince who formerly possessed the ground, which he voluntarily ceded to form our settlement, is Sianique. The extent of the possession of the place is one half league, included between the harbour and the great river. The chiefs reside in the town which I have formed, but their habitations are in the interior parts of the island. The property of the province of Antimaron belongs to the natives of the country; but they willingly surrender

surrender up lands, to engage the Europeans to settle among them, and cultivate the waste grounds. Messrs. the commissaries, may more particularly inform themselves in this respect, at the approaching assembly of the chiefs of the province, which I have invited, by their orders.

ARTICLE XII.

We demand a full list of the names of the principal Madagascar chiefs, who have acknowledged the authority of his Majesty, and have become tributary. What does the annual tribute consist of, to which they have submitted? What receipts have been made for his Majesty of these different tributes, or annual acknowledgments?

We demand of the Baron de Benyowsky, that he do convene, within the course of eight days, these different tributary chiefs, in order that we may ourselves assure them of the protection of his Majesty.

Answer to ARTICLE XII.

None of the chiefs have acknowledged the authority of the King; but they have attached themselves to us and the settlement, by treaties: their names are as follow;—Sianique, Mandingue, Raoul, Diamanongue, Manon, Manongamanon, Diamandrine; these chiefs have fifty other chiefs subordinate to them, who are all of the province of Antimarou: Raffene, a Sambarive chief, established at the village of Antianak, with four other chiefs; Raffangour, Cievi, Sancé, Dame, principal chiefs of the Sambarives, of Mananhar, having forty chiefs subordinate to them, of the people of Antavavi, Antivoitchou, Antivohibey, and Antimokol;

mokol; Lambarante, with twelve other chiefs, of the province of Laontoufou; France, Siloulout, with twenty chiefs, eftablifhed at Rantanbay; King Hiavi, with fifty chiefs, of the province of Foul Point, and Tamatava; Ramaraombe, Diamafie, with thirty chiefs, of the province of the Antifambarives to the eaftward; Rafidumoine, Diafaiche, Diaboulmaffou, with thirty chiefs, of the province of Angontzi; Lambouin, chief of the northern part of the ifland, with his family, confifting of twenty chiefs, at Voemara.

The chiefs and people of Madagafcar pay no tribute to the eftablifhment, but I have procured revenues to the fettlement, under the title of fubfidies: they confift of rice, cattle, and fome flaves. Before the laft war of Antimaron, the chiefs furnifhed, each for his own village, eight gamelles of rice, and four oxen. I have ufually accepted the value in timber, planks and flaves, as the accounts of the ftores will fhew. The amount of the fubfidies for this fourth year, is nine hundred and forty-two thoufand livres.

The chiefs fhall be affembled on the day fixed by the commiffaries.

ARTICLE XIII.

What treaties, or reciprocal engagements, fubfift between the French nation and the different Madagafcar chiefs?

What places do thefe laft inhabit, and what are their forces, and credit?

What is the nature of their revenues? Are they acquainted with the right of property in land?

Have

Have we any alliance with the King of the Seclaves, who is said to be the moſt powerful, and moſt warlike, of all the Madagaſcar chiefs?

Anſwer to ARTICLE XIII.

I have the honour to preſent to Meſſrs. the commiſſaries, the treaties and mutual engagements between the iſlanders and the French: they form only three articles;—1ſt. That the Madagaſcar nations ſhall permit freedom of trade in their country, and the erection of habitations wherever the ground is uncultivated: they willingly grant lands to the French. 2dly. That they ſhall ſupport the French ſettlements againſt all the enterprizes of their enemies. 3dly. That the French ſhall in no wiſe interfere in the private intereſts of the natives, unleſs they ſhall be required to act as mediators.

The forces of all the chiefs allied to the eſtabliſhment, may be eſtimated at one hundred and twenty-three thouſand warriors: this number varies according to the abundance of their harveſts. Their revenues conſiſt of ſugar, tobacco, indigo, cotton, rice, ſlaves, and cattle.

They are acquainted with the right of property; and a chief can be diſpoſſeſſed no otherwiſe than by the courſe of inheritance, or the chance of war.

We have formed an alliance with the chief of the Seclaves; but the chiefs which are ſubordinate to him, having interfered in the war of Antimaron againſt the eſtabliſhment, I have declared war againſt him, until he ſhall diſavow this proceeding, and render juſtice to the eſtabliſhment upon the chiefs who have taken up arms againſt our friends. The Seclaves, though they are very brave in war, have never poſſeſſed any ſuperiority over the reſt of the nation.

ARTICLE XIV.

Is there any national militia, or natives of the country, who have voluntarily submitted, as defenders of the settlement, to the orders of the Baron de Benyowsky? What is their number? How are they collected together? Under what conditions have they engaged in our service? Is it practicable, in case of need, to transport the free natives, of Madagascar, into India, to be employed in war?

Why did the Baron de Benyowsky adopt the project of introducing into the island of Madagascar, black slaves, purchased at Mozambique on his Majesty's account, as he has explained himself in his correspondence with the isle of France?

Answer to ARTICLE XIV.

In the infancy of the establishment, I kept a troop of armed natives in pay, who served in several excursions I caused my officers to make, upon discovery and observation in the internal parts of the island; but not having received the orders I demanded of the minister to this effect, and finding them to become chargeable, as I had no need of them since the commencement of this year, I have dismissed them, and have substituted in their place, black slaves from Mozambique, belonging to his Majesty, whose number though small, in the present situation of the establishment, may be sufficient in case of necessity.

The free blacks may likewise be employed in war; they may be had to the number of three, four, five, and six thousand from each province. Their discipline consists in obedience, without restriction; they are collected together
by

by sending a signal, which they know to belong to me. Their arms are musquets and sagayes. Their terms of engaging are, a musquet for forty days, and their provisions. Mr. La Bourdonnais and Mr. Laly, transported the free natives of this country to India, to serve in the war; but as the governors, instead of recompensing them, reduced them to slavery, I dare not promise that they will consent to leave their country, until their confidence in the French nation shall be again restored. The project of introducing Mozambique slaves into Madagascar, naturally presented itself, on account of the impossibility of their running away. As they are strangers in this country, they are more laborious; besides which, their assistance cannot be dispensed with in the sugar and indigo works.

ARTICLE XV.

Is it with pleasure that the inhabitants of Madagascar see us established among them? Would colonists from the isle of France, or Bourbon, if transported by Government to this island, be in any danger of being disturbed by the natives; or, on the contrary, would they be so far satisfied as to profit by our arts, and industry?

Answer to ARTICLE XV.

Messrs. the commissaries, will have an opportunity of ascertaining, in the assembly of the chiefs, whether the natives of Madagascar look with pleasure upon the French, who are established among them. French colonists transported hither, to form an European settlement, would be in perfect safety, throughout the whole extent of the island,

island, provided the colonial government made no attempts upon the liberty of the nation. The natives of Madagascar desire their presence, and their industry would increase by emulation. It is only by example that we can succeed in bringing the Madagascar people to submit to our regular form of government, and become civilized.

ARTICLE XVI.

What is the character of the people who live in the country round about the bay of Antongil?

Are they surrounded by nations, or numerous people, who are powerful rivals, enemies, or friends?

Are they sedentary; cultivators of the land; warriors? Have they any trade? With whom, and in what consists this commerce? Is the country wooded? To what uses can this wood be applied? What are the productions of the land; whether spontaneous, or by cultivation? Would corn thrive at the bay of Antongil?

Answer to ARTICLE XVI.

The character of the natives of Madagascar is the same throughout the island: curious, facile, superficial, superstitious, ambitious, revengeful, voluptuous, hospitable, compassionate, credulous, prodigal; one day sedentary, the next industrious cultivators of the land, and the next warriors. Their principal commerce is with us; but their interior trade consists of exchange of slaves for cattle or rice. The country is well wooded, and the wood may be applied to every imaginable use. The productions of the country are rice, sugar canes, indigo, tobacco, benzoan, incense,

incense, wax, honey, cotton, silk, wood, various pulse and fruit, and a large quantity of horned cattle. From my own trials, I am assured, that bread corn, barley, and oats, prosper at the bay of Antongil.

ARTICLE XVII.

Do the people of Madagascar live in society? Have they a form of government; or are they governed by usage, or follow the simple notions of the law of nature? Have they any religion, or at least a notion of a God? Do they adore him? Are they disposed to submit to the French government, to adopt our police, our usages, and our religion? Are they industrious, diligent, and laborious? Have they any arts and manufactures? Are they curious with regard to the productions of ours? What productions or merchandize are most acceptable to them? Are they imitators? Would it be easy to inspire them with a taste for instruction of every kind?

Answer to ARTICLE XVII.

The Madagascar people live in society, and have a form of government, which is Aristocratical: their laws are traditional; and they have a religion, and adore one God.

Their dispositions, by inclination, attach them to the French; but they are too jealous of their liberty, ever to submit with willingness to a foreign government. They adopt our usages and police; but I cannot venture to affirm any thing respecting a change of religion. The satisfaction of possessing a plurality of wives, is a charm which is too strong for them to think of adopting our religion:

the women seem desirous of embracing it; perhaps for the contrary reason, of having each an husband to herself. They are industrious, docile, and good workmen in metals and wood, such as goldsmiths, blacksmiths, armourers, and carpenters. Their manufactures consist in coverings, or cloths, for the waist, which are made out of the fibres * of the sugar cane, upon the eastern coast, and of silk and cotton, upon the west coast; they are, besides, very desirous of our productions, cloths, brandy, gunpowder, musquets, razors, hatchets, silver toys, mirors, knives, and pewter utensils. They are very fond of Galloon lace; are imitators, and disposed to learn trades.

ARTICLE XVIII.

Do the natives of Madagascar come willingly to settle near us? What is their manner of trading, and the articles exchanged between us and them?

Do the commodities annually imported by the Arabians, on the west part of the island, become dispersed over the whole island, and as far as the bay of Antongil? What are these? Would it be easy for us to extend communications throughout the whole island; and by what means? How and in what manner have the subjects of his Majesty, who formerly traded to this island, been informed of his intention, that such trades should be prohibited in those parts where the Baron de Benyowsky settled? Has any ordonnance been promulgated at the isle of France to this effect? What private vessels have been confiscated by the Baron de

---

* So I translate *Pagnes de Taffia*; perhaps improperly. E.

Benyowsky

Benyowſky to his Majeſty's uſe; and what is the amount of their cargoes?

Anſwer to ARTICLE XVIII.

The Madagaſcar people eſtabliſh their dwellings, by preference, near thoſe of the white men. The articles of exchange in this trade, confiſt of piece goods, brandy, and other merchandizes, mentioned in the preceding article; they furniſh rice, cattle, and ſlaves: they are likewiſe glad to receive piaſtres. The Arabians carry on a confiderable trade with them; but they only receive in exchange for their merchandize, benzoin, incenſe, a ſmall quantity of amber, a large quantity of tortoiſhell and rice: they bring waiſt-cloths from Surat, ſilver bracelets, gold ear rings, gold and ſilver in plates and hatchets, very ill made. The principal trade of the Arabians is with the nation of the Seclaves.

According to the plan of the ſecond principle which I have laid down, the communications from eaſt to weſt may be extended over the whole iſland: this may be done with moderate forces, but the confidence of the chiefs muſt be ſecured, in order that they may furniſh workmen and labourers.

The chiefs of the government of the iſle of France have informed the public of the interdiction of trade, and have promulgated this order upon the iſland. There have been no private veſſels confiſcated ſince my arrival on this iſland; ſeveral have been arreſted, carrying on prohibited trade, but I releaſed them, upon being aſſured that the owners and captains knew nothing of the prohibition. Such were the veſſels La Flore and Le Coureur.

ARTICLE XIX.

What is the most simple, the most certain, and the most advantageous method of trading with Madagascar for rice, cattle, and slaves, which we are in the habit of obtaining from thence? Are slaves plentiful in the country near the bay of Antongil, and upon the eastern coast? Would it be easy to trade in the interior part of the island? But if Government should think proper to establish a colony at Madagascar, would it not be more advantageous to forbear trading in slaves at all?

Answer to ARTICLE XIX.

The most simple, certain, and advantageous method of carrying on the trade of rice, cattle, and slaves, which are usually obtained from Madagascar, is to purchase these articles with ready money; and to open sales, at the storehouses of the established posts, for articles of merchandize, to be paid for in ready money; such, for example, as piece goods, musquets, gunpowder, brandy. In this way the money would return by circulation, which would be sufficient for the purposes of trade, by means of a moderate annual supply, even for the carrying on a very considerable commerce. The inhabitants of the bay of Antongil, being all husbandmen, never sell slaves; but, on the contrary, they make purchases of them every year. The whole of the east coast affords a very small number of slaves: they are brought from the interior parts of the island, from Ovou Antiasnak. The population of Madagascar is very moderate, in proportion to its extent; and in case Government should propose to export more than two thousand blacks annually, the country would soon be depopulated, if the supply were not kept up by the importation of Mozambique slaves, who, under the discipline of the European colonists, would form a particular militia, and by uniting with the Madagascar women, would produce a peculiar race, very proper for the formation of new establishments. It would, doubtless, be necessary to prohibit the trade of Madagascar slaves.

ARTICLE XX.

What may be nearly the total amount of the population of Madagascar, at present? Is the interior part of the island inhabited? Do all these people speak the same language?

Answer to ARTICLE XX.

The total of the population of Madagascar, in its present state, does not exceed two million five hundred thousand males. The interior part of the island is inhabited, and very populous. All the people of Madagascar speak very nearly the same language.

ARTICLE XXI.

What observations has the Baron de Benyowsky made upon that which is called the north part of Madagascar? Is it equally populous, abounding with cattle, and fertile as the southern part? For what reason did the Baron de Benyowsky prefer extending his settlement into the north, rather than towards the south part of the island, which, according to the received opinion, offers more resources

for

for trade, and is likewife better peopled, and more abounding with rice, cattle, and flaves?

Anfwer to ARTICLE XXI.

The obfervations which I have made upon the north part of the ifland of Madagafcar, are, that it abounds in cattle, timber, and rice, and has feveral harbours very well fituated for trading with the coafts of Africa, Surat, Mafcat, Baffora, Moka, and the Arabian iflands. The northern coaft is more fertile than that to the fouthward, and abounds with a greater quantity of cattle.

The reafons upon which I extended my fettlements into the north part of the ifland, are founded upon the affurance, that I fhould trade with people lefs prejudiced againft the French. I have always confidered it to be the intention of the minifter, in fending me to form an eftablifhment, that I fhould civilize the Madagafcar nation, and form alliances with them, by virtue of which the French would enjoy the advantages of commerce, and affiftance in favour of their fettlements in India, in cafe of war; and I have directed my operations accordingly. I cannot, even at this time, think that the intention of his Majefty and his minifter was fuch, as could lead them to expect me to act in any other manner. I have done my duty; and I can venture, on this occafion, gentlemen, to affure you, that my proceedings have been fuch, as would have been adopted and purfued by any other perfon who was jealous of the reputation of his Sovereign, under whom he ferved, and of the nation, whofe arms he had the honour to bear.

ARTICLE

ARTICLE XXII.

What in general are the productions of this immense island; and what are the speculations of trade, and the objects of importation, which might reasonably be attended to without excess, and with that prudence and wisdom which are necessary to prepare and determine the fate of every enterprize?

Answer to ARTICLE XXII.

As a military man, I have considered, that the island of Madagascar, civilized and attached to the interests of France, might have been advantageously recurred to in the construction of vessels, and to supply the other colonies with provisions; that its population being at length augmented, it might become a source of supplies for war; which, being in the neighbourhood of India, and the most extensive possessions of the English and other nations, would serve to keep them in respect. The islanders are accustomed to navigation; might be employed on board merchant vessels; and when, by different voyages, they had become capable of serving as mariners, in the navigation to and from India, and in the Indian seas, they would afford certain and necessary means for the preservation of the Europeans.

With regard to the present trade, it consists of rice, slaves, and cattle, wood in planks, with benzoin; these may now be exported. If in future the European or Mallabar colonists, transported into the island, should exert themselves to profit by the riches which nature presents, several other branches of trade would be opened, such as sugar, indigo,

indigo, tobacco, cotton, filk, wax, &c. The truth concerning Madagafcar, is, that the commerce is real, and fubfifts already; nothing more being wanted but the means of fecuring its extent. The merchant affirms, that his Majefty need only abandon the trade to individuals, and that emulation and exportation will increafe the culture of the land, and encourage the natives of the country; fo that by this means only, fubfiftence and riches will be fecured. He thinks himfelf in the right, but confiders himfelf only, becaufe he is interefted in the duration of his perfonal trade, which may laft a certain number of years, and he cares for nothing further. Speculating reafoners will fay, that it is beft to proceed gently; then the moft difficult enterprizes may be accomplifhed by mildnefs; that, by forming fmall eftablifhments, under favour of the treaties of the merchants and others, we may fucceed in gaining entirely the confidence of the natives; and that by this means the fmall colony will be augmented, and will at length become numerous, and as large as may be wifhed, without fatiguing the ftate by expences, or by any perceptible lofs of men. Thefe reafoners likewife fuppofe themfelves to be in the right. The firft, and the fecond of thefe projects, muft be eftablifhed upon toleration, the event of which is always unfortunate. I therefore leave it to you, gentlemen commiffaries, to decide what part ought to be taken, in thefe circumftances, by a chief to whom an enterprize of this nature was entrufted, and who is fent to form an eftablifhment in the moft convenient manner.

ARTICLE XXIII.

Have any mines of iron, copper, or other metals, been found at the bay of Antongil, or its environs? What are the

the interesting vegetables, or medicinal plants, which may be useful for our islands of France and Bourbon?

Does the country afford wood proper for ship-building, or to be used in dying?

What are the roots and oils of the country? What means are there of establishing to advantage, upon the coast, the fishery of whales, which are abundant in the neighbouring seas?

Answer to ARTICLE XXIII.

Ores of iron and copper are found, at the bay of Antongil; gold dust at the head of Angonaw; silver at Angontzi; crystal at Mananhar. But with respect to vegetables, I cannot venture to make any assertion, on account of my total ignorance of botany.

The country affords wood, very proper for building ships, or for masts of vessels: dying woods likewise grow here; the blacks use them to dye yellow, blue, black, red, green, &c. As to resins, they have arant, detamaca, and vohinata. The blacks make oil from the whale and the manata, or sea cow. The whale fishery will be always disadvantageous on the coast, unless a settlement be formed at St. Mary, sufficiently provided with vessels and men destined to this employ; but I consider a settlement at that place as impossible.

ARTICLE XXIV.

Where are the remarks and observations of the Baron de Benyowsky upon the navigation of the bay of Antongil? Do the south winds prevail here, as at the isle of France? Are they contrary to the passing of vessels out of the bay of Antongil? What time do veffels ufually require to pafs from this bay to fort Dauphin, on the fouthern part of the ifland?

Has the Baron fent perfons by fea to examine the northern part of the ifland of Madagafcar?

Has any fafe harbour been difcovered?

What are the navigable rivers of the ifland, and their fituation?

Is the country fubject to hurricanes or tempefts?

Anfwer to ARTICLE XXIV.

The winds from fouth-eaft to fouth-weft prevail from the month of March to the 15th of September, and fometimes to the end of the month; after which the winds from north-eaft, north-north-weft and weft prevail; but in the bay there is ufually a land and fea breeze, during the courfe of the twenty-four hours: the fea breeze begins to blow at eight, nine, or ten in the morning, and ceafes at fix, feven, or eight in the evening; and at eleven in the evening the land breeze ufually fprings up, by favour of which veffels can almoft always go out of the bay; obferving that, on the firft day after weighing, the iflands of Bats may be doubled, where they may anchor at the fetting in of the fea breeze; or if the pilot is fure of his veffel, he may turn to windward in the bay. In the evening they may again fet fail, and may get out the next day, at a certainty. By the obfervations I have made, in twenty-two voyages, of veffels which have failed out of the bay, none of them required more than four or five days for that purpofe, except the Grand Bourbon, which was three months in getting out, though feveral veffels failed from hence

while

while the commander amused himself in sailing from one side of the harbour to the other. I am ignorant whether this was the fault of the vessel, or of the captain; or whether it was in consequence of certain orders which Mr. Maillart gave him, to execute none of my commissions.

In order to sail to fort Dauphin, it is necessary to take advantage of the winds which blow between September and May. The usual passage, after quitting the bay, is four days. In the contrary season, it takes sometimes twenty-two, or twenty-five days, but no more than six or seven days to return.

I have sent people to explore the island, both to the southward and northward. Two harbours were discovered to the northward, the one at Angontzi, and the other at Voemar. To the southward there is only the anchoring place at Foul Point, and the road of Tamatava. The most considerable river in the north part of the island, is that of Tingballe, upon which the chief settlement is established. It is navigable for small boats, and the boats of the country. Voemar, and Louque to the northward, are likewise navigable for the vessels of the country. This island is exempt from hurricanes.

ARTICLE XXV.

Lastly, what are the reflections of M. the Baron de Benyowsky upon the pernicious influence of the air, during the winter, more especially at the bay of Antongil, and upon the coast? We pray that he will give us a memoir at large, upon this very essential point, which deserves the utmost consideration, on account of its tendency to preserve the lives of his Majesty's subjects.

The experience he has acquired, and the confiderable number of men he has loft at this place, during the three years following the eftablifhment of the fettlement, muft have fixed his ideas as well with regard to the precaution neceffary to be taken, and the means of preferving them.

Do the people who are found on the fea coafts during the healthy feafon, take refuge in the interior part of the ifland during the unhealthy feafon, to avoid the pernicious influence of the air? When they remain on the fea coafts during the unhealthy feafon, do they experience the fame diforders as the Europeans? It is in confequence of thefe confiderations, which are of the greateft importance to the fuccefs of the views that may be entertained by Government, that we demand of M. the Baron de Benyowfky, what inconveniences would arife from the formation of a folid eftablifhment, during the whole year, upon the peninfula of Tamatava;—the country is wholefome, fituated in the centre of the eaftern coaft, where the greateft abundance of rice, cattle, and flaves, may be furnifhed from all parts;—in this cafe, would it not be fufficient to fend, during the healthy feafon, managers of the trade to Foul Point, to the bay of Antongil, and principally to fort Dauphin, and to give the preference to Tamatava, as a place for the chief fettlement?

Moreover, whatever place may appear to the Baron de Benyowfky as deferving the preference to form the eftablifhment of a colony, admitting it to be healthy in itfelf, and during the whole year, we demand to be informed, what would be the forces, the means, and the expences to be made by Government, during the ten firft years, and what

would

would be the advantages which the nation would afterwards derive from thence.

We will carry this queſtion and reaſoning ſtill further. If the miniſter, and chiefs of the adminiſtration of the iſle of France, had acceded to all the demands which the Baron de Benyowſky has made, ſince his arrival in Madagaſcar, whether of men or money, or articles of trade, or any other ſupplies whatever; what advantages would the nation have derived from thence? It has already made efforts, which, for the firſt four years, 1773, 1774, 1775, and 1776, may amount to more than one million five hundred thouſand livres; we demand and requeſt that he will demonſtrate to us, what uſeful purpoſe has been anſwered by the employment of theſe firſt advances, or what ſucceſs in future may be hoped for from the diſburſement of ſuch a conſiderable ſum?

We are well convinced, that no perſon can better fill a charge of ſo delicate a nature than the Baron de Benyowſky; in the performance of which, it is neceſſary that all the qualities which he poſſeſſes ſhould be united, in order to diſcharge the duties, and ſupport the ſettlement, in the manner he has hitherto done. But the experience of the paſt, cannot but have enlightened his courage, and added to the force of his mind: it is from the one and the other of theſe, that we expect that diſplay of true information, which muſt fix the views of Government, the miniſter, and his Majeſty.

At the bay of Antongil, at the iſland of Madagaſcar,
September 20, 1776.

Anſwer

Anfwer to ARTICLE XXV.

Having addreffed to the minifter, conformably to his orders, an extract of my reflections upon the diforders of this country, I have now the honour to prefent a copy (annexed) of the fame to you.

The natives of the ifland ufually pafs the unhealthy feafon in the interior part of the ifland. The people of the interior parts, when they arrive at the fea coaft, are attacked by fevers, as well as the Europeans, but they are exempt from them at a diftance from the coaft. The eftablifhment, formed and concentrated according to my principles, would fuffer the following inconveniences:

The road of Tamatava being dangerous for fhipping, does not offer them the neceffary fhelter, and they would always run great rifks, becaufe the natives of thefe countries, being furrounded by enemies, would foon engage the fettlement in their quarrels. For the eftablifhment being prefent, and interefted in the poffeffion of the neighbouring territories, could not remain neutral; and its declaration in favour of the other fide, would engage the eftablifhment in a war, which could not fail of alienating the minds of their neighbours. Hiavi, firft chief of Foul Point, feeing the preference given to Tamatava, would be one of the firft to excite continual difcords, which would interrupt cultivation, and reduce the fettlement to the want of neceffaries. The Betalimenes, a numerous people at their eafe, and enemies to all the other nations of thefe countries, who are the richeft in flocks of cattle, would no longer dare to approach Tamatava, for fear either of

Fariavas,

Fariavas, or Hiavi. Lastly, the communication with the other posts would be very difficult, the road being overflowed at every new and full moon, by a high sea, and hurricanes, for near six days. Vessels at anchor, which would often be obliged to put out to sea, and would be driven by the current, could not regain the road, in some cases, in less than fifteen days. This circumstance, together with the difficulty of quitting the road, which is always dangerous, renders it absolutely impossible to fix the establishment of the chief settlement at Tamatava. The best that can be done, is to establish a factory, dependant on Foul Point: it would be of advantage, on account of the confluence of the natives, accustomed to the commerce of slaves, cattle, and rice. The salubrity of Tamatava, compared with that of Foul Point, makes no great difference; besides, the commissioners having judged on the one side respecting Tamatava, by themselves, and on the other, by considering my reflections on these subjects, may easily decide respecting this affair.

With regard to that paragraph of the present article, which begins with the words, "Moreover, whatever place "may appear to the Baron de Benyowsky as deserving the "preference," &c. in which the commissaries propose the question, What would be the forces and expences to be furnished by Government, during the first ten years; and afterwards, what would be the advantages which the nation would derive from thence—I have the honour to represent, that, in order to enable me to answer this question, it is necessary that I should have been previously apprized of the final decision of his Majesty, respecting the establishment at Madagascar. If the intention of his Majesty

jesty be, that the entire dominion of this island shall be the fruits of an establishment; or if the views of a general trade should interfere with the plan of the establishment, which by its nature will transform itself into a colony: or, lastly, if the mere subsistence of the isles of France and Bourbon, is to be the profit—Upon the first plan I cannot hazard an opinion; for former examples are sufficient to overthrow every violent enterprize upon the Madagascar nation. Besides which, the treaties and alliances I have formed with this nation, by order of his Majesty, forbids me from infringing them. I shall therefore proceed to the second.

To carry it into execution, as far as my knowledge extends, the following is my answer. If his Majesty, after supplying six hundred men, supported by a recruit of two hundred men at the end of each of the two following years, with permission to chuse husbandmen in the troop, and allowing them to marry with the women of the country, without any restraint on account of religion; and permitting me to import, annually, two hundred foundlings, of the age of twelve or fourteen years, and likewise Malabar and Chinese families from India; in this case, I say, Madagascar would at the end of three years form a colony, which, thus connected with the whole island of Madagascar, would begin to have some value. The expence would not exceed one million per year, except the additional expence of two vessels, one of six hundred, and the other of two hundred tons, fitted out by his Majesty, in order that the charge might not fall upon the colony; and also of six galliots, for the necessary communication of the posts and transports.

This,

COUNT DE BENYOWSKY.

This, then, is the plan of the forces, means, and expences to be made during three years, at the end of which the colony of Madagascar would support itself, and increase by the product of its principal, or united capital of three millions, until the tenth year, at which period it would be found to be a well established colony, sufficiently strong to be in no fear of a sudden revolution, and in a situation to reimburse, by the product of its commerce, the advances which might have been made.

To the paragraph which begins with the words, " We " will carry this question and reasoning still further," &c. I have the honour to reply, that if his Majesty had granted me the supplies which I demanded, and the isle of France had answered my requests, Madagascar *———the cultivation would have been increased, and the different departments of commerce explored, with national advantages. Lastly, the glory of his Majesty, in civilizing a whole nation, would have indemnified the sacrifice: and this nation, reckoned among the number of his allies, would have increased the force of his power.

Messrs. the commissaries, in consequence of information furnished at the isle of France, have valued the sum expended during the four first years, 1773, 1774, 1775, and 1776, at one million five hundred thousand livres. I must entreat them to be pleased to determine the true expences, by inspecting the balance of my account, and make a just comparison of the representation drawn up at the isle of France, by selecting the sums which were

* Here is a blank of one line and a half in the manuscript, which the Count has not filled up.

really employed for the formation of the establishment, and by separating them from those which are either pretended, or exaggerated. Besides this, as I have had the honour to present the receipts to the commissaries, by a former article, I think it unnecessary to repeat the state of the accounts.

Lastly, to shew the utility resulting from the application of the first advances, or what may be the supplies to be hoped for in future, I have the honour to represent to the commissaries, that having always directed my observations to the formation of the settlement, I have rendered it subordinate to the plan of securing the confidence of the natives of the country; and that commerce never entered into my views, but as an accessary, because I considered the national riches to arise from the product of the cultivation of a territory, the property of which I shall secure to Government; that the works which I have executed, to render the spot which I have chosen healthful, were indispensibly necessary, as well as the communication and establishment of the different roads, and enquiries concerning the interior part of the country, to direct the subsequent operations; and moreover, that as all these parts of my operations tend only to the same fixed purpose, which forms the basis of the whole, I admit that the greatest part of these expences will be pure loss, if the minister thinks proper to support the plan of conquering Madagascar; for the only consequence which will result from such an undertaking, will consist in the loss of men and money, uselessly thrown away.

For my own personal justification, and in order that I may have nothing to reproach myself with, I once more repeat

repeat my pressing request to the commissaries, that they will be pleased to read the instructions of the minister respecting my mission, and then I hope they will be convinced, that I have done nothing but what my duty and my zeal required me to do.

After having replied at length to the commissaries' questions, proposed to me by order of his Majesty, I take the liberty to represent to them, that in the present situation of the establishment, and in case his Majesty shall have deferred his final decision respecting the establishment, until the accounts came forward to him, no other means will remain in my power, than to secure the chief place, and its dependencies, by a suitable provision for the subsistence of the troops, which will be necessary, until the receipt of his Majesty's orders, and to suspend all the works whatever, which may occasion expence; and in this position to wait for the period which may determine the fate of the establishment at the bay of Antongil.

At the island of Madagascar, Sept. 22, 1776.

OBSERVATIONS UPON THE DISORDERS

OF THE

ISLAND OF MADAGASCAR.

UPON my arrival on this ifland, by his Majefty's orders, to form a fettlement, the fuccefs of which muft naturally depend on the prefervation of the people, I immediately applied my attention to acquire a perfect knowledge of the diforders of the country, which had been defcribed to me as very dreadful. But after all the enquiries I have made of furgeons, who frequented the ifland of Madagafcar, I find myfelf difappointed in my expectations. Out of fixteen, whom I have confulted, there were not two who agreed refpecting the caufe of the diforder, or the treatment of patients. The object of their voyages having been always that of trade, they embarraffed themfelves very little with this important affair, to which they ought to have paid the moft ferious attention. The informations which, on the other hand, I received from the natives of the country, have not led me to any difcovery concerning the nature of the diforder; though I think myfelf indebted to their method of treatment, which preferved my life, and that of my family.

Time

Time and experience therefore, alone, could give some information, which I have committed to writing, with the hope that my discoveries and observations might engage Government to cause them to be discussed, followed, and authorized, if they should be thought worthy of attention.

Here follow the OBSERVATIONS.

Every European, upon his arrival at Madagascar, who has not resided in hot climates, will be seized by the fevers of the country. The attack is more or less violent, according to the constitution of the individual, and they are retarded more or less, as well as attended with greater or less danger, according to the dryness or moisture of the place of settlement. This observation is grounded on,

1st. That out of three hundred and sixty-seven men, who came to Madagascar under my command, no more than fifty escaped the fevers of the country; and these men had been long inured to hot climates, by a considerable time of residence at Bengal.

2dly. There was no person of a full habit who did not experience burning fevers, followed by ravings, from which most of those who were of a strong constitution were exempt.

3dly. The fevers, after our arrival in 1773 and 1774, made considerable ravages. The men who had newly landed at Louisbourg, which was in the midst of a marsh, scarcely held up six months before they were attacked, and in general fatally. In the year 1775, after the greatest part of the marshes had been drained, the new-comers withstood the action of the climate for seventeen months, and were then attacked with less force. In this situation the sick did not suffer those dreadful ravings, followed by convulsions,

vulsions, and the mortality became essentially less numerous. The following year, 1776, was even more favourable; the fevers were of the usual appearance, and without any dangerous symptoms: I can venture to place them actually in the number of those which all hot and moist climates occasion.

The usual method of treatment adopted by the surgeons, in the fever, at Madagascar, is the following:

As soon as the first violence of the attack is over, they give a dose of emetic (tartar); the following day they give ipecacuanha, and afterwards quinquina and ptisan, until the fifth crisis. The patient at this period usually was in a lethargic drowsiness, and continual delirium, which gave way with difficulty to the application of blisters. Experience has unfortunately shewn that this treatment carried two-thirds of the patients to their grave. It was happy for those whose constitutions were strong enough to withstand this treatment for eight days, because the surgeons, at that period, gave them up to the course of nature, which very often produced better effects.

My own private observations are these:

When the Europeans first land at Madagascar, they have a strong appetite, and devour both animal and vegetable food indiscriminately, at the same time that their drink is nothing but lemonade. They are, besides, exposed to great heat, and breathe a moist air, occasioned by the exhalations of the marshes, and the mists or fogs, which arise from the rivers and woods. In this situation they are subject to continual sweats, which at length weakens the radical moisture, which is so necessary to digestion. Hence arise

arise those indigestions, which are so common in this climate, and produce convulsions on the slightest suppression of transpiration, which at length being dissipated in vapours, produce the most violent head-aches, most commonly attended with a dreadful delirium. The appetite is then lost, and gives place to a continual disposition to vomit, attended with a violent sensation of burning in the brain; the fever succeeds these symptoms, and is more or less violent, according to the constitution of the individual, or the nature of the place. As I found, from experience, that the treatment of the surgeons usually carried the patients to their grave, I availed myself of another method, in my own particular case, and that of my family, which was copied from the method of treatment adopted by the islanders; excepting only that I made use of theriaca to excite sweats, which they bring on by bathing, or by the use of simples, which are produced in the country. The method is as follows:

At the first indication of the head-ache, a dose of theriaca must be administered, and the patient must be kept warm, in a room with a fire in it, in order to re-establish the transpiration. The next day bleed in the foot, and on the third day purge with pure manna: afterwards the patient must every evening take a dose of confection of hyacinth, or some other cordial, and during the continuance of the disorder no other nourishment is to be given to the patient but soup and fresh eggs. It is to this simple treatment that I am indebted for my own life, and for the lives of most of those who have had the honour to serve his Majesty in this colony.

REMARKS on the means which I apprehend to be the moſt proper to prevent, and even to extirpate entirely, the diſorders to which the Europeans are ſubject in this country.

Firſt, the uſe of boiled fleſh muſt be entirely forbidden to all who have recently arrived; and their nouriſhment muſt be confined to ſoup and roaſt meat, with rice. It is likewiſe proper to forbid them the uſe of lemons, and to ſubſtitute vinegar in their ſtead. An allowance of ſome ſtrong liquor ought to be diſtributed morning and evening to every ſoldier, or workman, for the three firſt years, in order to preſerve them from the bad air occaſioned by the vapours of the marſhes, and the fogs which ariſe from the rivers and the woods.

Care muſt be taken to elevate the houſes in which they reſide, in order that the circulation of air may be facilitated. Fire-places, likewiſe, ſhould be built in them, to rarify the internal air, particularly during the night, when it is uſually moiſt and cold.

The reſt of the marſhes near the ſettlements ought to be drained: this buſineſs is already done in part, and the reſt may ſoon be finiſhed, provided Government ſhall think proper to make the neceſſary exertions and expence.

The places where poſts or villages are propoſed to be eſtabliſhed, within the iſland, ought to be at a diſtance from the rice plantations; and the places ought to be cleared ſix months before they are inhabited, that the putrid exhalations, which I have obſerved to abound upon newly cleared lands, may have time to diſſipate.

Experience has ſhewn me, that the time of planting was the ſickly ſeaſon; and likewiſe that the poſts eſtabliſhed in the

the uncleared woods, enjoyed a wholefome air, and were not attacked with fevers.

The men ought not to be employed in the works, until the fun has diffipated the vapours and fogs, which arife from the marfhes; for the heat is lefs pernicious than the morning exhalations.

The cultivation of red rice, which grows only in the marfhes, ought to be abolifhed throughout Madagafcar. The iflanders, in order to procure this grain with lefs trouble, make cuts in the month of December, which convey the water into the ground they defign to plant. They keep the ground under water, until it has acquired the confiftence of a bog, at which time they turn in a flock of cattle, to divide the foil by their feet, after which they fow the rice. It fhoots up in a very fhort time, and is again covered with water as foon as it is in the blade; which water they leave to evaporate fpontaneoufly. In many parts of the ifland they fave themfelves the trouble of digging canals, and making banks round the fields, by entirely damming up the rivers, and caufing them by that means to overflow their grounds. This is a very common circumftance upon the coaft; it is not, therefore, unworthy of credit, that this method of cultivation may be enough to poifon a whole country, and that the falubrity would be reftored by abolifhing it. It may be objected, that, by depriving the inhabitants of this method of cultivation, a great part of their productions would be taken away; but thofe who make this objection, know very little of Madagafcar, becaufe the cultivation of red rice amounts, at the utmoft, to no more than one-fourth of their whole product;

product; and the other three-fourths of white rice does not grow in the marshes, but upon the high grounds. And could not this loss be made up, by introducing the cultivation of wheat, and the use of the plough?

From my own experience, I am convinced that corn, barley, and oats, will thrive perfectly well here, and more especially maize.

REFLECTIONS

UPON THE

PROJECT OF A COLONY AT MADAGASCAR,

IN CASE ANY POWER SHOULD ADOPT

THE SYSTEM OF CIVILIZATION,

FOUNDED ON THE

BASIS OF AN ALLIANCE.

AN ESTIMATE OF THE IMPORTATION OF MEN, AND OF THE POPULATION.

AS the colony of Madagascar may be established in ten years, by means of an advance of three millions of livres; it will have consumed near eighteen hundred men during these ten years, supposing that seven hundred and twenty military were sent the first year; two hundred men for each of the two following years; one hundred and fifty for each of the seven following years; and that during the whole ten years, one year with another, there be imported one hundred and twenty European husbandmen, thirty creoles, and

and fifty natives, either of India, China, or from the coast of Malabar. The whole importation will amount to four thousand one hundred and seventy men: this number will annually produce six hundred children, the total of which, at the end of the tenth year, will amount to six thousand creoles, and three thousand three hundred and seventy Europeans; a sufficient number to fix the epoch of a colony.

COMMERCE.

Madagascar, in its present state, can consume three hundred thousand pieces of cloth, three thousand casks of brandy, at twenty-five veltes, twenty thousand musquets, one hundred and sixty thousand pounds of gunpowder, six hundred thousand knives, one hundred thousand looking glasses, fifteen thousand pieces of handkerchiefs, five thousand pieces of chintz, patnas, ginghams, &c. a large quantity of pottery, instruments, and tools of copper, iron, and tin; slight cloths of gold and silver, fine cloths, galloons, gold and silver laces; and this trade must produce to me, during the first and second year, a profit of one million four hundred and sixty-nine thousand pounds, all expences deducted, which in French money amounts to seven million eight hundred and sixty-nine thousand seven hundred and fifty livres.

In exchange for these merchandizes, the articles received will be skins, timber, and dying woods; gums, wax, honey, &c. And this trade of barter will in a short time increase, by affording coffee, indigo, sugar, pepper, and silk; and in the mean time, the advantage of one hundred per cent. will be constantly gained on the exchange of the value of

seven

COUNT de BENYOWSKY. 349

seven million eight hundred and sixty-nine thousand seven hundred and fifty livres. The property of these first merchandizes will open branches of commerce with Mozambique, Mascat, Baffora, and Surat; and these last imports will be always valuable in Europe, especially the indigo, which is of the best kind and quality. In a word, Madagascar, with her own productions, joined to assortments of those of Europe, will carry on the most advantageous trade to all the parts beyond the Cape, and will support her connection with Europe by virtue of her own productions.

REVENUES of the STATE.

The principal settlement of Madagascar will receive, during the first year, the revenue of the different provinces, consisting of four thousand oxen, one million three hundred thousand pounds of rice, two hundred and fifty thousand madriers or thick planks, fifteen thousand planks, and one hundred and eighty boats of the country; the whole valued at four hundred and thirty-eight thousand livres. This tribute will necessarily augment, as the peopling and cultivation of the land shall increase; so that it may, without any exaggeration, be set down at one million three hundred and sixty thousand livres for the third year.

INCREASE of the CULTIVATION by the COLONISTS and EUROPEANS.

This establishment, after the third year, will have formed one hundred and fifty European habitations, and the people will supply sixteen million pounds of sugar, five hundred thousand pounds of coffee, six million pounds of
tobacco,

tobacco, five hundred thousand pounds of cotton, and five million pounds of grain; one-tenth of which, passing into the public treasury, will amount to three hundred and five thousand livres. From the third to the tenth year, these habitations will increase, and consequently the product will be more considerable, especially when manufactories of cotton and silk shall have been established.

Every power allied to Madagascar will, moreover, enjoy the superior advantage, that, instead of exporting specie to India, to pass in the course of circulation into the hands of their rivals, they may purchase the necessary merchandize of their friends and allies, in exchange for the products of their own industry.

MINES.

The Island of Madagascar, abounding with mines of iron and copper, and having plenty of wood, offers likewise the advantage of furnishing these articles for the trade to India, the Persian Gulph, and the Red Sea.

MARINE AND NAVIGATION.

As Madagascar abounds with the best kind of wood for building, and affords resins and hemp of her own growth, and moreover possesses the advantage of excellent harbours, it offers every convenience for ship building. The islanders are very much disposed to navigation, and are accustomed to the sea by their own coasting trade; they will therefore be of the greatest service, after the first year, on board trading vessels in the Indian seas; and when become more skilful, they may be employed on board the King's ships.

There

There is no one that will not readily perceive the confiderable advantage of this circumstance, as well in the preservation of the European sailors, as in the facility of completing the crews of fleets of men of war, which are often under the necessity of abandoning their enterprizes for want of men. The island of Madagascar will, in a word, afford an asylum for shipping, will become a place of building and fitting out, and will be the general magazine for the subsistence of the fleets, and possessions of its protectors, beyond the Cape of Good Hope.

The STATE of DEFENSIVE WAR.

The extent of the island of Madagascar does not require a mass of fortifications of the first order: the first posts may be defended by simple works, intended only to cover the inhabitants from an unexpected landing. An enemy never can land so large a number as to drive them out of the country. I will even take upon me to say, that, at the tenth year after the formation of the establishment, the greatest forces which may be sent, will be unable to maintain their footing in any part of the island; and the result of their enterprizes will, in the end, be always reduced to considerable expences and loss.

I will take upon me to affirm, positively, that the island of Madagascar, after the expiration of the third year, will keep on foot upwards of twenty thousand fighting men, of infantry, well regulated and disciplined; and these twenty thousand men, led on by intelligent officers, will greatly exceed in force the small number of fatigued and exhausted Europeans, which might be sent to attack them. The experience I have acquired in this island, has convinced me, that the natives of Madagascar are as eminent for good principles and valour, when free, as they are for timidity and baseness when reduced to slavery.

The Madagascar people are naturally disposed in favour of the Europeans, and attach themselves to us with sincerity. If they are convinced, that by alliances they can secure equality of conditions, and the possession of their property, it will soon be seen that these islanders, confounded among the new inhabitants, will form but one people.

To obviate the objection which might be made, that all the different attempts to form establishments upon this island, for the course of a century past, have been attended with the most unhappy consequences, and that the present establishment upon the island might run the same risk; I answer, that the settlement will have nothing to fear, as long as the national chief maintains the prohibition of the slave trade; and that the Europeans, on their arrival, do not themselves raise disturbances, but endeavour to preserve the people from slavery. I have examined the conduct of the French officers, who were formerly entrusted with the conduct of the different enterprizes upon this island, and I am convinced that their avidity led them to injustice and oppression, which was the source of the misfortunes, that ended in the destruction of the ancient establishments. They were usurpers, and tyrants; who, with a view to increase their private fortunes, did not blush to attack the liberty of a people, to whom they ought to have been bound by the ties of gratitude.

The STATE of OFFENSIVE WAR.

The ifland of Madagafcar will victual the fquadrons of the power to whom fhe fhall be attached; will furnifh failors, who will ferve better in hot climates than Europeans; and will likewife afford men to be employed in the military fervice, as light troops. This people being able to fubfift upon rice and beef, the natural product of their ifland, will be lefs expenfive in their fubfiftence; and being inured to hot climates, they will be more able to fupport fatigue in the temperature of India.

Thofe who have ferved in India, inform us that the Englifh furpafs the French, by the number of Indians they keep in pay. But will any one prefume to make a comparifon between thofe feeble Indians, who have no idea of glory, and the free people of Madagafcar, led by affection and attachment to fupport the caufe of their allies, who have become their brothers and friends?—I can confidently predict, that the decided fuperiority which any power may acquire in India, will depend upon its connection with the ifland of Madagafcar.

ововорного# SUPPLEMENT,

TO

SERVE AS A SEQUEL

TO THE

MEMOIRS CONCERNING MADAGASCAR.

THE FAITH OF THE MADAGASCAR NATION.

THE Madagafcar nation believes in a Supreme Being, whom they call Zanhare, which denotes Creator of all things. They honour and revere this Being, but have dedicated no temple to him, and much lefs have they fubftituted idols. They make facrifices, by killing oxen and fheep, and they addrefs all thefe libations to God. It has been afferted, that this nation likewife makes offerings to the Devil; but in this there is a deception, for the piece of the facrificed beaft, which is ufually thrown into the fire, is not intended in honour of the Devil, as is ufually pretended. This cuftom is very ancient, and no one can tell the true reafon of it. With regard to the immortality of the foul, the Madagafcar people are perfuaded, that, after their death, their fpirit will return again to the region in which Zanhare dwells; but they by no means admit

that

that the spirit of man, after his death, can suffer any evil. As to the distinction of evil, or good, they are persuaded that the good and upright man shall be recompensed, in this life, by a good state of health, the constancy of his friends, the increase of his fortunes, the obedience of his children, and the happiness of beholding the prosperity of his family: and they believe that the wicked man's fate shall be the contrary to this. The Madagascar people, upon this conviction, when they make oaths, add benedictions in favour of those who keep them, and curses against those who break them. In this manner it is that they appeal to the judgment of Zanhare, in making agreements; and it has never been known, or heard of, that a native of Madagascar has broken his oath, provided it was made in the usual manner, which they say was prescribed by their forefathers.

Distinction of Kings, and Orders, which form the Government of the Country.

The Madagascar people have always acknowledged the line of Ramini, as that to which the rights of Ampansacabe, or Sovereign, belongs. They have considered this line as extinct, since the death of Dian Ramini Larizon, which happened sixty-six years ago, and whose body was buried upon a mountain, out of which the river Manangourou springs; but having acknowledged the heir of this line, on the female side, they re-established this title in the year 1776. The right of the Ampansacabe consists, in nominating the Rohandrians to assist in the cabars, at which all those who are cited are bound to appear, and the judgment of the Ampansacabe, in his cabar, is decisive. Another prerogative

prerogative of the Ampanſacabe is, that each Rohandrian is obliged to leave him, by will, a certain proportion of his property, which the ſucceſſors uſually purchaſe by a ſlight tribute, or fine. Thirdly, the Ampanſacabe has a right to exact from each Rohandrian, one tenth of the produce of his land, and a number of horned cattle and ſlaves, in proportion to the riches of the country poſſeſſed by each Rohandrian.

The ſecond order is compoſed of the Rohandrians, or Princes. Since the loſs of the Ampanſacabe, three of theſe Rohandrians have aſſumed the title of Kings—namely, the Rohandrian of the province of Mahavelou, named Hiavi; of the province of Voemar, named Lambouin; and the third at Bombetoki, named Cimanounpou.

The third order conſiſts of the Voadziri, or lords of a diſtrict, compoſed of ſeveral villages.

The fourth order conſiſts of the Lohavohits, or chiefs of villages.

The fifth order, Ondzatzi, who are freemen, and compoſe the attendants or followers of the Rohandrians, Voadziri, or Lohavohits.

The ſixth order conſiſts of Ombiaſſes, or learned men; and this order forms the warriors, workmen, phyſicians, and diviners: theſe laſt poſſeſs no charge.

The ſeventh order conſiſts of Ampurias, or ſlaves.

Having made enquiries from Bombetoki paſſing to the northward, and as far as Itapere, the reſult proved, that there are thirty-eight Rohandrians actually reigning, and two hundred and eighty-ſeven Voadziri. With reſpect to the Lohavohits, Ondzatzi, and Obiaſſes, it was not poſſible to obtain any accurate determination of their number.

These orders preserve a regular gradation, respecting which it would be very difficult to give a detailed account. They live in the manner we read of concerning the ancient patriarchs. Every father of a family is priest and judge in his own house, though he depends upon the Lohavohits, who superintend his conduct. This last is answerable to his Voadziri, and the Voadziri to the Rohandrian.

THE CONVENIENCES OF LIFE, AND THE STATE OF THE WEATHER.

The natives of Madagascar subsist on their flocks of oxen, sheep, and goats, which they maintain, together with poultry, of which they keep a vast quantity. Their houses are constructed of wood, but are very convenient, and wonderfully neat within-side. Their villages are surrounded with pallisades and ditches, and the habitations of the Rohandrians are well fortified and defended by cannon. They have *   and slaves; they cultivate the earth with industry, and it affords rice, millet, maize, and pulse, in large quantities: the soil likewise produces sugar, tobacco, indigo, coffee, and pepper; and the land is not sold, but given away. Erections of buildings cost nothing more than the trouble of fetching the wood. Fish and game are to be had for catching. The people of Madagascar have no reason to fear wild beasts, or venomous creatures, as there are none upon the island. Cold weather, frost, and snow, are unknown to them; and the hot weather is less troublesome here, than upon the islands which

* Blank in the Manuscript.

lie in the torrid zone, becaufe the nights are coo', and the heat of the day lafts only from nine to three, during which time the fea breeze prevails, and cools the air to fuch a degree, that it is feldom inconvenient. This heat lafts only four months, and during the reft of the year, one continued fpring prevails.

The Madagafcar people, having no communication with the main land of Æthiopia, have not altered their primitive laws; and the language throughout the whole extent of the ifland is the fame. It would be a rafh attempt to determine the origin of this nation; it is certain that it confifts of three diftinct races, who have for ages paft formed intermixtures, which vary to infinity. The firft race is that of Zafe Ibrahim, or defcendants of Abraham; but they have no veftige of Judaifm, except circumcifion, and fome names, fuch as Ifaac, Reuben, Jacob, &c. This race is of a brown colour. The fecond race is that of Zaferamini: with refpect to this, fome books, which are ftill extant among the Ombiafies, affirm, that it is not more than fix centuries fince their arrival at Madagafcar; and as it is the only one concerning which I have met with any accounts, I fhall proceed to give a fhort extract from that of the natives. With refpect to the third race of Zafe Canambou, it is of Arabian extraction, and arrived, much more lately than the others, from the coafts of Æthiopia: hence it poffeffes neither power nor credit, and fills only the charges of writers, hiftorians, poets, &c.

The Origin of Zaferamini. Translated from the Book Fassiri.

Rahimini, father of Imina, the mother of Mahomet, had two sons, the elder of whom was named Ramini, and was a great prophet. He went to seek Mahomet, at Mecca, and Mahomet was astonished at the wisdom of Ramini; but as Ramini would not eat the flesh of beasts, unless he had himself cut the throat of the animal, he irritated the disciples of Mahomet, who intended to spill his blood, because he proposed to introduce a new custom. But Mahomet, inspired by God, prevented the blood of the prophet from being spilled, and permitted him to cut the throats of the beasts he eat; and some time afterwards gave him one of his daughters, named Farafatema, in marriage. Ramini went with his wife, his disciples, and slaves, to Mongalor, where he lived the rest of his life, and was an Ampanfaca. He had a son, named Rehaurorud, and a daughter Ramini, who married together, and had two sons, the elder of whom was Rahadzi, and the younger Racovatzi. Rahadzi succeeded his father, and was King of Mangalor. Rahadzi being desirous of seeing his native country, and visiting the tombs of his ancestors, at Palmir, equipped two vessels for the voyage; and, as he had not any children, he gave orders that, in case of his death, his brother should be chosen Ampanfaca in his place: but he was scarcely arrived, before a great man, named Ambouhor, inspired Racovatzi with the design of assuming the title of King, and governing the country. Racovatzi, being naturally ambitious, convened

convened the great men, and declared that his brother was not gone to visit the tombs of his fathers, but to make an act of the profession of the law of Mahomet. Under this pretext he succeeded in his election; and out of all the great men, there remained only one, of the name of Amboulmasse, faithful to Rahadzi, who followed his master to Palmir, where he informed him of the sad news of his brother's transaction. Rahadzi, seeing himself thus dethroned, took the resolution of proceeding to an unknown land; and after sailing three whole months with his ships, he arrived at the island of Comorro, which he found inhabited; and from whence he passed to Malacass, and landed at Manghabey, where he was friendly received by the great men of the country. He married the daughter of a King, by whom he had two children, the elder of which, by his wisdom and the spirit of God, was chosen Ampansacabe. This King, whose name was Ramini Azoringhetzi, had several children, amongst whom he divided the provinces; but as they made war one against the other, the Rohandrians, governors of the said provinces, declared themselves Princes and Sovereigns of the country, and massacred the children of their Ampansacabe, except Ramini Mamere, who was then at the breast. It was to this Ramini Mamere that they preserved the title of Ampansacabe; and the following are his descendants:—his son Ramini Olive, from whom, in a regular series, issued Ramini Rohamado; Ramini Ragomin; Ramini Savatto; Ramini Panghare; Ramini Boamasse; Ramini Pangharzasse; Ramini Bohitz; Ramini Missava; Ramini Ravohe; Ramini Nong; Ramini Arive.

The

The Ampanfaca Arive had four sons; one legitimate, and three by his concubines. Ramini Benoule was the Ampanfacabe by inheritance; the three others were Dian Maninpele, Dian Tzianban, and Dian Raval. These three conspired against their elder brother, and slew him; and as he had only one daughter, they availed themselves of the confusion to erect themselves into Rohandrians, and established themselves in the southern part of Malacasse; for the northern provinces, being determined to revenge the death of their Ampanfacabe, made war upon them, and drove them out. The daughter of Ramini Benoule, married Dian Mihale, Rohandrian of the provinces of Mananghar, Antivoiezow, Antinokol, Antivohibey, Antimaroa, and these provinces elected and acknowledged Dian Mihale for their Ampanfabe, giving him the name of Ramini Mihale. Ramini Mihale had a son, who succeeded him; and his immediate descendants were Ramini Lubeton; Ramini Cievi; Ramini Lontazou; Ramini Refidzimon; Ramini Ravalou; and Ramini Larizon, the last of this second race of Ramini: he was slain in a war with the Rohandrian Milouzou, of Mahavelou, who was assisted by the French. The Rohandrian Milouzou slew the two sons of Ramini Larizon upon his tomb, and preserved only his daughter, whom he sold to a Dutch merchant, who carried her beyond sea. At the death of King Larizon, the title of Ampanfacabe remained extinct.

The descendants of Dian Maninpele, Dian Tzianban, and Dian Raval, who were settled at Mananzari, Itapoule, and Matatana, received the French alternately in their dominions, and were extirminated by them, except the line Tzerone, who avenged his family by a general massacre of all the French in the country. Thus far proceeds the detail of the Faffiri, a book which the Ombiafles, of the race of Zafleeanimanbou, have compofed; but as it is neceflary to bring it down to our time, the following may be added:

In the year 1776, the Rohandrians Voadziri, and Lohavohits, were perfuaded, that they had found a defcendant of the daughter of Ramini Larizon, upon whom they conferred the charge of Ampanfacabe, and entered into the oath of blood with him.

THE ARTS AND TRADES OF MADAGASCAR.

The Madagafcar nation being in want only of the neceffaries of life, have not applied themfelves to the invention of fo many arts and trades as are become indifpenfible in Europe. They are contented with fuch as are neceflary to make their moveables, tools, utenfils, and arms for defence; to conftruct their dwellings, and the boats, which are neceflary for their navigation: and laftly, to fabricate cloths and ftuffs for their cloathing. They are defirous only of poffefling the neceflary fupplies of immediate utility and convenience.

The principal and moft refpected bufinefs, is the manufacture of iron and fteel. The artifts in this way call themfelves Ampanefa vihe. They are very expert in fufing the ore, and forging utenfils, fuch as hatchets, hammers, anvils, knives, fpades, fagayes, razors, pincers, or tweezers for pulling out the hair, &c.

The fecond clafs confifts of the Goldfmiths, Ompanefa vola mena: they caft gold in ingots, and make up bracelets, buckles, ear-rings, drops, rings, &c.

The third are called Ompavillanga, and are Potters.

The fourth are the Ompanevatta, or Turners in wood, who make boxes called vatta, plates, wooden and horn spoons, bee-hives, coffins, &c.

The fifth, Ompan cacafou, or Carpenters. They are very expert in this bufinefs, and make ufe of the rule, the plane, the compaffes, &c.

The fixth are the Ompaniavi, or Rope-makers. They make their ropes of different kinds of bark of trees, and likewife of hemp.

The feventh, Ampan lamba, or Weavers. This bufinefs is performed by women only, and it would be reckoned difgraceful in a man to exercife it.

The Ombiaffes are the Literary men and Phyficians, who give advice only.

The Herauvitz are Comedians and Dancers.

Their DWELLING PLACES and BUILDINGS.

The Madagafcar people always live in fociety; that is to fay, in towns and villages. The towns are furrounded by a ditch and pallifades, at the extremities of which a guard of from twelve to twenty armed men is kept. The houfes of private people confift of a convenient cottage, furrounded by feveral fmall ones: the mafter of the houfe dwells in the largeft, and his women, or flaves, lodge in the fmaller. Thefe houfes are built of wood, covered with leaves of the palm-tree, or ftraw.

The houfes of the great men of the country are very fpacious; each houfe is compofed of two walls, and four apartments: round about the principal houfe, other fmaller habitations are built, for the accommodation of the women, and the whole family of the chief; but the slaves cannot pass the night within them. Most of the houses inhabited by the Rohandrians, are built with taste, and admirable symmetry.

Here ends the THIRD VOLUME, according to the division made by the COUNT; and in this place he has written the following in French.

"End of the THIRD and LAST VOLUME," with his cypher, or abridged signature, annexed; and underneath

"I, the undersigned, do certify, that the present work, drawn out in three "volumes, in twelve quires, is the true original."

Signed,

"MAURICE AUGUSTE Cte DE BENYOWSKY.

COPIES

(365)

COPIES

OF THE

MINISTERIAL LETTERS OF FRANCE,

OF

THE OATH OF THE MADAGASCAR NATION

TO THE

COUNT DE BENYOWSKY:

HIS ELECTION TO THE DIGNITY OF AMPANSACABE, HIS FULL POWER TO TREAT IN EUROPE, HIS DECLARATION MADE IN ENGLAND, AND HIS PROPOSALS TO THE ENGLISH GOVERNMENT.

Colonies. India Office.

Copy of the principal piece relating to the expedition to Madagascar.

Versailles, March 19, 1773.

SIR,

THE King, by attaching you to his service, is desirous of putting it in your power to give proofs of your zeal: in consequence of this disposition, his Majesty has made choice of you to form an establishment at Madagascar, which

which appears to him to be absolutely necessary, to procure the requisite supplies to the isle of France. This establishment may be productive of consequences of still greater moment, and more worthy of that zeal which animates you for the glory of the King. I cannot do better, in order to inform you of his Majesty's views, than to send you a copy of a letter, which I wrote by his order, to the Chevalier de Ternay and Maillart. It contains the instructions conformably to which you are to act. The correspondence which you will maintain with Messrs. De Ternay and Maillart, respecting the details of your operations, must not dispense you from rendering me a direct account of every step you may take for the success of the important and honourable mission his Majesty has been pleased to entrust to your care; and I beg that you will inform me of every thing relating thereto. I have the honour to be, very sincerely,

SIR,

Your most humble,

and most obedient servant,

To M. the Baron de Benyowsky.

DE BOYNES.

Copy

Colonies. India Of-
fice.

Nº E×E. Expedition
to Madagascar.

Copy of a Letter from M. *De Boynes to*
Messrs. *De Ternay and Maillart, dated*
March 19, 1773.

YOU are acquainted, gentlemen, with the project which Mr. De Maudave caused to be adopted in 1767, of forming a colony of Europeans at Madagascar, to civilize the inhabitants of that island, and accustom them to our manners and usages. It was soon perceived that this establishment was founded on false principles, and it was given up on account of the impossibility of affording the advances of every kind, which M. De Maudave required in favour of the new colonists.

Notwithstanding the bad success of this attempt, it cannot be disputed that the island of Madagascar contains very great resources, and that it would be useful to have an establishment there; but instead of a colony, the sight of which would too openly offend the rights of property, to be received with pleasure by a people composed of herdsmen and cultivators of the ground, nothing more ought to be attempted than a simple post, in favour of which, useful connections might be formed with the chiefs of the country, with whom a trade might be carried on in the way of barter, that would put an end to the abuse of purchasing with money. It will depend upon the abilities of the person to whom the care of this enterprize may be entrusted, to extend

tend his connections into the internal parts of the island, by which new branches of trade may be opened; and it is from his prudent conduct that we may hope to arrive at the end proposed by M. De Maudave, and form a colony so much the more firmly established, as it will be founded on the interest of the islanders themselves, and the confidence they may have been inspired with. Lastly, while our views are confined to the carrying on a trade, as has hitherto been done, by dismissing every idea of dominion and sovereignty, it will always be of importance to have a fixed post to direct the operations of individuals, and maintain a just balance between them and the natives of the country. No person has appeared more capable of carrying his Majesty's intentions into effect, than M. Baron de Benyowsky. In the course of his travels by sea, he has learned the manner of treating with savage people; and to a great share of firmness, he has joined that mildness of character, which suits a design of this nature.

It is therefore the King's intention to send him to Madagascar, with the forces over which he has given him the command; leaving him at liberty to chuse the most convenient place for the establishment which his Majesty has determined to form.

His Majesty excepts only fort Dauphin, notwithstanding the salubrity of the air, because this part of the island is very dry, and possesses no commercial resources. It is pretended, that Tamatava, on the east coast, is the most proper place for an establishment; as well on account of the goodness of the harbour, as the disposition of the inhabitants; together with the fertility of the soil, and the supplies of every kind which it affords. M. De Benyowsky will himself judge of these

these advantages; but in the uncertainty of the place where he may think proper to fix himself, it is indifpenfibly neceffary that he fhould have a fmall veffel, to run along the coaft, and make every neceffary fearch for infuring the fuccefs of the eftablifhment he is charged to form. It is with this view that his Majefty has purchafed the brigantine the Poftillion, which may be employed in tranfporting part of M. De Benyowfky's people to Madagafcar, and may afterwards remain fubject to his orders, with the Sieur Saunier. This officer has made feveral voyages to Madagafcar, and is therefore qualified to affift the operations of M. De Benyowfky.

As to the reft, M. De Benyowfky will find every other affiftance he may want, in his troops: they have been felected with the greateft care; are all ftrong and robuft young men, of different trades, in order that M. De Benyowfky may not find any embarraffment in the works he may undertake. On the other hand, I have given orders to forward to you, tents as well for the officers as for the foldiers, that they may encamp wherever M. De Benyowfky may think proper, without injuring the inhabitants. M. De Benyowfky will employ the geographical engineer, who accompanies him, to make exact plans of the coaft, with the courfes of rivers, and maps of fuch interior parts of the ifland as he may have accefs to. The King has likewife appointed a furgeon, for the treatment of the fick, to whom M. Maillart may give an affiftant; fo that there will be no other perfons wanting, but an officer of Adminiftration, a ftorekeeper, a treafurer for the order and management of expences, and an almoner for fpiritual fervice.

From the character which has been received of M. De Maisonville, he has been chosen to accompany M. De Benyowsky, and perform the functions of commissary; and his Majesty has been pleased, on this consideration, to grant him the brevet of sub-commissary. His Majesty refers the choice of a treasurer and storekeeper to M. Maillart, and that of almoner to the apostolical prefect. M. Maillart will consider, whether one person may not have the charge of the cash and the stores.

Such is the plan, according to which the operations of M. De Benyowsky are to be conducted. It will occasion no extraordinary expence to the King, and will produce a real assistance to the isle of France, as the troops of M. De Benyowsky may be maintained much more easily and cheaply at Madagascar, than on the isle of France. As soon as M. De Benyowsky shall arrive in the colony, the Chevalier de Ternay shall supply him with recruits, which are designed for him, according to the lists drawn out at their embarkation, to be formed into a new troop, which M. De Benyowsky shall exercise; and you will be pleased afterwards to give him, upon his request, the necessary orders for transporting them to Madagascar, and disembarking them at the place which shall be determined upon by M. De Benyowsky.

Notwithstanding the necessity of abstaining, with the greatest care, from every attack upon the inhabitants of Madagascar; and though the express orders of M. De Benyowsky are to employ no other means with regard to them, but those of mildness and negociation, and to maintain his people in the most exact discipline; yet it would not be prudent to expose him in the midst of those islanders,

who

who are jealous of their liberty, and naturally reftlefs and fufpicious, without putting it in his power to repel any act of violence on their part.

The forces he may be fupplied with, may likewife enable him to gain, with greater facility, the confidence and friendfhip of fuch chiefs as may have occafion to require his affiftance in their own domeftick quarrels.

He demands twelve pieces of cannon, fix twelve-pounders, four eight-pounders, fix pateraroes and two fmall mortars, with their bombs; five hundred granades, three barrels of gunpowder, one of battle powder, five hundred pounds weight of fulphur, and the fame quantity of faltpetre, with four thoufand weight of lead, and moulds for making bullets. You will fee whether it be practicable, in the prefent fituation of your ftores, to deliver thefe articles to him. Some of thefe may be employed in his trade with the natives; and it would be of advantage that you fhould add, with the fame intention, other articles equally fought after by the inhabitants of Madagafcar, fuch as mufquets, piftols, hatchets, nails, bars of iron, copper, fome pieces of cloth; and, in general, every thing fuitable to the trade. M. De Benyowfky will require, for his own ufe, a fet of carpenter's and cabinet-maker's tools. The ftorekeeper, whom M. Maillart may chufe, fhall charge himfelf with all thefe effects, and account for them in the ufual form.

As it may be prefumed, that it will be near the bad feafon of the year when M. De Benyowfky and his people may arrive at Madagafcar, it will be of confequence to provide for the fubfiftence and payment of his troops, during the time in which they can hold no communication with the ifle of France; M. Maillart will therefore remit a fufficient fum to the treafurer for fix months pay, and provide the ftorekeeper with wine and brandy for the fame time; together with flour, and falt provifions, for three months only, becaufe refources of this laft kind will not be wanting at Madagafcar, as foon as they fhall have fixed their eftablifhment. Other articles of confumption may be afforded from the magazine, according to the tarif which you may draw up before the departure of M. De Benyowfky.

If this expedition be attended with the fuccefs, which there is reafon to expect from the zeal and intelligence of M. De Benyowfky, it will procure very plentiful fupplies to the ifle of France; taking care, neverthelefs, to prevent the fhips of private traders from approaching that point of the ifland where M. De Benyowfky fhall have fettled, and to fend only fuch veffels as are appointed to fetch the flaves and cattle, collected in confequence of the trade carried on on the King's account; and, at the fame time, without fuffering the officers who command thefe veffels to carry any private trade. The orders of M. De Benyowfky are pofitive in this refpect, and he is charged to fee them put ftrictly into execution. By this means, the augmentation of price, which is produced by the concurrence of veffels, will be prevented, and an end will be put to the pernicious abufe of paying in money, by feizing thofe times when the iflanders are in want of our merchandizes, which cannot be done by private veffels that fail along the coaft, and aim at little more than to cover the expences of fitting out.

M. De Maifonville being empowered, in quality of Commiffary, to direct all the operations of the commercial intercourfe tercourse upon the King's account, at the place where M. De Benyowsky may settle, it is of importance that he should have with him a trusty person under his orders, with two interpreters, who may serve at the same time in the negociations which M. De Benyowsky may enter into with the chiefs of the country.

M. De Maillart will please to be no less careful in the choice of these persons, than of the others, whose nomination have been left to him; because their influence may equally affect the success of the views I have explained.

Of all the means which could be imagined to procure the necessary supplies to the isle of France, which are wanting to increase its cultivation and insure its subsistence, there are certainly none better adapted to the purpose, and at the same time less chargeable to the King; and his Majesty depends upon your seconding the efforts of M. De Benyowsky with the greater earnestness, from the reflection, that if the continual residence at Madagascar should effect a happy revolution in the minds and manners of its inhabitants; and if success should follow the attempt to inspire them with a taste for our productions, our works, and our manufactures, a market will be formed at the isle of France for a trade which will be an abundant source of riches and prosperity. These motives ought to excite all your zeal; and you cannot act more agreeably to the wishes of his Majesty, than by restoring to the isle of France those resources, of which it has been deprived by the abuses which have crept into the trade of Madagascar, and by that means to clear it of its dependance on foreign colonies for subsistence. I have the honour to be, &c.

Versailles,

Colonies. India Office.
Provisions.

Versailles, July 2d, 1775.

GENTLEMEN,

I Send you, by his Majesty's corvette, La Sirene, an assortment of victualling stores, furnished by M. to whom I have given a commission for that purpose.

This forms only a part of M. De Benyowsky's demand; but I propose to forward the rest by the ships which sail at the end of the year. M. Des Assizes, or the officer of Administration who may represent him, must be careful that the effects be carried to the storehouse, and duly acknowledged by a receipt from the storekeeper; after which they may be distributed in the colony, care being first taken to examine them by the invoice which accompanies this. He will likewise see that they be not delivered out, except to his orders, which will prevent abuses in the consumption.

As to the rest, you will find no difficulty respecting the conduct it is necessary you should adhere to, provided you conform to the common instructions which you have received in my dispatches. I have the honour to be, very truly,

GENTLEMEN,

Your very humble, and most obedient servant,

DE SARTINE.

To Messrs. Baron de Benyowsky,
and M. Des Assizes.

Colonies. India Office.

In form of Instruction relating to past and future Conduct.

Verfailles, July 17th, 1775.

THE commander of the Postillion has brought me all your dispatches, from your arrival at the bay of Antongil until the 24th of last September. I have very minutely attended to the detail of your operations, during the first eight months; and I see, with satisfaction, that Government may conceive favourable hopes from your prospects, and your first proceedings with the inhabitants of Madagascar.

The success of this important enterprize, in effect, depends on the prudent and conciliatory means which you have continued to employ with the natives of the country. They are gentle, laborious, and disposed to trade, and associate with us; but the different attempts which have hitherto been made on the island, and which have either been attended with great violence to the natives, or expence to Government, puts you under the present necessity of continually multiplying your precautions, to prevent treachery, and every inimical enterprize, on the part of the Malgachee, who, like all uncivilized people, are jealous of their liberty. These islanders will be always disposed to be apprehensive of the consequences of a permanent establishment, if they be not treated with kindness, or if any humiliating

miliating diftinction be made between them and the Europeans. The temptation of a commerce, which is become agreeable and advantageous to them, may have feduced them at firft; but it is to be feared, that they will become jealous of the advantages which the fuperiority of our knowledge and power muft give us over them: you cannot, therefore, be too attentive to the manner in which you behave to them.

These confiderations have always entered into the views of utility, which have determined the miniftry to entruft you with the care of an enterprize, which may actually require confiderable affiftance; but his Majefty has determined to referve the communication of his intentions until the end of the year. In the mean time, I fend the corvette, La Sirene, to bring you the firft fupplies of officers of health, workmen, money, provifions, and merchandize, as much as the tonnage of the veffel would admit. I confined myfelf, therefore, to the indifpenfible, until I can enter more fully into the fubject, and comprehend all the parts of the fervice which an eftablifhment of this nature requires; you will then receive recruits, which I have already ordered to be raifed, with a greater quantity of provifions, and other articles requefted in your difpatches, to which I fhall more particularly reply in future.

His Majefty, by his determination of fitting out the corvette, La Sirene, and approving that I fhould fend you an almoner, two furgeons, with fome foldiers and workmen, fufficiently apprizes you that his intention is, that you fhould continue to apply your whole attention to the eftablifhment at Madagafcar, and the prefervation of his fubjects, in order that you may be able to adminifter, with
fuccefs,

success, that assistance which shall be necessary, to such as still feel the effects of the intemperature of the climate, which has hitherto been so fatal to your people. I wait with great impatience for news concerning the return of this season; and am continually apprehensive that the sickly time of the year has taken off the greatest part of your people, and forced you to abandon the bay of Antongil, and retire with your people to the place you distinguish by the name of the Plain of Health. I am persuaded, however, that you will make every effort to preserve, to the utmost of your power, all the posts you have established within the island, or upon the coast. Besides which, I invite you to continue firm and constant in your enterprize, notwithstanding the obstacles and inconveniences you have experienced, which are always inseparable from an infant establishment. The more pressing your situation may become, the less I shall lose sight of you; and you may depend upon my attention, and the dispositions of his Majesty with respect to you: he has authorized me to assure you of the same, and has charged me to exhort you to proceed with unabated zeal. His Majesty, however, disapproves your having sent Madagascar slaves to the Cape of Good Hope. He recommends to you to be more circumspect in your operations, especially with respect to the colony of the isle of France, with which you ought to endeavour to trade, in preference to any other of his Majesty's colonies, and more especially to a foreign colony; so that all your dispositions should be subservient to the good of his Majesty's service. I cannot too strongly recommend to you, to use the greatest œconomy. in your expences, and to give M. Des Aſſizes every explanation which may be neceſſary to regulate thoſe which preceded his arrival; to leave entirely to him the adminiſtration of the finances, and the diſpoſition of the ten thouſand piaſtres, which the corvette, La Sirene, will bring; and, in a word, to conduct yourſelf towards him with that reſpect and delicacy, which are neceſſary to maintain that good union and harmony, which are ſo eſſential to the welfare of his Majeſty's ſervice.

I have the honour to be,

Very truly,.

S I R,.

Your moſt obedient Servant,

DE SARTINE.

P. S. In the hand of his lordſhip.

I have received your letter of the 1ſt of November. When you ſhall have received the two ſurgeons I ſend you, you may return thoſe to the iſle of France who have been ſent by Mr. Maillart, if you find that thoſe who come from France are better informed in ſuch matters as may be uſeful to you. I ſhall provide for the reſt of your affairs without delay; but I cannot too ſtrongly recommend to you, that
your

your accounts be regularly kept; œconomy be attended to; and that you keep on good terms with the commiſſary. I do not ſay any thing with regard to the preſervation of his Majeſty's ſubjects, as you cannot but be aware of its importance, and are more ſtrongly intereſted in it than any one elſe.

Colonies. India Office.

Relating to the Death of several Officers, and of Messrs. Marin, the father and son.

Versailles, July 23, 1775.

SIR,

I Have received your letter of the 20th of September, 1774, in which I cannot, without the most sensible regret, observe the considerable loss you have suffered of your officers. The loss of your lieutenant-colonel, M. Marin, afflicts me more sensibly, as well on account of the reputation he had acquired in Canada, as because he might have contributed, together with yourself, to the success of the establishment at Madagascar. Though I am sensible of the necessity of speedily replacing this officer, I have not been desirous of precipitating my choice, because it is essential that he who is appointed to second and to share your labours, ought to possess the talents necessary to an employment of this importance. It will be the end of the year before I can send you a lieutenant-colonel; but I promise you before-hand, that I will use the utmost attention to send one who shall be capable of imitating the example of courage and firmness you will set him.

Your letter of the 18th of September, 1774, in which you propose persons to the vacant employments, is likewise come

come to hand. I refer to the same time, the formation of a new corps of officers under you, in which, however, it will not be possible to comprehend all those whom you propose; not only because I have a great number of reformed officers, whom it will be just to employ in preference, but likewise because the advancement you propose for several of your volunteers, would be much too sudden. But I shall pay every respect to your proposals which circumstances and principles will allow.

  I have the honour to be,

    Very truly,

      SIR,

  Your very humble, and most obedient servant,

        DE SARTINE.

Colonies. India Office.
N° 18.

Versailles, March 30, 1777.

SIR,

I Received your letter of the 2d of June, 1776, N° 4, in answer to mine of the 17th of July, 1775. My fears left you should be forced to abandon the bay of Antongil, are happily dissipated; and I see, on the contrary, that you have increased and extended additional posts, by making new conquests. Although success has hitherto always crowned your attempts, I should be much better satisfied to hear that you avail yourself of the means of mildness and persuasion, to subject the islanders: military exploits exhaust your troops, are expensive, and may some time be attended with unhappy consequences. I know, on the other hand, that you have not always had the power over events; but from the details contained in your letter, I see, with pleasure, that your warlike expeditions are at an end; and I have reason to believe that you will now employ yourself, solely, in the care of keeping the peace, and civilizing the people subject to your command. The principal object of your mission being agriculture and commerce, you must be sensible that you cannot make either flourish, but by the exertions of the natives. Now, in order to turn their attention to those objects, it is necessary that, by

avoiding

avoiding the troubles of war yourself, you prefent to them the view of greater advantages, to arife from a fure and lafting union, than from rendering each other flaves.

I have the honour to be,

Very truly,

SIR,

Your very humble, and moft obedient fervant,

DE SARTINE.

Verfailles,

Colonies. India Office.

N° 19.

Verſailles, March 30, 1777.

SIR,

THE letters you wrote on the 10th and 24th of April, 1776, have arrived. Annexed to the former, I find the diſcourſe which you pronounced at the aſſembly of officers of your corps; and to the ſecond, the manifeſto and declaration of war, which you have thought proper to publiſh againſt the   Your poſition at that period was moſt critical. I ſee that you had only a ſmall body of troops to oppoſe to the multitude of your enemies; and I conſidered, with regret, that the ſupplies I had ſent you by the Sirenne, had not then arrived. Though that veſſel brought no recruits, yet the money on board, and my diſpatches, would at leaſt have diſpelled your anxieties. The policy you have employed on this occaſion, and the reſolution you adopted to march out and meet the enemy, rather than wait for him in your lines, are very honourable, both to your prudence and your courage. I muſt particularly acknowledge the pleaſure I received from the account of your march, and the plan of your campaign; alſo the ſtill greater pleaſure I received from hearing of the ſucceſs of your operations.

I have the honour to be, very truly,

SIR,

Your very humble, and moſt obedient ſervant,

To M. the Baron de Benyowſky.
N° 14.

DE SARTINE.

Colonies. India Office.

N° 20.

Verfailles, April 6, 1777.

SIR,

I Learn with pleasure, from your letter of the 1st of January, 1776, that you have had the good fortune to escape the influence of the climate of Madagascar, and that your convalescence has placed you in a situation to give me a more ample account of your operations, than those which you have addressed to M. De Boines, by the Sieur Saunier.

His Majesty being informed of the measures which you had taken to dissipate the league which threatened the settlement at Louisbourg, appeared satisfied with the zeal you shewed on that occasion. This confederacy shews that you have, perhaps, depended too much upon the pacific dispositions of several chiefs, whom you considered as the friends of Government. These chiefs, who do not behold without concern the exertions we make to form an establishment in their country, will, on their side, employ every manœuvre to drive us thence. You ought, therefore, to be continually on your guard against their snares; to mistrust even those who appear to be the most sincerely devoted to you; and to maintain no post which you cannot defend against the sudden attacks you will be exposed to for a long time to come. The object of your mission, is not

not so much that of extending yourself in the island of Madagascar, as of maintaining your footing there. As soon as you shall be firmly established in the post, which you actually possess in the bay of Antongil, I hope that the neighbouring inhabitants, attracted at first by trade, will perceive the mildness of our laws, and will of themselves submit to a Government, whose superiority they will perceive, and of whose advantage they will be desirous.

These are the only means which his Majesty authorizes: every thing which tends to destruction, is repugnant to his benevolence; and he would rather wait for the voluntary submission of the Madagascar people, instead of owing it to his arms; and he does not approve of the wars you have to support, except so far as you may be able to justify them in his sight, by the necessity of a lawful defence. I exhort you, therefore, Sir, not to depart from these principles; and acquaint you, that I shall always receive much greater satisfaction from the news of a solid treaty of peace, than of a brilliant conquest. The impatience you express respecting the supplies, which have been announced to you, is very natural; but the King, before he permits them to be forwarded to you, is desirous of being informed of the present state of the settlement, at the bay of Antongil; the certain advantages which may be derived therefrom; and more especially of the possibility of forming it without engaging in wars, or too evidently exposing the lives of his subjects. The inspection of Messrs. De Bellecombe and Chevreau is directed to this object; and I daily expect their observations that I may propose to his Majesty, either to support it in an effectual manner, or to abandon entirely the works you have made.

I do

COUNT DE BENYOWSKY. 387

I do not conceal, that the diforders which prevail in the place where you are fettled, and have carried off fo many of your men, give me the greateft uneafinefs; and I am not fully fatisfied with what you have done to deftroy them. The filling up of the marfh, is doubtlefs a very wife precaution; but the fuccefs is not infallible, and it may, at the utmoft, ferve to correct the influence of the climate in a flight degree, if the diforders depend on that caufe. This is a point which remains to be cleared up, concerning which I have not yet received fufficient explanation; for though your loffes have been lefs confiderable during the latter years, this may perhaps arife not from the air of the bay of Antongil having become purer, but merely from its being lefs pernicious to men who are accuftomed to it. Eftimates fhould be made from thofe who newly arrive; and it is from them that the effects of your operations may be afcertained, by an exact calculation.

I fee with pain, Sir, the contefts you have had with the Adminiftration of the ifle of France; and the King has expreffed great difpleafure on this head. They have not only injured the fervice of his Majefty, but have given rife to letters, on your part, which were not fufficiently weighed and confidered. It is not from obfcure reports that you ought to form a judgment of the fentiments of Meffrs. Ternay and Maillart. If you had reafon to complain of them, you were fure of finding me divefted of all prejudice, and difpofed to render you juftice: befides which, your reafons, if well founded, would have loft none of their force for being urged with lefs bitternefs; and you would have obferved that politenefs, which men in place mutually owe to each other, and which cannot be laid afide

D d d 2 without

without giving juſt cauſe for reprehenſion. I have thought this obſervation neceſſary, in order that you may conduct yourſelf in future in a manner more conformable to my views; and that, by ſtifling every ſecret reſentment in your breaſt, you may attach yourſelf to do and to write nothing, but what may conciliate the affection of the adminiſtrators, with whom you correſpond, and contribute to accompliſh his Majeſty's intentions, in the command he has been pleaſed to entruſt to you.

    I have the honour to be,

        Very truly, &c.

M. the Baron de Benyowſky.

       DE SARTINE.

India Office. } N° 21.

(No date in M.S.)

SIR,

I Have received your letter of the 2d of June, 1776. The anxiety you exprefs refpecting his Majefty's flute La Sirene, was unhappily too well founded. You muft have fince heard of the lofs of that veffel; and what is ftill more diftreffing, of the greateft part of her people. With regard to the effects and money, which I forwarded to you by that conveyance, Mr. Maillart has been attentive to replace them; and Meffrs. De Bellecombe and Chevreau muft have brought a fupply for the immediate wants of the fettlement. I hope, therefore, that the fupplies you have received will enable you to proceed, until I can declare his Majefty's determination concerning your final operations, if they are intended to take place. The uncertainty which ftill remains in this refpect, engages me to write only fhort anfwers; but when his Majefty fhall have given me his final orders, if his intention be to continue the eftablifhment at the bay of Antongil, I will then give you the moft ample inftructions concerning the conduct you ought to follow, with refpect to the accounts, which makes the principal object of your letter; and I will fend you fuch people, as I am fenfible you muft be in want of, in order that this effential part of the fervice may not be neglected, but invariably kept with exactnefs and regularity. In the mean time, I recommend to you to keep accurate

accounts

accounts of your expences; to look to the preservation of his Majesty's property, and not to permit any disposal of the same, without your consent; in order that you may be enabled to give me reasons for the uses to which it shall have been applied, and that I may judge whether the œconomy I have ordered is punctually attended to.

I have received, together with your letter, the memoir you mention, concerning the fevers of the bay of Antongil; but the ink you have made use of is so bad, that the writing is almost entirely obliterated, and cannot be made out; I therefore beg you will send me another copy the first opportunity.

I have read, with pleasure, the reflections you have presented to me, respecting the colony at Madagascar. I think with you, that the slave trade would be its ruin, and that all the views ought to be directed to trade and agriculture. I had already consigned these truths in the particular instructions of Messrs. De Bellecombe and Chevreau, so that you will not have had any difficulty in bringing them to approve your principles, which do not differ from mine. I do not much differ from you with regard to the Europeans; but this question will not be entirely resolved, until I can positively assure you that his Majesty intends to have a colony at Madagascar.

I have the honour to be, very truly,

SIR,

Your very humble, and most obedient servant,

DE SARTINE.

To M. the Baron de Benyowsky.
N° 15. Immediately

⁎ Immediately after the correspondence there follows, in the M.S. a copy of the ACT OF OATH, with the names of the chiefs present; and also a copy of the FULL POWERS. These agree with the same copies at pages 268 and 280 of this volume; excepting a few immaterial verbal variations, and the dates. The date of the Oath, in the last copy, is October 1, 1776; and of the Powers, October 3, 1781. Whether the difference between these and the dates in the Memoirs, be intentional, or founded in mistake, I shall not attempt to conjecture: it did not appear necessary to re-print them in this place.

DECLARATION

OF THE

COUNT MAURICE DE BENYOWSKY.

THE Count de Benyowsky, Magnate by birth of Hungary, who has the honour to present the annexed propositions to his Britannic Majesty, has been charged, on the part of his late Majesty Lewis XV. to form an establishment upon the island of Madagascar, in the year 1772, with orders to contract treaties of commerce and friendship with the natives of the country. He followed his mission for five years, and having accomplished it, he acquainted the Court of Versailles with his success; but the French ministry, being desirous of changing the treaties of commerce and friendship into an unlimited submission, on the part of the chiefs and people of the island, sent orders to the Count de Benyowsky to change the system agreed upon, and to establish an unlimited superiority, which could not be executed without infringing the primitive treaties concluded with the natives of the country: he thought proper, therefore, to forward his resignation

COUNT DE BENYOWSKY.

to the Court, which immediately sent Messrs. Bellecombe and Chevreau, in quality of commissaries and inspectors for the King, to examine the conduct of Count de Benyowsky, who was found to be fully justified by the original instructions; and the commissaries of the King could not refuse him a justificatory act. As soon as he had obtained this, he gave up his charge of Commandant and Governor-General, by entirely renouncing the service of France. The chiefs and people of Madagascar being informed of the mortifications the Count De Benyowsky had received, and being desirous of testifying their gratitude, assembled, and conferred upon him the charge of supreme Judge, and supreme Chief of the nation. Furnished with this title, he has obtained authority and power to treat in Europe, for the establishment of connections, either of trade, interest, or friendship, in order to accelerate the civilization of the inhabitants of Madagascar. With this charge, the Count de Benyowsky returned to Europe, where he experienced a violent persecution, on the part of the French ministry; to avoid which, he passed into the service of his Majesty, the Emperor, in hopes of obtaining from that Sovereign, the assistance he was in want of for Madagascar. But having soon received information, that the interests of his Imperial Majesty were not calculated to accomplish his engagements, he regularly quitted that service; and, during two years, has employed himself in the execution of his charge. It is with this intention that he has the honour to present the annexed proposals to his Britannic Majesty.

His good fortune will be complete, if he fhould fucceed in interefting his Majefty, and fhall obtain the affiftance he is in need of, to accomplifh the defires of an amiable and worthy nation, which has given him their unbounded confidence.

PROPO-

PROPOSALS

OF THE

COUNT MAURICE,

TO THE

MINISTRY OF HIS BRITANNIC MAJESTY.

TO BE PRESENTED AT LONDON, DECEMBER 25, 1783.

THE Count de Benyowſky, having obtained the powers and conſent of the chiefs and people of Madagaſcar, who have confided to him the charge of ſupreme Chief of the nation, being convinced of the advantages which would reſult to the intereſt of his Britannic Majeſty, the augmentation of the trade of his kingdoms, and the particular advantage of the civilization of the Madagaſcar people, in caſe a commercial intereſt were eſtabliſhed between the ſubjects of his Britannic Majeſty and the inhabitants of the iſland of Madagaſcar, PROPOSES, and submits unto his said Britannic Majesty, to cause him to be acknowledged Suzerain of that extensive and vast island; the interior civil and political government, and all the other regulations of civilization, high police, cultivation, and commerce, remaining independant. It is in this only quality of vassals to his Majesty, that the chiefs and people of Madagascar engage themselves:—

I.

To furnish his Majesty, in case of any war in India, with five thousand fighting men, led and commanded by their own officers; who shall be, in every respect, subject to the orders of the commander in chief of his Majesty's forces, during the whole time they shall be absent from the island, and employed against the enemies of his Majesty.

II.

They oblige themselves likewise to victual the squadrons of his Majesty; and to furnish, if required, the contingent of two thousand seamen, to serve on board his Majesty's ships in India.

III.

They stipulate, that they will constantly import such European merchandizes only, as are of the product, or manufacture of England. The population of Madagascar amounting to three millions of souls, their consumption must necessarily augment the advantages of trade in favour of England.

IV.

As an acknowledgment of their liege homage, the chiefs and people of the island of Madagascar, oblige themselves to pay annually a stipulated sum, to serve as an appanage to one of the Princes, sons of his Majesty; but this acknowledgment cannot be paid until the fourth year after the signing of the treaty. In return for these advantages, the Count de Benyowsky demands, in the name of the united chiefs and people of Madagascar;—

1st. That his Majesty do grant, in case of a foreign invasion, supplies of arms, shipping, and warlike stores; the forces of Madagascar being, in other respects, sufficient to repel any enemy on shore.

2dly. That his Majesty do permit the free embarkation, in all his harbours, of such foreigners (the French excepted) as shall be desirous of passing to Madagascar, in order to dwell upon the said island. With regard to French subjects, they cannot be received, but with the consent of the representative of the nation.

3dly.

3dly. That his Majesty do grant to the Count de Benyowsky, one vessel of four hundred and fifty tons; another of two hundred and fifty; and a third of one hundred and fifty tons; with cargoes and supplies of warlike stores, effects, and merchandizes, to the value of fifty thousand pounds sterling. The amount of this sum will be placed to the account of the island of Madagascar; and its Administration will pay the interest for the space of four years, and at the end of that term the capital sum shall be reimbursed to his Majesty. On these conditions the Count de Benyowsky offers to stipulate his submission, conformably to the articles herein before announced, on both sides; and it will depend only on the pleasure of his Majesty, to nominate, and send one or more commissaries with the Count de Benyowsky to Madagascar, to conclude the definitive treaty.

  Done at London, the year, month, and day, as herein before written.

After

⁎ After the copy of this inftrument, the Count has written the following with his own hand, in French:

" NOTA. M. De Magellan, for his direction, will obferve, that henceforth every idea of Suzerainety muft be banifhed; and that, in future, it will be proper to attend only to treaties of alliance, intereft, and trade. It is with this fole view that we have configned to him the prefent regifters.

" Done at London, the 24th of March, 1784.

" Signed,

MAURICE AUGUST. AMPANSACABE."

FINIS.

DIRECTIONS TO THE BINDER.

Place the Plates according to their Titles in the following Order.

Vol. I.

The Map to face the Title Page.

The Grütlin Matte	to face p.	99
The Mufic of the Kühreigen	—	100
The Valley of Lauterbrunn	—	111
St. Peter's Church	—	300
The Coloffeum	—	320
Outfide View of the Coloffeum	—	322
The Campo Vaccino	—	325
The Circus of Caracalla	—	353
The Interior of the Pantheon	—	424
Outfide View	—	427

Vol. II.

Grotta di Matrimonio	—	97
View of a rocky Valley near Sorento	—	105
Temple of Neptune	—	111
Winter Huts, two plates,	—	131
Ruins of a Grecian Temple	—	262
A View in Trapani	—	268
The Tree called Dei Cento Cavalli	—	485
Two Views in the Ifland of Ifchia	—	530

www.ingramcontent.com/pod-product-compliance
Lightning Source LLC
Chambersburg PA
CBHW022120290426
44112CB00008B/749